D1131277

Designing the New City:
A Systemic Approach

Wiley Series on Systems Engineering and Analysis
HAROLD CHESTNUT, Editor

Designing the New City:
A Systemic Approach

J. E. Gibson

Commonwealth Professor and Dean
School of Engineering and Applied Science
University of Virginia

A WILEY-INTERSCIENCE PUBLICATION

JOHN WILEY & SONS, New York • London • Sydney • Toronto

309.262
G449d

Copyright © 1977 by John Wiley & Sons, Inc.

All rights reserved. Published simultaneously in Canada.

No part of this book may be reproduced by any means, nor transmitted, nor translated into a machine language without the written permission of the publisher.

Library of Congress Cataloging in Publication Data

Gibson, John E.
  Designing the new city.

  (Wiley series on systems engineering and analysis)
  "A Wiley-Interscience publication."
  Bibliography: p. 282
  Includes index.
  1. Cities and towns—Planning—United States.
2. System analysis. I. Title.
HT167.G5   309.2'62'0973   76-44899
ISBN 0-471-29752-6

Printed in the United States of America

10 9 8 7 6 5 4 3 2 1

191197

SYSTEMS ENGINEERING AND ANALYSIS SERIES

In a society which is producing more people, more materials, more things, and more information than ever before, systems engineering is indispensable in meeting the challenge of complexity. This series of books is an attempt to bring together in a complementary as well as unified fashion the many specialties of the subject, such as modeling and simulation, computing, control, probability and statistics, optimization, reliability, and economics, and to emphasize the interrelationship between them.

The aim is to make the series as comprehensive as possible without dwelling on the myriad details of each specialty and at the same time to provide a broad basic framework on which to build these details. The design of these books will be fundamental in nature to meet the needs of students and engineers and to insure they remain of lasting interest and importance.

To Nancy

Preface

This book attempts to develop a coherent, complete, and, in a word, systemic methodology with which to approach large-scale societal problems. The particular example chosen to illustrate the method in some depth is the design of a large freestanding new city to be built in the United States in the near future.

The particular methodology proposed in this book is deliberately non-mathematical insofar as is possible. I believe that the general methodology should be accessible to all interested persons, professional and layman alike. Mathematics has an important place in carrying through the analysis of well-defined and specific details, of course. But too early a reliance on mathematical formalism may alienate many interested and potentially valuable contributors. Moreover, mathematical formalism is all too often a Procrustean bed; the problem is trimmed and stretched to fit the mathematics, rather than the reverse.

In Part I the proposed methodology is set forth, along with a short survey of the background to the urban problem. Chapter 1 will be recognized as what we call at a later point the descriptive scenario. Then the methodology itself along with a discussion of the problems involved in working with an interdisciplinary system analysis team is covered in Chapters 2 and 3.

Part II initiates the system analysis of the problem of urban revitalization. The first three phases of the systemic approach are to develop the goals, to agree upon evaluation criteria, and then to state alternate solutions. These three phases are discussed in Chapters 4 through 6.

Part III initiates the analysis of one revitalization option, the freestanding new city. One could argue that the final four chapters are too little and too late. They do not provide enough detail with which to form a definitive judgment on the viability of the proposal. Why would it not have been preferable to omit the first six chapters, or at least Chapters 4 through 6, start with the new city concept, and devote the entire book to that issue? This criticism, although reasonable enough on the surface, must be rejected on systemic grounds. One must generalize the problem and place it in context if a valid solution is to be assured. Perhaps in a subsequent volume the new city planning process will be continued to the next level of detail, but detailed analysis must follow, not precede, goal development.

To whom is this book addressed? It has been written, first, for urban system analysts, and then for the wider audience consisting of all large-scale-system analysts and regional and urban planners, whatever their methodological persuasions may be. Finally, a system analysis should result in an action phase. Thus I hope that the concept of the freestanding new city will prove attractive to clients and decision makers.

I wish to acknowledge the help and support of the National Science Foundation under Grant GK-41907, and the Battelle Memorial Foundation for support at the Summer-Systems Science Workshop at their Seattle Center in 1970. Oakland University provided me an administrative summer leave for work on this book. J. N. Warfield has read and commented on much of this manuscript as have H. Chestnut, J. D. Hill and A. P. Sage and a large number of my graduate students. To all my thanks.

J. E. GIBSON

Charlottesville, Virginia
September 1976

Contents

Designing the New City:
A Systemic Approach

Part I

BACKGROUND

1

Introduction to the Problem

We have an image of America which overemphasizes the importance of the small town and the open country neighborhood. Our folk heroes are the Tom Sawyers and Huckleberry Finns of a lost America; our literature is replete with Thoreaus, Emersons and Faulkners, who write of another world.

SCOTT GREER
Governing the Metropolis
John Wiley, N.Y., 1962,
p. 9

In one sense, we can trace all the problems of the American city back to a single starting point: We Americans don't like our cities very much.

JOHN V. LINDSAY
The City
W. W. Norton and Company, N.Y., 1968, p. 47

The traveler from the United States or the industrial cities of Europe or Japan goes each summer to visit the remnants of preindustrial civilizations. That is because Athens, Florence, Venice, Seville, Agra, Kyoto and Samarkand, though they were infinitely poorer by the standards of modern Nagoya, Dusseldorf, Dagenham, Flint or Magnitogorsk, included, as part of life, a much wider aesthetic perspective. No city of the postindustrial era is, in consequence, of remotely comparable artistic interest. Indeed, no traveler of predominantly artistic interest ever visits an industrial city and he visits very few of any kind which owe their distinction to architecture and urban design postdating the publication of Adam Smith's *Wealth of Nations* in 1776.

J. K. GALBRAITH
The New Industrial State
Houghton Mifflin Company, Boston, 1967, p. 347

1.1 What Is a City?

Cities came into existence concurrently with the agricultural revolution of neolithic times 12,000 years ago. Thus the city is an artifact that predates

3

the industrial revolution. Although most of those ancient cities were small, a few were quite large. We know of at least one city of a million persons that existed 3000 years ago and several others that large 2000 years ago. Almost a dozen such megapolises waxed and waned, some several times, before A.D. 1000.

Although cities seem permanent to man with his short lifetime, they are in constant growth and decay. Economic forces and sometimes military force can cause cities to change, but only within the past four or five decades have the forces of technology united against the city. It is a truism that cities are in trouble. American visitors in Europe watch with sorrow as the great classical cities allow themselves to be crippled by technology. Tokyo has caught up with and now passed Europe in its headlong rush to emulate the United States. Even Moscow seems to be following the same path. What can be done? Are cities doomed? A recent survey in St. Louis indicated that 25 percent of all housing units are abandoned. Pruitt-Igoe, its (in)famous high-rise, low-income housing project, which received the gold medal of the American Institute of Architects when it opened a decade ago, seems to be a paradigm of the urban condition. Pruitt-Igoe has been abandoned and is now, in its turn, the object of a massive slum removal effort. Perhaps nothing can be done. Perhaps we should turn away from cities. Perhaps they are not needed any longer.

Yet, while cities destroy themselves, the world becomes more urbanized. The ratio of urban population continues to rise in the United States. Remote counties grow more slowly than urban counties, and some rural areas exhibit an actual population loss. It appears that the situation is ripe for a careful, objective analysis, stripped as free of polemics and narrow subjectivity as possible. Perhaps in this way we can find what is worth saving and what should be altered in the city of the future. To start with we will provide some definitions.

A city is a group of people and a number of permanent structures within a limited geographical area, so organized as to facilitate the interchange of goods and services among its residents and with the outside world. But, as we probe more deeply, we find that this or any other definition of a city fails in one or another important respect. Gibbs[1] gives approximately 30 different definitions of a city. One can talk of the urban, built-up area as a city, or the political boundaries can be used. One can use the Standard Metropolitan Statistical Area (SMSA) of the U. S. census or the region of urban economic influence, the so-called service area. One conventional population definition is as follows: the cordon that encloses the area in which the density is 2500 people per square mile. Table 1.1 gives a few densities to establish a feeling for this number.

Table 1.1 *An Urban Population Density Comparison*

Region	Approximate Population Density (people/mile²)
Manhattan	76,000
New York City	24,000
N.Y.–N.J. SMSA	3,700
United States	50

There is a wide latitude for argument about various specific definitions of urban agglomerations based on size. What is a hamlet, a village, a town, a city? The various terms are imprecise, and local usage varies. In the United States a "town" is bigger than a "village" but smaller than a "city," whereas in England "town" does not necessarily indicate a specific size at all. A group of buildings on a farm could properly be called a town in Britain. Table 1.2 gives some possible city definitions based on population.

"Megalopolis" is the term coined by Jean Gottmann[2] to designate the central eastern seaboard stretching from Boston southward to Norfolk, Virginia. We might call this whole area Eastern City. According to Constantinos Doxiadis,[3] a Great Lakes Megalopolis is developing below the southernmost tip of Lake Michigan and stretching along the southern edge of Lake Erie. This Midwestern City includes Milwaukee, Chicago, Detroit, Toledo, Cleveland, and Pittsburgh and is separated from Eastern City by the Allegheny Mountains. Similarly, Western City is growing between San Francisco and San Diego, including Los Angeles. Of these three, Doxiadis maintains, only Midwestern City is not limited in growth by natural barriers such as mountains or deserts.

Thus we can conclude that there is no one definition of a city. One must adopt a definition commonly accepted for the purpose to which he wishes to put it. Furthermore, the user must make very clear his precise definition if this plays a pivotal role in his argument.

1.2 How Did Cities Originate?

The rise of cities is interwoven with the agricultural revolution. In the fertile crescent of the Near East the agricultural revolution process began

Table 1.2 *Possible City Definitions*

Definition	Examples	Land Area (miles²)	Population[a]	Density (people/mile²)	Reference	Comment
Planet	The Earth	58 × 10⁶	3 × 10⁹	52	2	McLuhan's global village concept
Megalopolis	Great Lakes (U.S. and Canada)	89,200	35,900,000	402	1	Gottmann's megalopolis
	East Coast of U.S.	53,575	37,000,000	700	3	
Metropolis	New York SMSA	3,930	14,759,428	3,756	2	Doxiadis Class C city
	London	617	7,763,820 (1968)	12,587	2	Doxiadis Class B city
	Tokyo	784	12,270,000 (est. 1970)	15,647	4	Center of communication
Regional trading center	Hot Springs, Ark.	9	28,337	3,148	5	Doxiadis Class A city
	Portsmouth, N.H.	15	26,900	1,793	5	
	Carlsbad, N.M.	8	25,541	3,192	5	
Village	Vassar, Mich.	2.0	2,680	1,340	5	Not a city as generally accepted
	Sugar Creek, Mo.	1.2	2,663	2,219	5	
	Chaska, Minn.	1.8	2,502	1,390	5	

[a] All data as of 1960 unless otherwise noted.

1. C. A. Doxiadis, *Emergence and Growth of an Urban Region*, Vol. 1: *Analysis*, Detroit Edison Co., 1966.
2. L. H. Long (Ed.), *The World Almanac and Book of Facts*, Enterprise Association, Inc., N.Y., 1969.
3. Jean Gottmann, *Megalopolis: The Urban Northeastern Seaboard of the United States*, Twentieth Century Fund, N.Y., 1961.
4. Guiness, McWhirter, Norris, Ross, *Book of World Records*, Sterling Publishing Co., N.Y., 1968.
5. *County and City Data Book*, U. S. Department of Commerce, 1967.

during the neolithic era about 13,000 B.C. To this era also we can trace the earliest known fixed habitations. A study of the available remains of these neolithic villages indicates that many had no walls. Excavations[4] on the Rhine River near Cologne in the 1930s (the so-called Köln–Lindenthal site) also serve to demonstrate this. Danubian I people settled in a fortified neolithic village of 35 houses about 4000 B.C. Directly beneath this village on the same site, however, a previous settlement of the same people was discovered; this earlier settlement of 27 houses was unfortified.

Wheeler points out that open villages existed in northern Iraq in the fifth millennium B.C., and a substantial town without walls stood at Catal Huyuk, near Konya in southern Turkey, not later than 7000 B.C. On the other hand, Jericho with its walls has been dated by Carbon-14 techniques as of the early eighth century B.C.[5]

These "open" villages cause Mumford to speculate[6] that tribal defense was not the main purpose in the origin of a fixed settlement. He argues there were three reasons for establishing these first villages: first, as sanctuaries and places for rites of the dead; second, as ceremonial centers for magic, religious practices, and social enjoyment; and only thirdly as a means for promoting the safety of the tribe.

It would seem that Mumford has overlooked the most obvious reason for a fixed settlement. It is a great deal of trouble continually to pick up one's life and follow the herds and the seasons. In all probability it gradually became clear to a tribe that the fixed agricultural life is easier than the wandering hunting–gathering mode of existence. Adams[7] calculates that in pre-Hispanic Mexico approximately one-half man-year of labor was required to maintain the average family in the agricultural mode, and he estimates about the same for Mesopotamia. Hardoy[8] goes further. He states, "In approximately two months, the Maya farmer of the Classic Period [A.D. 300–900] produced the quantity of food necessary to feed himself and his family, as well as his share of the community tribute payment." In the hunting–gathering mode of life, on the other hand, almost all of the energy of the tribe must be devoted to staying alive. Occasional surpluses become available, of course, but to preserve and transport such surpluses is an effort.

We need not limit our search for the origin of fixed habitation and its relation to the agricultural mode of life to the neolithic period. In our own era and on this continent, evidence abounds of the superiority of the fixed agricultural mode over the older, wandering hunting–gathering mode of life. By the early seventeenth century the Five Nations of the Iroquois had established their domination over the whole northeast quadrant of the

North American continent. Numbering at the peak of their power perhaps 4000 braves,[9] they controlled the far more numerous Algonquin.

Except for the detached nation of the Tuscaroras, and a few smaller tribes adhering to them, the Iroquois family was confined to the region south of the Lakes Erie and Ontario, and the peninsula east of Lake Huron. They formed, as it were, an island in the vast expanse of Algonquin population, extending from Hudson's Bay on the north to the Carolinas on the south; from the Atlantic to the Mississippi and Lake Winnipeg on the west.[10]

The Algonquin were a nomadic people and subsisted by hunting, fishing, and gathering. In general, we could say they were a neolithic people who had not passed through the agricultural revolution. The Iroquois, on the other hand, had an agricultural economy. They lived in comfortable, permanent lodges behind carefully constructed defensive ramparts. For a distance as great as 5 miles out, their villages were surrounded with maize fields and apple orchards. They had abundant stores of corn, beans, squash, and fruit in storage by the time winter approached. This advanced agriculture was carried on by the women and children, leaving the warriors free to engage in art forms such as the dance and elaborate rituals, to develop a complex political structure, and most of all to engage in offensive war. Whereas the Algonquin needed all their energy to maintain each small wandering band through the cold winter, the Iroquois gathered, nation by nation, in their warm lodges, supported by their ample stocks of food and fiber, and planned their raiding parties for the approaching spring.

The surplus human energy released by the agricultural revolution can be argued, as it has by Adams, to have triggered the rise of cities. Mumford would agree and go further, pointing out that in turn this encouraged an attitude of special sanctity toward property rights and indeed the invention of aggressive war. And Carneiro[11] connects the rise of agriculture to the rise of the state.

1.3   What Are the Functions of a City?

The functions of a city are related to its size. An agricultural village exists for the mutual convenience of the families cultivating the nearby fields, but larger agglomerations such as seaports and caravan and trade route intersections develop more specialized functions.[12] For the large city of a million or more people, some special force must come into play over and above that of regional trading center. Doxiadis maintains[13] that for thousands of years the regional trading center, which he calls a Class A settlement, was the largest kind to exist.[14] This is the "natural-size" settlement if the dominant mode of transportation is by foot. A Class A city was approximately 2 kilometers (1.25 miles) on a side and contained a maximum of approximately 50,000 persons.[15] Such size permitted a citizen to walk between any two points within the city in about 10 minutes. By a similar argument Doxiadis holds that the region of natural influence of the ancient city was the radius that a man could walk in 1 day, or about 50 kilometers (30 miles).

Exceptions to this rule are the capitals of empire (Doxiadis' Class B settlements). Such cities as Rome, Constantinople, and Peking grew to 10 kilometers (6 miles) on a side and contained as many as 1 million people at their peak. As Doxiadis points out, such cities are too large to negotiate on foot and the residents began to use horse-drawn carts. Thus straight, paved city streets became a necessity. This is the first of a series of conflicts brought on by exceeding the "natural" size of an organization. Doxiadis writes:

These great cities of the past are remembered more for their conquests than for their organization. They were easily disorganized, tended to deteriorate into slums, were often controlled by mobs; they usually shrank to normal size after the empire was dissolved. Rome and Constantinople are examples.[16]

"Center of Empire" could describe the first of three functions we will postulate as the driving force behind the establishment of Class B centers. These three functions are also roughly sequential in time, although remnants of early Class B type centers still exist. Most major cities of the world before the eighteenth century were centers of empire. Because rapid communication was impossible, the reins of government had to be gathered together in the capital. A major portion of the army was stationed nearby, and the greater part of the empire's business was conducted near the capital. All of these conditions combined to cause the capital city to swell beyond the limits of a regional trading center to become a Class B city.

After the industrial revolution and the growth of the factory system, new pressures for agglomeration developed. Thousands of employees were needed in the newly developed large mills, and in addition many independent suppliers chose to locate in the factory cities. Thus centers of industrialization sprang up. Often these grew out of what were originally centers of empire, although many of these older cities never became industrialized, but rather entered a stage of arrested development or decay. Many European cities, however, and almost all American cities, Washington being an exception, grew up from their beginnings as centers of industry. Mumford, for one, has never accepted the industrial city, and it is true that many are dirty and ugly. This is not the reason, however, that the centers of industry are now in the process of decay.

Because of rapid and ubiquitous transportation by modern motor vehicles and the rising costs encountered by urban industries, the Class B city as a center of industry has outlived its need. Rarely, if ever, nowadays is a new factory constructed within city limits. Often, in fact, a corporation will extract a promise from nearby city government never to annex the area on which a plant is to be built before it will even consider locating *near* an existing city. Not only must a new factory avoid high city taxes, but also it cannot afford the high cost of urban land. This is the reason why proposals to replace urban slums with modern factories prove infeasible on a purely economic basis.

The third and most recent Class B city function is to serve as the center of commerce and communication.[17] To act as a center of communication remains one of the few viable functions performed by a major city. New York City is an example. Despite rising land costs and other difficulties, major business activities locate their main communication functions there. The stock market cannot leave. The Pan-Am building is fully occupied, and the International Trade Center has recently been completed. The elements necessary for a successful center of communication are not entirely clear, since this new role for the city has become dominant only in the past several decades. Such a determination is important, however, if effective planning for the future is to be possible.

The concept of the center of communication seems to be implicit in Vernon's description of why certain industries are attracted to or remain in New York City despite high rents and wage rates.[18] Vernon directed a 3-year New York Metropolitan Region study late in the 1950s, the results of which occupy approximately 10 volumes. He explains the apparent paradox in economic location of manufacturing activity in terms of external economics in overcoming uncertainty and unpredictability. In other words, a New York City location is valuable to organizations that need rapid communication with many diverse sources of information. Examples cited by Vernon are the fashion industry with its rapid and unpredictable shifts and turns, advertising, printing, publishing, and specialist electronic producers; for all these, access to market information more than compensates for the high cost of a New York site location.

1.4 What Are the Mechanisms of Urban Growth?

The growth of Class A regional trading centers seems clear enough. Doxiadis has commented on the natural region of influence of such centers, and in a later chapter we will see Petrie's observation on the remarkable regularity in the spacing of the regional trading centers in the Nile Delta of ancient Egypt, based on similar observation.

Christaller developed the central place theory[19] to relate the size and spacing of such regional trading centers. The lowest ranking of his hierarchical arrangement are towns that purvey goods in daily use to their surrounding regions or so-called hinterlands. The radius of the hinterland depends on the prevailing mode of transport. In rural China, where much travel is by foot, the hinterland of a village is smaller than it is in the Great Plains of the United States. Recently the network of central places in the Midwest has been rearranging itself as farm-to-market roads are paved and high-speed highways become common. Towns die out as the hinterland of a regional service center expands and overlaps with formerly exclusive hinterlands of nearby towns. The second level of the central place cities is spaced more widely and is supported by providing retail outlets for major purchases and by county seat government. Still more widely spaced, larger cities are loci for wholesaling, warehousing, railroad junctions, state capitals, and so on. But, as we have suggested, an entirely different mechanism from the optimization of personal satisfactions of the inhabitants of a region must be sought to explain the growth of Class B metropolises.

City after city around the world has grown to the 1-million mark. In 1960 more than 112 cities in the world had populations exceeding 1 million. By 1970 this number was over 130 with 33 in the United States alone. Ancient Babylon had a population of almost 1 million in 1000 B.C. Rome and Constantinople reached this number, as did Hangchow, Peking, and possibly Anuradhapura, Ceylon, under the Sindalese before A.D. 1000. Other early large cities were Mexico City under the Aztecs (1519), Alexandria, New Delhi, Tokyo, Paris, and Moscow. Most of these ancient cities were "capitals of Empire" in the sense of garrison cities or cities of massive central administration. Most were also trade centers and foci of culture and affluence. The growth of such a center can often be traced to a unilateral decision by a ruling autocrat or dynasty.

The development of post-industrial-revolution "centers of industrial empires," however, cannot be as simple. Is geography the determinant? Or chance? Consider New York City, for example. Are not its port facilities and the opening of the Erie Canal the determining factors in its growth? Jean Gottmann in Part I, called "The Dynamics of Urbanization," of his beautifully done book, *Megalopolis*,[20] devotes four chapters to a consideration of this question. He follows in some detail the development of the northeast portion of the United States. He points out (p. 61, italics in original):

Both past and present experiences show there is no guarantee that wealth and a large money market will remain where they are now. For their retention and growth a region needs other resources—*resources of the spirit,* which may, perhaps, be summarized briefly as *knowledge* and *the will to take risks and fight to win.*

We could characterize this as the entrepreneurial spirit. Later (p. 69) in a section titled "The Tradition of Promethean Endeavor," Gottmann states:

The various companies that financed the first settlements in this area [east coast of the United States] certainly had in mind materialistic considerations of profit as well as the charitable intent of helping persecuted people to a haven. But for the settlers, and especially for their leaders, *the idea of being on a mission* dominated their removal to the wilderness of America. It was not just a refuge these people were seeking. They were on a mission to conduct an "experiment" or an "errand" in the new environment.

This mystical interpretation of Gottmann may at first seem out of harmony with modern explanations based on that academic creature, "economic man," but it has a ring of truth.

Gottmann recognizes that to aspire to be a regional market center is to be satisfied with a small population. He points out quite clearly (p. 106):

Within a generation of their founding, Boston, New York, and Philadelphia had developed into substantial metropolises, by the standards of the time. This growth, and that of a dozen smaller seaport towns on the same coast, could not have taken place had the towns served only as regional markets supplying the surrounding rural population and exporting their surplus produce. This is well illustrated by developments in the southern English colonies [in America] which were, from the point of view of the motherland, a much greater asset [than the northern cities for they supplied large quantities of tobacco and naval stores].

The reader will recognize these regional market centers as Doxiadis' Class A settlements.

The rate of growth and the rank of the major cities on the U. S. eastern seaboard are as follows. By 1699 three had populations of more than 4000—in order, Boston, Philadelphia, and New York. By 1800 these cities plus Baltimore were at greater than 25,000 persons, with New York well in the lead, followed by Philadelphia, Boston, and Baltimore. Boston and Baltimore slowed their rate of growth, but by 1850 New York City and Philadelphia had more than 300,000 people each. Thereafter New York's magnificent natural harbor plus the development of the Erie Canal and the entrepreneurial spirit of New York merchants combined to allow New York to move ahead more rapidly.

Do men make the times? Did entrepreneurs build these cities, or did the opportunities create the entrepreneurs? The probable answer, of course, is a combination of the two. Without the proper opportunities and the right leadership, growth would not take place. The opportunity for growth may be a political realignment, the opening of new territory, or the discovery of a new natural resource. More and more often in modern times, however, this special opportunity results from a new technological development. Even in the nineteenth century spectacular growth of a city was often spurred by the opening of a new canal or railroad. Most large midwestern cities in the United States owe their present sizes to technology: Pittsburgh to steel, Detroit to automobiles, and Chicago to railroads bringing grain and livestock for processing. To summarize, we argue, then, that small regional trading centers with 20,000 to 50,000 persons can develop from a confluence of "natural" causes. But which of these regional centers will develop into large metropolitan complexes depends on the resources of the spirit that Gottmann mentions and the presentation of opportunity.

One could argue that, since "the opportunity" is often a unique event isolated in time, it is impossible to predict when and whether it will occur. Furthermore, we can predict nothing about the possible behavior of the specific, individual risk takers who may be present when "the opportunity" presents itself. Perhaps one entrepreneur, more or less, does not make the difference. It is the spirit of the region and the flavor of the times that count. Robert Albion makes this clear in his book on the development of the port of New York.[21] He points out that New York outdistanced Philadelphia, as well as its other early rivals such as Boston and Charleston, advancing from fourth rank in 1770 to first in 1797 and developing a commanding lead after the close of the War of 1812, by a series of bold entrepreneurial strokes, any one of which could have been duplicated or anticipated by its rivals. Remember that all of this occurred more than a decade *before* the opening of the Erie Canal. In fact, one might go so far as to argue that, rather than the Erie Canal causing the rise of the New York port, it was the same spirit which caused New York to drive for prominence that sensed the possibilities in the canal and effected its construction.

Here are several of the more important entrepreneurial successes recounted by Albion.

- New York became the main U. S. market for British goods after the War of 1812 by providing effective brokerage at the "Pearl Street auction."
- New York became such an effective middleman and financial resource it even serviced New England textile mills to the exclusion of Boston.

- In 1818 the first regularly scheduled sailing packet service began with the Black Ball Line between New York and Liverpool.
- Because of superior quality, New York flour sold at a premium even in Philadelphia, its major northern rival for this trade.
- New York dominated the southern trade even though it was faster and cheaper to ship directly from southern ports to England. Cotton was New York's most valuable export by far, accounting for about 40 percent of the port's $9 million domestic exports in 1822. Northern flour accounted for less than a third the value of cotton, and southern tobacco equaled flour in value. In all, more than 55 percent of New York's exports represented southern trade. It has been said that $0.40 of every dollar paid by English mills for southern cotton stayed in New York.
- After the Erie Canal was opened, New York merchant bankers invaded the Ohio Valley to buy wheat futures, thus diverting wheat from its natural course down the Mississippi to New Orleans.

So much for geography!

In the city of the future with ubiquitous transportation and instantaneous communication, small differences of geography will be further devalued. The citizens of the city will command its future, as they probably always have, though they have not always realized it.

1.5 Growth of a Center of Industrialization: Detroit

We have considered Gottmann's rather metaphysical view of the growth of New York and the somewhat different, though harmonious, perspective of the economic historian, Albion, of the same process. Both studies seem to indicate the importance of entrepreneurial endeavor in the growth of Class B centers of industry. Now let us continue this same discussion from still a third point of view, that of the geographical or regional scientist. And let us switch our attention to Detroit for several reasons.

- Detroit is a somewhat more typical metropolitan city than New York, which might be said to occupy, along with Tokyo and London, another class of still larger cities.
- Although no city is completely average, Detroit comes as close as most to being a typical large industrial city. It has a somewhat higher than average number of corporate headquarters, but until recently this has had no discernible positive impact on the milieu. Detroit, along with Pittsburgh and Seattle, have somewhat lower industrial diversity indices than other large American industrial centers. On the whole,

however, Detroit is representative of large centers of industry. Below we will consider the statistics of smaller cities of about 1 million population.

• Detroit could be called a lake port, but it does not carry on extensive shipping activities and its port facility underdevelopment has been a bone of political contention for many years. Detroit's specific location seems not to have been a special factor in its growth. Any other location on navigable water would provide equivalent cheap bulk-raw-material transport to serve its manufacturing activities.

Greater Detroit contains more than half the total population of Michigan and spreads its economic influence over a radius of several hundred miles. The three counties of Wayne, Oakland, and Macomb are considered by the U. S. Bureau of the Census as the Detroit Standard Metropolitan Statistical Area (SMSA). See Figure 1.1. However, a Doxiadis study shows that neither the SMSA nor the six-county area consisting of the SMSA plus Livingston, Washtenaw, and Monroe, which is usually regarded as Greater Detroit by planners, marks the boundary of the urban influence area. Doxiadis maintains[22] that for practical purposes the urban Detroit influence includes 25 counties in Michigan, 9 in northern Ohio, and 3 in Canada, an area of 23,000 square miles.

Greater Detroit spreads along the river that connects Lake Erie with Lake Huron. It is a natural confluence of trade routes and has been inhabited continuously from well before the American Revolution. Founded in 1701 by French fur traders led by Antoine Cadillac and later captured by the British, by 1920 it was an important rail and manufacturing center and had a population of over 1 million. See Table 1.3. After 1910 the automobile manufacturing industry assumed greater and greater importance to the growth of the city. Detroit enjoys good lines of communication by rail and water and access to the raw materials required by industry, but it is an entrepreneurial accident that the automobile industry grew up in this specific location rather than at any other point on the Great Lakes.

In 1910 Chicago, another Great Lakes metropolis, was three times larger than Detroit, yet by 1960 it was only 43 percent larger. Both cities continue to grow linearly in population at the same rate. Both showed the same relative hiatus in the depression years and for the past 50 years have maintained an almost constant population differential of 2 million persons. See Figure 1.2. This is not to say, of course, that growth is inevitable. The Cleveland–Pittsburgh area, for example, kept pace with Chicago and Detroit from 1910 through the depression years, lagging behind the former and leading the latter, but from 1940 through 1960 fell behind its

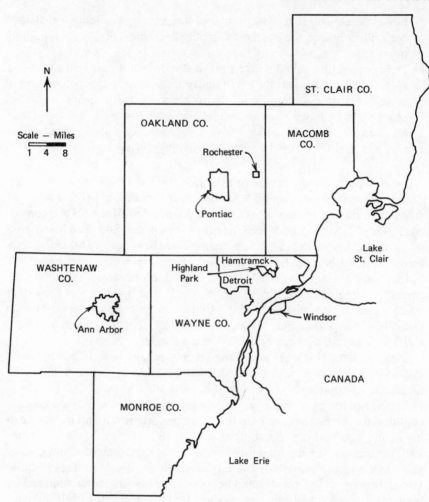

Figure 1.1 Geographical Detroit, showing several possible definitions for a city.

rivals in growth rate and now is about equal in population with Detroit. It could be concluded that Cleveland–Pittsburgh has 1.2 million fewer people than we would expect if it had kept pace.[23] Of course, it is for the people of that region to say whether the reduced industrial tax base that has resulted is compensated for by the reduced population pressures. The slower growth pattern of Cleveland–Pittsburgh is probably due to the failure of the city leaders to appreciate the effect on the local iron and steel industry of the exhaustion of the nearby Appalachian coal fields and

Table 1.3   *Population of Detroit (SMSA) (The Detroit Standard Metropolitan Statistical Area is defined as Wayne, Oakland, and Macomb Counties.) (*SOURCE: *U. S. Department of Commerce, Bureau of the Census)*

Year	Population	
	SMSA (2005 mile²)	Wayne County (625 mile²)
1840	57,535	24,173
1850	89,556	42,756
1860	136,651	75,547
1870	187,531	119,038
1880	239,590	166,426
1890	330,172	257,114
1900	426,829	348,793
1910	613,773	531,591
1920	1,305,798	1,177,645
1930	2,177,343	1,888,946
1940	2,377,329	2,015,623
1950	3,016,197	2,435,235
1960	3,762,360	2,666,297
1970	4,199,931	2,666,751

a subsequent entrepreneurial failure to exert the effort required to find replacement industries.[24]

It is perhaps worth noting in passing that Pittsburgh's situation, though intensified by its heavy reliance on a single industry, is typical rather than unique. No amount of effort in attracting basic or heavy industries such as chemicals, oil, rubber, iron and steel, or aluminum can have a major effect on employment in any region of the United States. This is true because these are precisely the industries that are most susceptible to automation. For example, the number of man-hours required to produce a ton of steel in the United States has been cut in half in the past 10 years. Indeed, one can go further and say that heavy industries in the United States *must* automate if they are to maintain their place in international commerce in the face of foreign competition.[25]

One way of illustrating the dynamics of growth of an urban area is to plot contours of land use as a function of time. Such land-use contours probably provide as valid a definition of a city as any. Suppose we choose a contour that encloses the land area that is less than 65 percent devoted

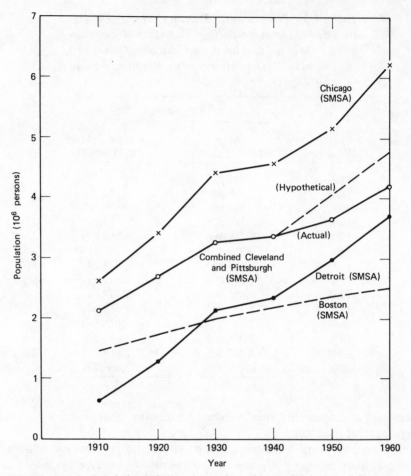

Figure 1.2 Populations of several American cities as a function of time.

to agriculture. Any other percent contour would serve equally well to illustrate the point, of course. In Figure 1.3 these contours are shown for southeast Michigan for the period from 1900 to 1959. Detroit can be seen to be growing out on a line toward the northwest and enveloping first Birmingham, then Pontiac and Rochester, and thereafter extending out past Flint to Saginaw and Bay City. To the south, Toledo is soon to become a satellite city, as Windsor, Canada, has long ago. By examining Figure 1.4, which shows the results of the latest study of land use, one can detect new growth vectors, one aimed due west, enveloping Ann Arbor, Jackson, and Battle Creek, and another pointing northeast toward Port

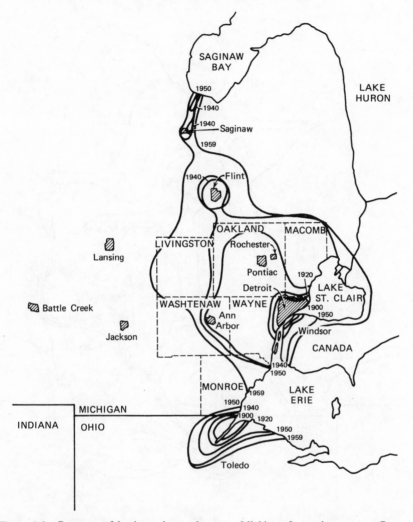

Figure 1.3 Contours of land use in southeastern Michigan for various years. Contour encloses the region in which less than 65 percent of area is devoted to agriculture. (SOURCE: Doxiadis, *Emergence and Growth of an Urban Region.*)

Huron and Sarnia, Canada, on Lake Huron. These new growth vectors to the west and northeast are not yet visible by on-site inspection, and hence this analysis has some predictive value.

Doxiadis[26] goes further and projects two additional vectors: one through Windsor into Canada and one northwest through Lansing. A new interstate highway from Detroit through Lansing follows one proposed

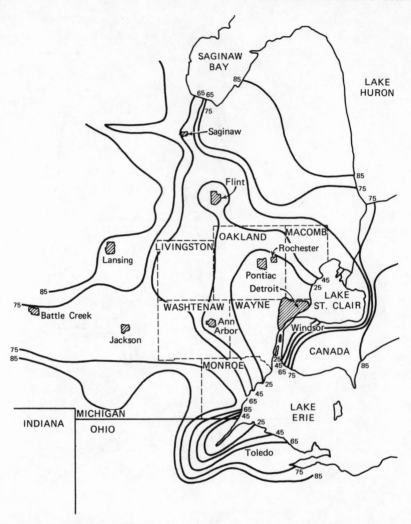

Figure 1.4 Land use in 1960 for Greater Detroit region. Contours enclose given percentage devoted to nonagriculture. (SOURCE: Doxiadis, *Emergence and Growth of an Urban Region,* loc. cit.)

vector of Doxiadis. It will be interesting to see the effect of this highway on growth. There is no "natural" reason to anticipate such growth, and it seems likely that a major reason for connecting the state's capital and its major population center with I-696 was for the convenience of state officials. Thus, if growth occurs, it can be attributed to this highway.

There is no doubt that city, county, and state boundaries, not to speak of the international border, will continue to interfere with the regional planning of the Urban Detroit Area (UDA), as they have in the past. Some improvement is noticeable, however, in that various regional governing units in greater Detroit are beginning to communicate with each other. Here are several items of concrete evidence of this dialogue.

- The interstate highway system ties together the region and follows the growth vectors outlined above.
- The Detroit Edison Company supplies electrical energy to most of the region and is closely affiliated with Consumers Power, which serves Flint and the region west of Detroit.
- The Detroit Water Supply System soon will serve the region up to and including Flint and Port Huron, as well as Ann Arbor in the west.
- Sewer interceptors that will tie most of the separate township sewer systems together are under construction.
- A regional Transportation and Land Use Study (TALUS) is essentially complete.
- The Michigan legislature approved in 1967 a bill authorizing metropolitan transportation authorities, thus encouraging the formation of the Southeast Michigan Transportation Authority (SEMTA).
- A Southeast Michigan Council of Governments (SEMCOG) has been formed.

Let us turn back now to the one major growth vector of greater Detroit which has been apparent for 40 years and about which there can be little argument: the one thrusting slightly west of north through Pontiac and Flint to Saginaw and Bay City. Why does it exist? Why has not the growth been along the Detroit River and the edge of Lake St. Clair, for example? Or why not directly west toward Lake Michigan and Chicago? Both of these routes have obvious advantages in transportation and accessibility. The band of counties along the southern border of Michigan to the west of Detroit contains the best land in the state for agriculture, by far the best-educated labor force available for manufacturing employment, and by far the largest per capita income. There is nothing new in this observation; it has been apparent for 150 years. In 1837 the Michigan state legislature agreed to build and operate two railroads "as part of a broad program on internal improvements designed at once to build up the interior of Michigan and advance the commercial interests of its cities, particularly Detroit."[27] In 1846 the railroads were sold to private interests, and by 1857 both had reached south of Lake Michigan to Chicago. The construction routes of these two lines, shown in Figure 1.5, demonstrate how clear the trend of development was to early legislators and commercial interests.

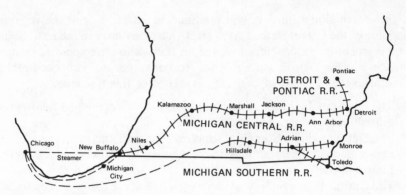

Figure 1.5 The routes of early Michigan railroads. (SOURCE: Hirschfeld, *loc. cit.*)

One might argue that there is now some mystic "center of gravity of the state" which directs the Detroit growth vector up through the lower peninsula (LP), but this seems unlikely. The population of the western portion of the upper peninsula (UP) is oriented to Wisconsin rather than to Detroit, which is 500 miles away by automobile, while the eastern half of the UP is sparsely settled land of poor quality and exhausted natural resources (lumber and copper). The upper half of the LP is more accessible than the UP but has only slightly greater endowments. Its land is worthless for agriculture, it is lightly settled with a poorer and less well-educated population than that of the southern half, and by far the greater part of the land remains forested. In fact, although Michigan as a whole recently has registered the highest population gain of the five Great Lakes states, 23 percent per decade, the upper half of the LP has fallen behind the national average of about 15 percent per decade and the UP has shown an actual loss in population. The major use of both these areas appears to be to provide vacation country for the population of the larger cities, all of which are in the lower half of the LP. Why, then, this anomalous growth vector tending toward Saginaw Bay and nowhere, away from good land, population resources, and links with the rest of the United States? Why do Pontiac and Flint seem to attract developing Detroit, and not the more "natural" choice of growth directly west toward Ann Arbor, Jackson, and Kalamazoo or even slightly north of west toward Lansing and Grand Rapids?

It is quite apparent that jobs attract people. Natural beauty, recreation opportunities, and the presence of family and friends have little to do with population trends in any large-scale, primary sense. California boomed after World War II because the aircraft industry found it convenient to settle there, not because it has a nice climate. Pittsburgh has declined because the local steel industry has fallen behind and no other industry has replaced it. The Gulf Coast Crescent from Houston to Cape Kennedy has been undergoing a boom in recent years because a federal decision was made to locate the plants and facilities of the space program along it. Thus we should examine the behavior of Pontiac, Flint, and Saginaw toward fostering industry, and that of Ann Arbor, Jackson, and Lansing toward discouraging it, for a clue as to the growth of the Detroit metropolitan region.

Although these viewpoints regarding the growth of a large city seem to rest on different bases—Gottmann's on the human quest or sense of mission, Albion's on economic history, and Doxiadis' on regional science and demographics—all are harmonious.

- Each authority accepts geographic factors as important but only in the broadest sense as determinative. In other words, cities that depended largely on the British–American trade would spring up on the east coast of the United States in the eighteenth century, but their exact positions on the east coast were not determined by geography. Similarly, great steel cities and manufacturing cities would develop in the Midwest in the nineteenth century along the Great Lakes, but geography does not mandate exactly where.
- Major urban centers are not merely "central places." To be content with the role of regional trading center is to remain relatively small.
- The amount and the direction of growth depend on economic factors, that is, jobs. And jobs are provided by entrepreneurs or risk takers.
- To say "All the best locations for cities are taken" is nonsense. With very few exceptions cities wax and wane independently of such factors as "best locations." Why is Detroit a "better location" than Port Huron or Toledo? Why did Pittsburgh stop growing in 1940? Why did New York outdistance Boston, Philadelphia, and Baltimore? Why did not "King Cotton" cause Savannah to grow to rival New York?
- If one plans a large new freestanding city, its geographic location will contribute somewhat to its success, but much more important will be the ability to attract and hold growth industry to provide an economic base.

1.6   Statistics on Six Medium-Size U. S. Cities

Detroit is perhaps a typical U. S. industrial metropolis. But metropolises themselves are not typical U. S. cities. Let us consider data that appears relevant to our purposes on six medium-size U. S. cities: Boston, Cincinnati, Dallas, Memphis, Norfolk, and San Francisco.[28]

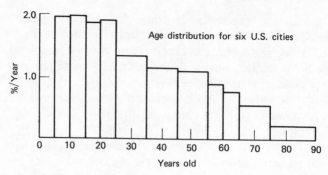

Figure 1.6 Age distribution of population in six U. S. cities (SOURCE: *U. S. Census of Population and Housing*, 1970).

Age distribution averaged over these six cities is shown in Figure 1.6. We note the recent decline in births and consequently the reduced need for lying-in hospitals and schools, as well as decreased demand in the future for four- and five-bedroom homes, even among the well-to-do. In a city of 1 million, from 20 to 24 percent of the population are between 6 and 18 years of age. This sets an upper limit on schoolroom spaces. If instructional television is widespread, this number can be reduced significantly. Approximately one-half of the 8 percent between 18 and 22 will want post-high-school education. These 40,000 people will be divided evenly between junior colleges and the university if present national trends continue. Thus 20,000 spaces should be provided in community colleges and the same number in the university.

In Figure 1.7 is shown the *distribution of jobs*. Notice that only about 28 percent of the jobs in the city are directly concerned with manufacturing a product. Yet it is generally assumed that these are the jobs that provide the driving force for the city. All the other jobs (construction, retail trade, services, etc.) derive from the activity provided by manufacturing. Why is this so? Because only manufacturing is considered to provide a product for export from the city. All other jobs provide a product or service consumed on site. This is not true in detail, however; Hartford, Connecticut, is an important insurance center, for example, and most of the workers in that activity export a service from Hartford. Transportation centers export transportation service in the same sense.

In regard to *families,* persons per household, according to the census, are not the same as persons per family. See Table 1.4. If primary individuals (people living alone) are not considered as a family, then total population divided by number of families is higher than the average number of persons per household. The number of families divided into

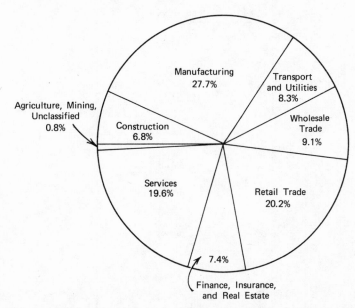

Figure 1.7   Job distributions in five U. S. cities, Boston excluded because data are incommensurate.

total population shows an average of 4.1, yet the average number of persons per household is about 3.25. Approximately 12.8 percent of the households are headed by females in our six cities. This seems to indicate a large need for day-care centers if these women are to be able to work to support their families. Perhaps neighborhood day-care centers, each staffed by a professional person assisted by local mothers in rotation, constitute a good arrangement. If so, jobs should be arranged to fit this schedule. Primary individuals are in significant number. Their housing needs are different from those of families. Another significantly large group consists of people on Social Security benefits, and their impact on the society should also be considered.

In respect to *housing,* a vast majority of Americans express a preference for single-family housing that they own if they can afford it. Since many can't a large portion of our population live in rented multiple-family dwellings. Figure 1.8 shows that just over 56 percent of the housing in our six sample cities is owned by the occupant. It is not surprising that the average income of home owners is significantly higher than that of renters.

The 56 percent figure fails to show the rapid growth in the mobile home category. Some years ago *Business Week* said:

Table 1.4 Selected Population Characteristics for Six Cities From the 1970 United States Census

Population Characteristics	City						
	Boston	Cincinnati	Dallas	Memphis	Norfolk	San Francisco	Average
Total population	2,753,700	1,384,851	1,555,950	770,120	680,600	3,109,519	1,709,123
Number of whites	2,602,741	1,228,776	1,296,469	478,709	504,471	2,574,802	1,447,661
Number of blacks	127,035	152,333	247,181	288,913	167,943	330,107	217,252
Number of persons per family	3.09	3.15	3.10	3.3	3.24	2.79	3.22
Total population Number of families	4.16	4.16	3.9	4	4.25	4	4.08
Percentage of female heads of families	14	11	10	16	14.5	12	12.8
Percentage of primary individuals	7	6	6	5	4.5	10	6.4
Percentage on Social Security	9.9	9.5	7.2	8.4	6.8	9.2	8.5
Percentage aged between 18 and 22 years	8	7	7	8.5	11	8	8.25
Percentage aged between 6 and 18 years	22	30	23	30	26	25	26

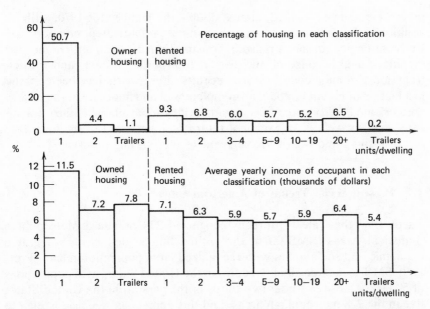

Figure 1.8   Housing characteristics of six U. S. cities (SMSA). (Source: Table A-6 HC(2)-152, *U. S. Census*, 1970.)

This year, [mobile home] sales will near the $3 billion mark. One in every two single family homes sold (1970) will be a mobile home—up from one in five in 1966. . . . Industry officials now expect to sell 475,000 units in 1970, and 1 million in 1975. . . . Last year (1969) over 90% of all new single family homes under $15,000 were mobile homes.[29]

Three implications of this trend appear important to designers of the new city:

● Privacy is important to purchasers of so-called mobile homes, which actually are not mobile at all.

● Mobile homes are financed in the same way as automobiles, rather than being mortgaged like conventional houses. This added flexibility is important.

● The industrialized housing industry is in existence, selling to a well-developed market, and is called the mobile home business.

Despite a slow start, industrialized production of housing parts appears to be another rapidly growing segment of the housing industry. The National Association of Building Manufacturers estimates it is presently a $7 billion industry with a growth potential of 20 percent annually. *Business Week* estimates that approximately 500,000 prefabricated housing units were shipped in 1972, almost double the number for 1970, with an additional 500,000 units containing some prefabricated components. Early attempts at industrialized construction of complete homes or modules failed because of unexpected transportation costs and recalcitrant local zoning codes. More recently the growth has been in the production of precut lumber and complete wall and floor panels, as well as prefabricated utility cores. Significant savings are available to the ultimate consumer, as well as an excellent return on investment to the manufacturer, in this rapidly growing segment of the housing industry.[30]

1.7 Present Social Trends of American Cities[31]

As of 1967 the Census Bureau recognized 228 Standard Metropolitan Statistical Areas (SMSAs) in the United States, defined as integrated economic and social units with recognized large population nuclei. Presently SMSAs include all of the cities in the United States with populations of 50,000 or more.[32] About two-thirds of the persons in the United States live in the 228 metropolitan areas, and this percentage seems destined to increase to about 71 percent by 1985. Forty-one percent of the nation's population is concentrated in the 38 largest SMSAs, and these account for one-half of *all* local government finances. Although direct federal aid to cities is increasing, about 95 percent of local government expenditures comes from local taxation, with about one-third of this amount from property taxes. Although cities are expensive to govern (about one-third more costly than local government outside of metropolitan regions), they contribute much more to the state and federal coffers than is returned, according to the Douglas Commission. In other words, state and federal governments make a "profit" from the cities.[33] Within the 228 metropolitan areas, 20,745 separate local governments exist—an average of 91 governments per SMSA. Some SMSAs have a single government (so-called metropolitan rule), whereas others such as Chicago have as many as 1313 separate jurisdictions. Sixty percent of the SMSAs cover areas smaller than 2 square miles, and 80 percent have less than 4 square miles. The series C census projection estimates a 40 percent increase in U. S. population from 179 million in 1960 to 252 million in 1985. The nonwhite increase will be 37 percent in this same period.[34] Eighty percent of the projected growth of 65 million will occur within the 228 SMSAs if present trends continue.

The central cities already contain half the nation's nonwhite population and will have an even larger share in the future. If past trends persist, by 1985 more than three-fourths of all U. S. Negroes will live in metropolitan areas, and 58 percent in central cities. It is expected that by 1985 New Orleans, Richmond, Chicago, Philadelphia, St. Louis, Detroit, Cleveland, Baltimore, and Oakland will join Newark, Gary, and Washington, D. C., in having a black majority in the central city. Black migration from the rural South to northern cities will continue but at a much slower pace, and so also will the white migration to the suburbs. In 1960 the central cities held a small numerical advantage over their surrounding suburbs. By 1968 the central city population was only 85 percent of that of the suburbs and by 1985 will decline to 58 percent.

Even with a declining birth rate, the United States will have an increase in the total population by 1985. . . . There will be a sizable increase by 1985 in the number of young people, especially nonwhite young people, at the most vigorous age. Taken with the projected continued concentration of the poor and the nonwhites in the central cities, this is one of the most potentially important domestic trends of the next several decades.[35]

While the number of poor is declining in the United States, both proportionally and numerically, the white poor are declining more rapidly than the nonwhite poor. Thus, while the urban black may be better off than he was some time ago, he sees himself as losing ground with respect to his white suburban neighbor. Although in 1967 there were twice as many white poor as black poor,[36] 41 percent of the nonwhite population was poor and only 12 percent of the white population was so defined. The proportion of relatively well-off families has increased among blacks in recent years, but there has been a similar rise among whites. See Figure 1.9.

For 20 years nonwhite unemployment has consistently been twice as great as white unemployment, with young blacks at a still further disadvantage. Although the poor are concentrated in central cities, not only because housing costs are lower but also because lack of mobility requires that they live near their jobs, an increasing number of jobs are located in the suburbs. The trend of commercial and industrial construction out of the central city is increasing. More than half of commercial construction and 60 percent of industrial construction was outside the central city in 1968. Census data for five large metropolitan areas show an increase of 28,000 new jobs from 1951 to 1965 in the central cities and over 1,000,000 new jobs in their suburbs. Not only does it take longer for the poor city resident to commute out to these suburban jobs, but also transportation may cost $10 to $15 additional per week.

Subsidized housing for the urban poor is a controversial subject, but the actual balance of benefits is not widely appreciated. Up to 1968 over $7 billion of federal funds had been spent on urban renewal. What has been

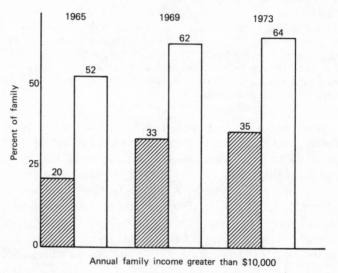

Figure 1.9   Proportion of U. S. families with annual incomes above $10,000. (SOURCE: U. S. Bureau of the Census.)

the distribution of benefits? To take at random one year, 1962, the federal government spent an estimated $820 million to subsidize housing for the poor. This includes public housing, public assistance, and savings from income tax deductions. Of the entire U. S. population the poorest 20 percent received this $820 million in housing subsidies, while the richest 20 percent received $1700 million in tax deductions for housing. In the 20 years after World War II, 24 percent of all housing starts in the nation or over 7 million units were aided by FHA and VA financing. Less than 10 percent of this help went to poor and near-poor families (below $6000 annual income). Essentially *none* of this aid went to those with less than $3600 annual income. Thus it seems fair to say that most federal housing aid has gone to the *non*poor.

It seems likely that the public housing controversy is based more on a clash of values than on any objective rationale. For example, outcries against graft, shoddy construction practices, lack of maintenance, and the like in public housing projects have attacked the program, and some of these complaints have been justified. Yet, as early as the Housing Act of 1954, Congress began to require careful neighborhood planning and mandated a move away from isolated "projectitis," and in 1961 the requirements for planning, dubbed "workable programs," were stiffened. The seven elements of a workable housing program were defined by the Department of Housing and Urban Development (HUD) as follows:

- A plan for orderly growth of the city.
- Identification and analysis of neighborhoods that would include (but not be limited to) blighted or slum districts or those with defective housing.
- Modern and well-enforced police power measures controlling urban development, that is, building codes.
- Adequate organization for administering construction and operation.
- Financial capability to meet requirements for local grants and costs of improvement.
- Arrangements for relocating displaced families and businesses.
- Means of assuring public participation in planning.

Many communities would not or could not meet these requirements, however, and it was necessary to adopt a policy of gradual enforcement if action was to be obtained. It was estimated by the Douglas Commission that a minimum total need of about 11 million housing units existed in 1968 to replace dilapidated shelter and to relieve the stress in adequate but overcrowded units. In other words, about 40 million U. S. citizens presently exist in unsatisfactory shelter. Only about 20 percent of the estimated housing needs of the poor have been addressed by actual programs through 1968, the Douglas Commission estimates.

Even so, massive and disruptive demolitions and housing removals have taken place. The commission reports a National Home Builders Association estimate that 2.38 million units were demolished by public action from 1950 to 1968, and private action added 2.35 million units to this list. The demolition of approximately 5 million housing units in this period displaced approximately 20 million persons—mostly poor and black, one can estimate. Relocated families found their rents higher and were forced to allocate an increased portion of their means to rent. Urban renewal, plus the construction of urban freeways through neighborhoods, surely contributed to urban unrest in the recent past. Up to 1968, of some

21,000 families known to have been displaced by urban freeway construction, only 12 percent had applied for relocation assistance. Of this small percentage a still smaller portion actually received financial aid.

Although claims of lavish public aid to the urban poor are manifestly out of proportion and indeed facts show that the middle and upper classes have profited more than the poor from federal largesse, large sums *have* been spent and the cities continue to deteriorate. It was estimated in 1972 that 25 percent of all dwelling units in central St. Louis have been abandoned. Block after block in this city could now represent the no man's land envisioned for sometime in the future by the science fiction writer Heinlein in his pessimistic novel.[37] Pruitt-Igoe, for example, a high-rise renewal project for 3500 families, built at an estimated cost of over $50 million, has been completely abandoned for several years, although, as stated earlier, it received the prize of excellence from the American Institute of Architects upon its opening less than a decade ago. It was recently suggested that more money be spent on explosives to blow off the top several stories of each building and thus convert the project to low-rise and lower-density units. Obviously, urban renewal has gone wrong. Why? The following are some possible answers.

- Until recently, federal standards enforced racial segregation.[38]
- High-rise, low-cost public housing has been crowded into the central city, thus contributing to its racial and financial segregation.
- Urban freeway construction failed in almost all cases to consider neighborhood integrity.
- Urban freeway construction proceeded in almost all cases without regard to displaced families, and with but few exceptions no relocation assistance was rendered.
- Widespread graft and deliberate embezzlement in low-cost housing rentals and sales, with the connivance of HUD officials in many cities, has been admitted by former Secretary Romney.
- The Douglas Commission specifically indicts public housing construction for the "unconscionable amount of time consumed in the process."
- More than 75 percent of the projects took over 10 years to complete.
- Another major Douglas Commission indictment of urban renewal is that it has failed to help the poor and near-poor who have been displaced by renewal projects.

To describe the status quo with a few broad, sweeping generalizations is a necessary evil, although it cannot fail to annoy the expert. The thrust of the paragraphs above is that the large cities in the United States are becoming bigger, blacker, and poorer. There are countertrends of course, but these countertrends are generally minor and do not contradict the main thesis. Moynihan points out, for example,[39] that some urban blacks are making it. Young (husband 35 or under) black families outside the South in which both husband and wife work for a short time had *higher* incomes than equivalent white families. But Moynihan is not trying to tell us thereby that all is well. Indeed, by 1973 the short-lived advantage of this relatively small group of blacks had disappeared.

1.8 Why Is the American City in Trouble?

It seems that an economic analysis is all that is needed to yield the answer; nothing metaphysical or psychological is required. Industry and citizens have moved out of the city to save money. It is cheaper and more profitable to move to the suburbs, given present accounting rules for individuals and corporations. This is only an accounting artifice, however, and the artifice cannot be sustained indefinitely.

For industry a location outside the city limits permits it to avoid city taxes while still buying the services it needs. On a marginal accounting basis it may even appear to the city authorities that this is a good bargain. For example, an industry approaches a mayor of a small or medium-size city with the following proposition. "We will locate just outside the city line and thus avoid city taxes. However, we will pay for our utilities. Furthermore we will bring needed jobs to your city. Do you want us on those terms?" Chamber of Commerce members, most of whom are engaged in retail trade, can be counted on to endorse the proposition. Even if the fallacy of ignoring all but marginal costs is explained, the short-run benefits will be difficult to turn down. In larger cities no such explicit bargains need be struck.

A second benefit of a suburban location to industry is the lower cost of land and the absence of zoning restrictions. American industry must automate so as to minimize the labor content of its products. This dictates straight-through materials handling on a single floor. Thus plant floor space per worker continues to climb. Ancillary benefits such as free parking for employees are also important but not determinative.

Suburban plant locations would not be economically feasible, however, if transport costs incurred thereby counterbalanced the savings in taxes and land. Such is not the case for most industry. Indeed truck transport is often more economical than transport by rail or water, although this is not always obvious from a simple comparison of mileage rates. Nevertheless many other transport costs are reduced by truck transport, as the following examples indicate.

- Warehousing costs in regional distribution centers can be reduced by overnight door-to-door truck delivery.
- Pilferage at rail centers and docks is greater than need be expected in owned or leased highway trucks.
- Fixed transportation costs are minimized. No expensive rail sidings or docks need be maintained. The cost of maintaining the highway system is largely paid for by gas taxes on private automobiles.
- Flexibility is maximized. Only the transport that is needed at any time must be maintained.
- Trucks generally are faster, and thus perishables and market-volatile items go best over roads.

For the individual citizen a suburban home is also cheaper than an urban one. Housing contractors find suburban land cheaper to buy, and this translates into a lower-cost home. Lower taxes are also a factor in housing, as in industrial site location. Ancillary benefits such as having grass to mow and the availability of recreation opportunities are important but not determining. But what about increased transport costs? The typical auto owner does not amortize total costs. He is inclined to count only marginal operating costs. Moreover, gasoline costs for the typical journey to work are paid for by 5 minutes of labor. Surveys show that auto commuters perceive their costs as *cheaper* than those of mass transit,[40] as indeed they are on a marginal cost basis. A survey in Detroit a few years ago showed that typical auto commuters would have to be paid $2 to $5 daily to abandon their cars and utilize mass transit (i.e., a negative transit fare!).

Thus we can say that, for the individual family seeking housing and for the industry seeking a site, the value of a suburban location is much greater than its price, whereas the reverse is true for central city locations. Now that central cities have deteriorated so far, even free central city land would be too expensive to accept. Safety costs are higher, congestion and pollution costs are higher, and aesthetic values are lower in the central city.

Yet this is not a stable situation. The economic advantage of a suburban location for the individual and the corporation is based on the freedom to externalize many costs that should in fairness be borne. To put the matter more plainly, individuals and organizations that remain in the city and pay taxes subsidize in some measure the flight of others to the suburbs. Suburban dwellers do not pay their fair share of total costs if they are permitted to participate in urban benefits while paying only marginal costs. And this situation is bringing city after city to its knees.

Proposed solutions to the urban problem must account more fairly for total urban costs. New-towns-in-town or whatever other proposals are put forward should fairly reflect in their balance sheets the additional burden they place on the surrounding city. All too often federal funds are so restricted that they do not cover the full cost of accomplishing the project for which they are granted. If the grantee city realizes that its own funds must make up the deficit, this is perfectly fair. However, on a number of occasions the grantee fully recognizes its obligation only after the project is well underway. Thus a number of urban renewal efforts have stalled or failed entirely because the grantee city has been unable to fund its share of the effort. The various scenarios discussed in the following chapters must be subjected to this important economic validation if they are to avoid the same fate.

Notes and References

1. J. P. Gibbs (Ed.), *Urban Research Methods*, Van Nostrand, Princeton, N. J., 1961.
2. Jean Gottmann, *Megalopolis: The Urbanized Northeastern Seaboard of the United States*, Twentieth Century Fund, N. Y., 1961.
3. C. A. Doxiadis, *Emergence and Growth of an Urban Region*, 3 vols., Detroit Edison Co., Detroit, 1966.
4. G. Bibby, *The Testimony of the Spade*, A. A. Knopf, N. Y., 1956, p. 256.
5. Sir M. Wheeler, *Civilizations of the Indus Valley and Beyond*, McGraw-Hill Book Company, N. Y., 1966, p. 9.
6. L. Mumford, *The City in History*, Harcourt, Brace and World, N. Y., 1961. See also K. E. Boulding, "The City as an Element in the Instructional System," *Daedulus*, Fall 1968, p. 1111.
7. R. M. Adams, *The Evaluation of Urban Society*, Aldine Publishing Co., Chicago, 1966, p. 42.
8. J. E. Hardoy, *Pre-Columbian Cities*, Walker and Co., N. Y., 1973, p. 227.
9. F. Parkman, *The Conspiracy of Pontiac* (1891), The Macmillan Co., N. Y., 1962, p. 49.
10. Parkman, *loc. cit.*, pp. 53, 54.
11. R. L. Carneiro, "A Theory of the Origin of the State," *Science*, Vol. 169 (August 21, 1970), pp. 733–738.
12. A fairly complete theory of the size and spacing of regional service centers, called central place theory, has been developed by Christaller and is discussed in more detail below.
13. C. A. Doxiadis, *Ekistics*, Oxford University Press, N. Y., 1968.
14. Perhaps the first city to which we can put a name is Ur, in the Mesopotamian Valley. Archaeological evidence seems to indicate that in 3000 B.C. Ur had a population of about 10,000.
15. Mohenjo-Daro in the Indus Valley at about 2500 B.C. was 3 miles in circumference and is an example of a Class A settlement. This is the oldest known example of systematic town planning and had basically a gridiron shape. See Wheeler, *loc. cit.*, p. 19. See also A. Morris, *History of Urban Form*, G. Godwin, London, 1972.

16. C. A. Doxiadis, "Man's Movement and His City," *Science*, Vol. 162 (October 18, 1968), pp. 326–334.

17. See also R. L. Meier, *A Communication Theory of Urban Growth*, M.I.T. Press, Cambridge, 1962.

18. R. Vernon, *Metropolis 1985*, Anchor Books, Doubleday and Co., Garden City, N. Y., 1963, p. 99 et seq.

19. W. Christaller, *Central Places in Southern Germany*, Prentice-Hall, Englewood Cliffs, N. J., 1966.

20. Jean Gottmann, *Megalopolis*, Twentieth Century Fund, New York, 1961.

21. R. G. Albion, *The Rise of the New York Port, 1815–1860* (Scribners, 1959), Archon Books, Hamden, Conn., 1961.

22. C. A. Doxiadis, *Emergence and Growth of an Urban Region*, Vol. 1, p. 144. The Doxiadis Study of Detroit, now complete in three volumes, cost 5 years and $3 million. It is claimed to be the most complete study of an urban region ever made. The Doxiadis volume is the basic source for this section.

23. In certain respects Detroit is more similar to Pittsburgh in its dependence upon one industry than it is to Chicago. Detroit is the luckier of the two in that, whereas steel has not been a growth industry in the last few decades, the automotive industry has.

24. Pittsburgh now seems to recognize its problems. See *Economic Study of the Pittsburgh Region*, 4 vols., University of Pittsburgh Press, Pittsburgh, 1963.

25. This is not to say that a region should automatically reject the entry of basic industry. Such industry adds to the tax base *without* consequent heavy increase in local school levies due to an influx of new workers. However, one cannot count on such industry to solve existing unemployment problems.

26. Doxiadis, *Emergence and Growth of an Urban Region,* Vol. 1, p. 160.

27. C. Hirschfeld, *The Great Railroad Conspiracy*, Michigan State Press, East Lansing, 1953.

28. *U. S. Census of Population and Housing*, Government Publications Nos. PHC(91)-29 Boston, PHC(1)-44 Cincinnati, PHC(1)-52 Dallas, PHCCD-127 Memphis, PHC(1)-148 Norfolk, PHC(1)-189 San Francisco; *Census of Housing*, 1970, No. HC(1)-A1; *County Business Patterns*, CBP-70-06 California, CBP-70-23 Massachusetts, CBP-70-45 Texas. United States census data are available in great detail, and the difficulty is to avoid being swamped with them.

29. *Business Week*, January 24, 1970, p. 74.

30. *Business Week*, February 10, 1973, pp. 43, 44.

31. Most of the data in this section are drawn from *Building the American City*, Report of the National Commission on Urban Problems, the Douglas Commission, U. S. House Doc. No. 91-34, U. S. Government Printing Office, Washington, D. C., 1968. This is one of a number of excellent government studies on urban affairs. In the years since publication the urban situation has changed in some details but not generally for the better.

32. The Bureau of the Budget (!) establishes the definition and names for SMSAs. For details see the most recent issue of its publication, *Standard Metropolitan Statistical Areas*, U. S. Government Printing Office, Washington, D. C. 20402.

33. Revenue sharing, as initiated in 1972, partially redresses this imbalance.

34. Indigenous births in 1972 fell below the replacement level, but immigration maintained the population growth as positive. Even at or below replacement-level birth rates, the

population will continue to grow for some decades, until a stable age distribution is reached.

35. Douglas Commission, *loc. cit.*, p. 44.

36. As defined by the Social Security Administration. In 1967 a family of four with an annual income of less than $3335 was classified as "poor." By 1972 the poverty income level had climbed to $4137.

37. R. A. Heinlein, *I Will Fear No Evil*, G. P. Putnam Sons, N. Y., 1970.

38. See, for example, C. Abrams, "Discrimination, Federal Housing," in *The Language of Cities*, Viking Press, N. Y., 1961, p. 92.

39. D. P. Moynihan, "The Schism in Black America," *The Public Interest*, Spring 1972, No. 27, pp. 3–24.

40. P. M. Williams, "Low Fares and the Urban Transport Problem," *Urban Studies*, Vol. 6, No. 2 (February 1969), pp. 83–92.

2

System Analysis Methodology

The Peace Corps had no definition. Love or production, no one could tell which. The fact that everyone should be so confused struck me. There were a lot of general ideas about peace without specific ideas of what to do with the Peace Corps. . . . I believe the new directions have saved the Peace Corps overseas. Within six months [of the goal analysis] the regions were doing their jobs and we were getting more requests [for volunteers] from the countries.

JOSEPH BLATCHFORD, Peace Corps Director,
quoted in AP wire service article by Tom Seppy,
November 8, 1972

System: a complex unity formed of many often diverse parts subject to a common plan or serving a common purpose: an interdependence: a set of units combined by nature or art to form an integral, organic or organized whole: an orderly working totality: a coherent unification . . . .

Webster's Third International Dictionary, unabridged
Merriam-Webster, 1969

Major urban processes lending themselves particularly to systems analysis today are physical activities, such as transportation, waste disposal, and land use. The most important areas for future development will increasingly involve the human aspects of broad systems.

F. A. LINDSAY
Daedalus, Fall 1968, p. 1222

2.1 What Is a System?

A system is an interconnection of elements so organized as to aid in driving toward a defined goal. There are three operative elements to this definition. The first is the existence of a set of elements, that is, a group of objects with some characteristics in common. All the passengers who have flown in a Boeing 747 or all the books written on system theory form a set, but mere membership in a definable set is not sufficient to form a system according to our definition. Second, the objects must be interconnected or must influence one another. The members of a football team then might qualify as a system, since each individual's performance influences the other members. Finally, the interconnected elements must have been formed to achieve some goal or object. A random collection of people or things, even if they are in close proximity and thus influence each other in some sense, would not by this criterion form a meaningful system.

Implicit in the definition is an index of performance or a measure of accomplishment. It must be possible to estimate how well the system is doing in its drive toward the goal. Proper choice of an index of performance is crucial for successful system design. A measurable and meaningful index of performance is simple enough in concept, although one sometimes has difficulty in conveying its importance to a client. It may be complex in practice, however, to establish an index that is both measurable and meaningful. The temptation is to count what can be counted if what really matters seems indefinable. Much justifiable criticism has been directed at system analysts in this regard.[1]

Our definition of a system certainly permits components or, in fact, the entire system to be of living form. The complexity of biological systems and social systems is such that complete mathematical descriptions are difficult or even impossible with our present state of knowledge. We must content ourselves in such a situation with statistical or qualitative descriptions of the influence of elements one on another, rather than analytic and explicit functional relationships. This presents obvious objective obstacles, but also more subtle subjective difficulties. It requires maturity by the system team members to work across disciplinary boundaries when their disciplinary methodologies are different not only in detail but also in kind.

From the definition above we are forced to conclude that the words "system," "subsystem," and "parameter" do not have objective meanings independent of context. The electric utility of a region, for example, could be a system, could be a subsystem, or could establish the value of a parameter, depending on the observer's point of view of the situation. An engineer for the Detroit Edison Company could think of his electric utility as a system. Yet he would readily admit that it is a subsystem in the Michigan Utility Pool, which in turn is connected to the power pool covering the northeastern portion of the United States and eastern

Canada. On the other hand, the city planner can ignore the system aspect of Detroit Edison and think merely of it as supplying energy at a certain dollar cost. This is so if it is reasonable for him to assume that electricity can be provided in any reasonable amount to any point within the region. In this sense, then, the cost of electricity is a regional parameter.

That the function of an object and its relationship to neighboring objects depend on the observer's viewpoint must not be considered unusual. Koestler, for example, argues persuasively that this is true for *all* organisms as well as social organizations. For these units, which we have called systems, he coins the term "holon."

Koestler says:

But *"wholes" and "parts" in this absolute sense just do not exist anywhere,* either in the domain of living organisms or of social organizations. What we find are intermediate structures on a series of levels in an ascending order of complexity: sub-wholes which display, according to the way you look at them, some of the characteristics commonly attributed to wholes and some of the characteristics commonly attributed to parts. . . . The members of a hierarchy, like the Roman god Janus, all have two faces looking in opposite directions: the face turned towards the subordinate levels is that of a self-contained whole; the face turned upwards towards the apex, that of a dependent part. One is the face of the master, the other the face of the servant. This *"Janus effect"* is a fundamental characteristic of sub-wholes in all types of hierarchies.[2]

Simon Ramo, a very successful early practitioner of the system method, has written a small book in which he defines the method simply and directly and speculates on its application to urban problems we now face. *Cure for Chaos*[3] is highly recommended as a nontechnical introduction to the system method and its applications.

Case 2.1 Terminology Confusion. Because one often is introduced to system analysis in a specific context, it may be confusing to find subsequently the method used in an entirely different context. Engineering students, for example, may follow a "systems" curriculum that specializes in automatic control, communications theory, computer science, information retrieval, and the like and entirely excludes general system planning. Students of management may think of fiscal control or filing "systems" when they use the term "system analysis." We have sewage systems, social systems, and horse players' systems. Perhaps Koestler was wise to avoid the word "system" entirely, but then again he only renamed the problem. Here is an example of a dual use of the word "system" which resulted in initial confusion by members of a government advisory panel.

A panel of engineers was requested by the federal government to establish the future research and development needs in the field of high-speed ground transportation (HSGT).[4,5] The main panel originally conceived the study in a number of categories as shown in Figure 2.1. It soon became apparent to the "system" subpanel, however, that a number of the tasks which they were asked to consider fell into the category we have called general system planning. Such items as system integration, reliability, and system management surely must be so considered. Yet what about communications and control, the question of a single, overall control computer versus many individual machines, or the reporting of the position and velocity of individual vehicles? Just as surely these are more specific "systems." Thus the final report of the HSGT panel was organized as shown in Figure 2.2. This was a more functional arrangement and provided a simpler and more useful report.

2.2   The System Analysis Method: Six Major Phases

There are six major phases in a properly conducted system study.

- Determine goals of system.
- Establish criteria for ranking alternative candidates.
- Develop alternative solutions.
- Rank alternative candidates.
- Iterate.
- Action.

Determine Goals

The requirements governing a proposed system investigation are often unclear to the client.[6] Thus this problem definition phase is particularly critical to the ultimate success of the project. It may seem unlikely to the novice system analyst that the client would not understand his own problem. Perhaps an analogy to the patient–physician relationship will clarify matters. Most of the time, although not always, the patient knows he is sick. He has a list of symptoms, although he has no way of telling

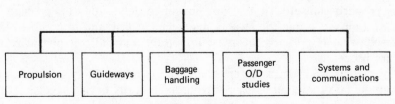

Figure 2.1   Original HSGT study concept.

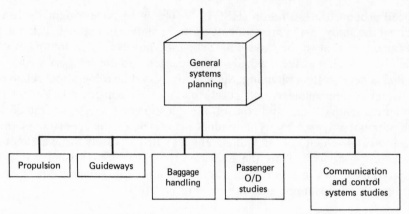

Figure 2.2   Final HSGT report formulation. Note dual use of the term "systems."

which are critical and which are less basic, though perhaps more obvious. But he does not know what questions to ask or data to gather or treatment to apply. The same is true in large-scale systems with major societal components.

A good example of the difficulty in extracting the real crux of a societal problem is the Appalachian program initiated by the President's Appalachian Commission Report of 1964 and funded by the Appalachian Regional Development Act of 1965. It would seem apparent that the problem in Appalachia is poverty and rural isolation, yet Rothblatt[7] points out that it took 2 years for the states within the Appalachian planning region to discover and articulate their planning goals. In the meantime over $450 million was expended on activities that were not necessarily integrated into the overall goals and plans that were finally accepted.

The fact that the client cannot define his own problem is particularly exasperating to the young theorist who may have been taught that one cannot handle a problem until it is completely defined. In practice the converse is true. *The system analyst must expect to engage in a dialogue with his sponsor to arrive at a suitable statement of a large-scale system problem.* The sponsor cannot present the analyst with a well-defined problem for analysis; rather, the analyst must expect to define the problem properly himself. To ask the sponsor to define fully his problem is to ask him to assume the system management task and to complete for himself what is perhaps the most important and difficult phase in the entire process.

Specialists who join a system team are especially likely to attempt to avoid the task of definition by referring to authority or by suggesting that other specialists be added to the team to address each new aspect of the overall problem as it becomes evident. Indeed the generalization process implicit in goal determination becomes so threatening to some specialists that they are unable to participate effectively and must withdraw from the team.

Establish Performance Criteria

To measure the performance of various candidate solutions one must have clearly established goals and constraints. The basis of comparison should be set before the search for candidate solutions is launched. This will often help to direct the search for candidates. Furthermore, if the candidate solutions are assembled before the performance criteria are set, there is a danger that analyst bias for or against a particular solution will unconsciously influence construction of the index of performance so as to influence the choice.[8] The client must be involved in developing the criteria and must give his final approval of those chosen. However, it is unlikely that the client will appreciate initially the centrality of establishing the criteria and to force this view upon him will be unproductive.

Examine Alternatives

This examination includes alternative solutions and alternative questions. Functional alternatives should be examined as well as technological ones. Walking, the horse, and the automobile may be functional alternatives, although they have little common technology. The videophone may be the functional equivalent of much business travel, yet the technology is quite unlike. A system analysis, to be effective, must order the alternatives by function rather than being limited to technical alternatives in the early, general planning phase. Finally, as the alternatives are narrowed, one generally arrives, of course, at specific comparisons among technological alternatives.

Rank Alternatives

The indices of performance and constraints are next applied to the list of candidates, and a rank ordering of their acceptabilities is developed. At this point a number of additional concerns, which are not normally listed as performance contraints, must be considered. Here are some examples of nonperformance concerns.

- *Effect on nonusers.* Questions such as noise insult and pollution come readily to mind, but more generally the analyst must ask whether a particular candidate solution results in a differential disadvantage to some group.

● *Effect of incremental introduction.* Many large-scale systems are so large that they must be introduced piecemeal. This can provide opportunities as well as disadvantages. A candidate that is critically dependent on complete installation before performance begins is very vulnerable.

● *Impact on existing system.* It is rare for an important system to be considered *de novo.* No doubt the existing solution is in many senses unsatisfactory or else the study would not have been authorized, but the cost of ignoring or removing the existing solution could be major. A plan that ignores such situations lacks contextual integrity.

● *Sensitivity of performance index to parameter variation.* Often a pseudo-optimal candidate appears that suffers significantly if certain of its parameters or constraints are revised slightly. Such a candidate lacks robustness and should not be highly ranked.

● *Ratification procedures.* The technical man sometimes imagines that he can fight free of political pressures and select the "best" system in a vacuum. This has probably never been the case, and most rational men know it. Indeed, one could argue that democracy demands a public ratification procedure.

● Other.

Iterate

After obtaining a group of prime candidates, one can initiate a more careful analysis of each and a more precise definition of the problem for the next iteration. One cannot expect to have a full appreciation of a meaningful system problem a priori. An attempt to do general system planning on a straight-through basis will generally delay project initiation, result in premature loss of options, waste money and time on portions of the problem later found to be irrelevant, reduce the probability of selecting the optimum candidate, and sometimes cause outright failure of the effort.

In a well-directed system study one expects to see a smooth and orderly narrowing and deepening of the analysis. A study that does not begin broadly enough, that fails to deepen in intensity of analysis as weak candidates are rejected, or that exhibits abrupt leaps from a general level to an extremely specific solution is generally suspect. A common question concerning this approach is, "How many times should we iterate?" The iteration process should narrow in smoothly to an optimum result. Each iteration clarifies and refines the solution but costs additional money. One stops when the additional cost of another iteration exceeds the probable benefit of the additional clarification. The suggested time scale of these iterations will be discussed further in Chapter 3.

Action

A systems study that ends with a report must be considered a failure. To achieve the client's real goals is the real success indicator. Thus the systems final report must have a strong action orientation as described below.

Notice that this is a problem-centered or a *goal-centered approach*, rather than a *technologically centered approach*. The classic story told and retold in operations research textbooks to clarify the distinction concerns the arming of Allied merchant vessels against enemy submarines in the North Atlantic during World War II. After several years it was noted that very few of these gun crews had actually sunk a submarine, and it was therefore proposed to remove them. A goal-centered operations research study, however, asked the purpose of the guns; was it to sink subs or rather was it to guard the freighters from surface attack by subs, thus reducing the freighters' vulnerability? The latter, of course, was the proper criterion, and the gun crews were found to be very effective in this sense.

We have just compared the goal-centered approach with a technology-centered approach. Another possible trap is the step-by-step or *chronological approach*. The goal-centered approach is, in a sense, a completely backward way of going at things. Instead of starting at the beginning, one starts at the end! What could be more logical than starting at the beginning of the problem and enumerating a list of chronological steps to be taken in order to solve it? This chronological or so-called laundry list approach involves, however, several major difficulties.

- Unless the goal is known precisely, the step-by-step approach may waste effort in developing task segments that turn out to be unneeded.
- Without the end point set for each subtask, a subtask may be elaborated upon to an unnecessary degree, thus wasting resources.
- Without a known end point, the specification of a vital subtask may be underestimated, thus incurring a performance deficiency.

Thus it seems that a goal-centered approach is superior to the two alternative methods more commonly utilized.

2.3   Seven Steps in Goal Development

The most difficult, unfamiliar and tension-producing phase in system analysis and the one to which ultimate success is most sensitive is the first: goal development. To organize this process we propose seven detailed steps.[9]

1. Generalize the question.
2. Develop a descriptive scenario.
3. Develop a normative scenario.
4. Elaborate the axiological component.
5. Prepare an objectives tree.
6. Validate.
7. Iterate.

Generalize the Question

The general system planner generalizes the question because he knows that the client seldom, if ever, understands his own problem. Generalization is needed to phrase the question correctly and, even more important, to place it properly in context. Lack of contextual integrity often frustrates planners who limit their concerns to technical solutions of socially relevant problems. The designer who applies a conventional engineering approach to urban freeways or high-powered automobiles or supersonic aircraft cannot help feeling a sense of bafflement when he completes his assignment successfully, only to have it rejected on other than technical grounds. He says, "But I gave you what you asked for!" Society is equally frustrated in this situation since, if it is honest, it realizes that it *did* ask for what the designer produced. Yet all concerned realize, after the fact, that something is very wrong. The client misinterpreted the problem, and the designer failed to appreciate this fact in time. Generalization attempts to avoid this difficulty.

Develop a Descriptive Scenario

Describe the situation as it is. Tell how it got that way. Point out the good features and the unacceptable elements of the status quo. This exercise will help to broaden and deepen one's understanding of the generalized problem. This is another attempt to give the work contextual integrity. One way to initiate this process of generalization and description is a group "brainstorming" session. A list of descriptive phrases can be generated quite quickly, and then the full prose narrative can be elaborated at leisure. Chapter 1 of this book is a descriptive scenario for a system study of the city.

Develop a Normative Scenario

Describe the situation as it will be when the project is fully operative. The normative scenario will preserve the positive features of the descriptive scenario and change as many of the negative features as possible. Thus the normative grows out of the descriptive. It need not be limited, however, to correcting existing deficiencies. In fact, the real purpose of dwelling on the preparation of this section is to encourage the group to build innovatively upon the descriptive scenario and to surpass it. We need encouragement to visualize the potentialities of the situation. This is not to say that we should ignore financial and physical limitations, but rather to point out that imaginative combinations will often reveal entirely new possibilities not contained in mere extrapolations. Here again a group interaction session with the usual prohibition on expressing negative thoughts is one way of obtaining an initial list of normative phrases.

Elaborate the Axiological Component

The normative scenario lists conditions as they should be when the project is complete. Thus it contains within it a value system. This set of values initially may be implicit and possibly incomplete or conflicting. Furthermore, many people initially find it somewhat difficult to articulate such matters. To talk about values may seem to some to be attacking them. Others may find such a discussion boring or irrelevant. Indeed, for some well-specified problems such a discussion would be unnecessary, but the well-specified problem is the *result* of general system planning and does not precede it. After an initial difficulty in starting the discussion, we would expect to have an intense involvement and possible disagreements within the group. Since it will be apparent to all that the initial value set is inadequate, it will be difficult to proceed to the next phase. Maximum progress seems to occur, however, if the group rapidly passes on to the fifth step and does not resolve any tensions incurred by the value discussion. It may seem that a more logical way of proceeding would be to set down a consistent set of operative values and from them to deduce a normative scenario. Then one could note the differences between specific items in the normative list and the existing situation and from this list form specific action tasks. Unfortunately such a consistent set of values does not exist.

An important reason for articulating the values implied in the normative scenario is to sensitize the analysis group to its members' values. It must be remembered that the client's values are not to be overridden by those of the analyst. Caution is advised, however, in opening the discussion of values with the client in the early phase of analyst–client interaction, since the client may feel more threatened by questions of value than by nonaxiological matters. If the analyst places too great an emphasis on questions of value early in his relationship with the client, he will risk being thought impractical and possibly incompetent.

Prepare an Objectives Tree

The objectives tree is a chart of objectives, having the most general at the top and becoming more specific as it branches below. The statements in the boxes should be action statements or goals. Questions, difficulties, and the like are out of place in the chart. The objectives chart should be a graphical presentation of the goals and values obtained in the previous steps. However, we usually find that this elaboration reveals new goals or values that were not apparent previously. Generally speaking, the system group will experience little difficulty in beginning the objectives tree, but problems grow as the work progresses. Thus the situation is the reverse of that encountered with the axiological component. Among the things to watch for are the following:

- Make the general goal concrete and related to the problem. Do not let it become merely a vague platitude.
- Allow space for future expansion of the tree by including an "other" box at each level.
- Do not become sidetracked by including goals of the group or of the study. The objectives tree should show the client's goals and be action oriented.

Validate

The first five steps should be developed quickly, possibly in a single group session. Then at a more leisurely pace a validation phase may be completed. Initially, validation may merely be individual evaluation of the material produced by the group. In later iterations the client should be allowed to react to the objectives, and consideration should be given to open hearings on the objectives of a public system.

Iterate

The results of the first group session on objectives or norms must not be expected to be useful as is. A group should not feel obligated to the material that it has developed in the first iteration. The first run-through should be regarded merely as a thought starter. Thus the group should not allow itself to be bogged down in the first run-through. Several iterations on goal development constitute an important feature of the first phase in general system planning.

2.4   Graphics in System Analysis

To this point we have been discussing system philosophy and the general system analysis strategy (see Figure 2.3). Now we turn to detailed tech-

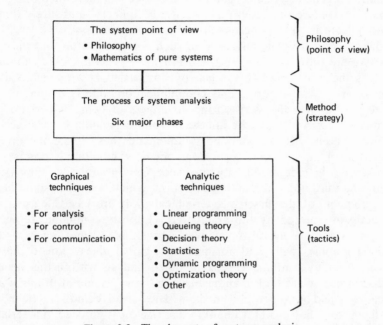

Figure 2.3   The elements of systems analysis.

niques or tactics. Techniques can be divided into two broad categories, graphical and analytic. Graphical tools can be made to serve three different and distinct functions.

● Communication.
● Analysis.
● Management and control.

Graphics for Communication

One of the marks of an intellectual discipline is the code that its members develop for communicating with one another. Sometimes it is obvious that a code is in use. Special words or symbols have been invented, the meanings of which are revealed only upon initiation. Mathematics is a well-developed example of this sort. A more subtle communication code is the sort that is not obvious as a code at all. It uses standard symbols but in a special way, so that a surface meaning seems clear to the layman but a deeper meaning is inferred by the cognoscente. Rock music lyrics are said to contain primitive elements of this style.

Communication within a system study presents a special problem. By definition a general system planning effort involves more than one discipline. The study group itself may be interdisciplinary, and surely it must communicate its results across disciplinary boundaries.

Three codes are generally used in such communication, but only the first two are fully accepted as such. For most of us the third, although perhaps the most powerful, is generally regarded as a mere auxiliary. First is the narrative form. This communication code is redundant and imprecise but has the very strong advantage of being understood, in elementary form at least, by almost the entire population. The second form is the analytic or symbolic. Mathematics has almost the inverse properties of the narrative form. Mathematic symbology is precise and compact but is understood only after specialized training. Graphics constitute the third and often underrated form, which combines some of the best elements of the first two. Graphical tools are easily learned and correctly interpreted by the uninitiated. Graphics communicate across disciplines and are useful for analysis as well as in reporting.

Good graphics will yield an immediate global impression to the observer, and they continue to repay detailed analysis with further insight. Perhaps this is what McLuhan means by a "cool" medium. It might also be called a field or holographic medium. The narrative and analytic modes are linear (or "hot" to McLuhan) in that one must proceed in a serial or linear fashion to the end whether he wishes full details or not.[10]

Certain professions are critically dependent for their successful continuation on communication across group boundaries. It seems more than a coincidence that in the two professions in which communication across professional boundaries is vital to continued existence the graphical mode of communication has been raised to the status of a high art form. In any architectural presentation or brochure, multicolored pictures abound. Maps, charts, and pictorial renderings form the heart of such documents. Robert Sommer, an industrial psychologist often called upon to consult with architects on spatial arrangements, remarks that he has found by experience that one must show pictures if he is to communicate with architects. He says[11] that he has learned to carry with him a book of photographs to illustrate his meanings in such consultations, although he admits puzzlement as to just why they should be needed.

For the advertising man the client presentation is the payoff, and the attention he pays to every nuance of this activity is a modern-day legend. Graphics form a major portion of such presentations and, indeed, of advertising in general. Thus, in architecture and advertising, both professions in which communication is recognized as essential, graphics are paramount.

Graphics for Analysis

Large-scale systems are usually so complex and contain so many constituent elements that it is difficult to understand the interrelations among these elements without graphic aids. In the process of constructing the various graphic portrayals of a system under analysis, it has been the almost universal experience that one will begin to perceive new and perhaps unexpected insights. One's span of perception broadens to capture a feeling of the system as a whole. Different charts portray the whole from different but not conflicting points of view. Almost universally, however, the early forms of the various charts will later be found to show great gaps and conflicts. These gaps indicate initial faulty understanding and show that the graphical analysis has developed and improved understanding.

Graphics for Management and Control

As the graphics are developed, they reveal to the group and its leader the status of the project, the things that must be done next, and the percentage of accomplishment, along with the time remaining for various activities. This is a valuable aid for reducing the tension produced in a group that knows itself to be rapidly using both time and money and yet is unsure of its chance of successfully meeting the client's goals.

Many charts and diagrams will find their way into system analysis reports. Line graphs, bar graphs, and pie charts, for example, are familiar tools for representing statistics or numerical data. Organization charts are valuable for displaying organization hierarchies. In the following sections, however, we will stress four kinds of charts that are especially valuable in large-scale system analysis and at the same time are probably unfamiliar to the reader.

2.5 The Objectives Tree[12]

The objectives tree is a graphic display of the goals of the system study. A particular form of intent structure in the sense of Warfield, it will be found especially useful for helping the analysis team and the decision makers to clarify and organize a rational set of goals in the early stages of the effort.

Then in later phases the objectives tree helps in reporting progress and in maintaining a goal-directed effort while discouraging nondirected excursions. Let us first examine the theory of construction and then give several examples.

An objectives tree is a special form of a hierarchical logic structure, and it falls within the area of mathematics called graph theory. It is possible to develop an algorithmic approach to the construction of a hierarchical tree, once elemental goal statements are given.[13] This procedure may be desirable in exceedingly complex analyses that contain dozens of elemental goal statements. It is also recommended as a check on the correctness of the formal logic in a graph constructed by hand. We will not pursue the pure theory of trees beyond referring to Warfield, however, for the following reasons:

- Manual construction of the objectives tree serves to stimulate the analysis team to broaden its concept of the problem and to create an attitude of initiation and creativity among the team members.
- To construct an objectives tree is also to begin thinking about interactions of activities and the relation of objectives to a value structure. Both these matters will become team concerns in subsequent phases. In effect we recommend here that one not let the computer do his thinking for him.
- To aid in communicating the goals of a large-scale planning effort to decision makers, interested observers, and involved citizens, it is desirable to keep the tree simple. Hand construction of the tree serves this purpose by causing the participants to think through and compress their objectives during analysis.

Statement Format

A first step in tree construction is to state tentative elemental objectives in proper form. Warfield suggests the following semantic structure:

To (ACTION WORD) + (OBJECT) + (QUALIFYING WORDS)

Here are several elemental objectives expressed in proper form:

(a) To (Kill) (Rats) (In the city).
(b) To (Improve) (Urban life-style) (For all Americans in this decade).
(c) To (Eliminate) (Racial Prejudice) (In the cities).
(d) To (Prevent) (Police brutality) (   ).

Each of these examples of elemental objectives is semantically acceptable as an isolated statement and would be processed by a computer algorithm for objectives tree construction. They are typical also of early thinking by inexperienced urban analysts in that they are disordered, vague, improperly qualified, incomplete, and subjective. We will see momentarily how the process of tree construction will address the questions of incompleteness and possible conflict. Now, however, let us improve these statements by making each tighter, more objective, and more specific. We need not strain for perfection, since the whole system analysis process is iterative. The specific goal statements and their hierarchical arrangement should be subject to continual examination and improvement as the study progresses. Even at this early stage we can see that one wants to kill rats with minimum side effects and low cost, that to aspire to improve the life of all citizens is a lofty but unattainable goal, that it is more practical to seek to "reduce" objective discrimination than to "eliminate" a prejudicial mind set, and that "police brutality" is a rather inflammatory term. Here are suggested revisions for each of the original four examples:

(*a'*) To (Reduce impact of) (Rats) (Economically and safely).

(*b'*) To (Improve) (Urban life-style) (For many Americans in this century).

(*c'*) To (Reduce) (Racial discrimination) (In housing patterns).

(*d'*) To (Ensure) (Fair, equitable law enforcement) (For all groups).

Here are some aids to constructing elemental objectives:

- Use of proper semantic form will assist in developing action-oriented statements.
- Difficulties are not goals, nor are non-goal-oriented studies acceptable.
- Do not be concerned with possible conflicts among suggested objectives or with polishing elements once they are in proper form.
- Do not worry that some goal statements are too general or too specific.
- Goals that display biases of specific team members are acceptable initially.

Tree Structure

The second step is to arrange the elemental goal statements in hierarchical order. This is almost sure to be a difficult task initially but is often eased by asking the team members to print their statements on 3-inch by 5-inch cards and arranging the cards on a table. Some teams prefer to break up into subgroups of two or three members each to work on separate trees before combining the trees. What is sought is a hierarchical ranking of the goals with higher and more general goals above and more specific ones below. One should expect to experience difficulty in generating broad goals that at the same time do not become vague or fuzzy and promise all things to all men. Conversely, as the objective elements become more specific, one must guard against becoming too detailed in certain sectors while ignoring other sectors entirely. To satisfy the graph-theoretic definition of a tree, the objectives structure must not reenter or close. Rather, from one very general goal the structure opens outward as one proceeds down through branches showing more specific objectives. Sometimes one finds a specific objective that seems to fit into several branches, possibly at different levels. In such a case it is advisable to cast the two or more similar statements in somewhat different words to reflect the different higher objectives they serve, rather than closing the diagram on one statement. This not only seems to aid clarity but also permits computer verification of the logic should this be desired.

Four Tests of Objective Tree Logic

After the first few elemental objective statements have been written on cards and arranged in hierarchical order in accordance with the generality of the statement, one can apply four tests to the tree. These tests can be applied repeatedly as the arrangement is modified and statements are added. Each test should be made on each statement in the tree.

- Each goal statement should provide a more explicit and detailed goal than the statement above it in the hierarchy. It tells how one proposes to reach the immediately higher goal. Thus, reading *down* any branch, each goal statement must answer *how* for its immediately superior goal.
- Reading *up* any branch, each higher statement must answer *why* the goal below it is needed.
- Reading *across* the goals at a given level under any one general goal, ask whether *all* these more specific goals are needed to accomplish the more general goal.
- Reading *across* the goals at a given level under any one general goal, ask what *other* specific objectives at this level are needed to accomplish the more general objective.

Case 2.2   An Objectives Tree for Planting a Garden. Take a trivial example of an objectives tree to illustrate the method. We start by writing down objectives in planting a home garden as they occur to us.

(*a*) Buy fertilizer.
(*b*) Get hose out of cellar and connect up to outside water tap.
(*c*) To reduce food cost for family.
(*d*) To get regular, moderate exercise.
(*e*) Borrow George's rototiller.
(*f*) Plan garden layout and timing for planting.
(*g*) Buy seed.
(*h*) Get to work.

Before organizing a first hierarchy we can rewrite the statements in proper form.

(*a'*) To (buy) (fertilizer) (of proper kind and amount).
(*b'*) To (provide) (irrigation) (as needed).
(*c'*) To (reduce) (food costs) (for family).
(*d'*) To (provide) (exercise) (of proper kind and amount).
(*e'*) To (prepare) (soil) (properly).
(*f'*) To (plan) (layout and timing) (as needed).
(*g'*) To (buy) (seed) (of proper kind and amount).
(*h'*) To (follow) (plan) (expeditiously).

We now write the statements on cards and arrange them. Usually, but not always, the final qualifier of each objective is obvious and may be omitted for simplicity after the first conception. Also, it would seem that (*a'*) and (*g'*) could be merged, since both relate to obtaining raw materials, but we will leave them separate momentarily.

In Figure 2.4 is shown a first grouping of the objectives; analysis reveals some possible generalizations. Figure 2.5 shows a possible objectives tree that includes the generalizations evident from Figure 2.4. We have merged economy and exercise as a general goal, and rather than exercise we now use the term "healthful recreation." Note that planting a garden is not the only way of accomplishing this general objective. For example, one could accomplish it by adopting a stricter food purchasing plan and buying hiking shoes or bicycles or tennis rackets. Not only does the tree clarify the existence of alternatives; it also precludes other possible false goals. No objective has been included that permits use of the garden as a disciplinary measure for the children, for example. Notice also that over specific mechanisms tended to disappear as the iterations went on; George's rototiller is not mentioned in Figure 2.5. It still may be the best bet, but "prepare soil" allows for alternative approaches and specific means would appear in reading down from that box and asking, "How"? We note within the "labor" sector some timing interactions; one should

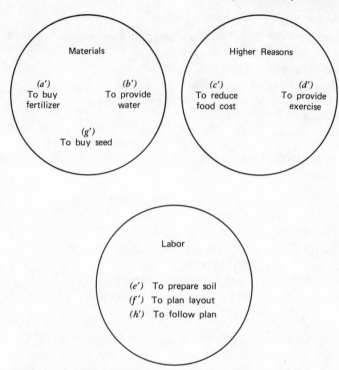

Figure 2.4 A first grouping of eight objectives in planting a garden.

"prepare soil" before "plant seed." Note also interactions at this level with other activities. For example, one should "buy seed" before "plant seed." But the objectives tree fails to reveal these interactions and the required time sequencing in a systematic way. Such information is available from the interaction matrix and the Gantt chart.

Case 2.3 Preliminary Objectives Tree for the New City. In a later chapter we will consider in some detail the system planning for a new city (NC). Here let us list some of the objectives for the new city that might be suggested in an early planning effort on this topic.

To develop a viable community.
To determine NC design parameters.
To develop multidisciplinary group planning methods.
To make money in land investment.
To select a site.
To prepare a NC development proposal for a federal agency.
To attract industry.

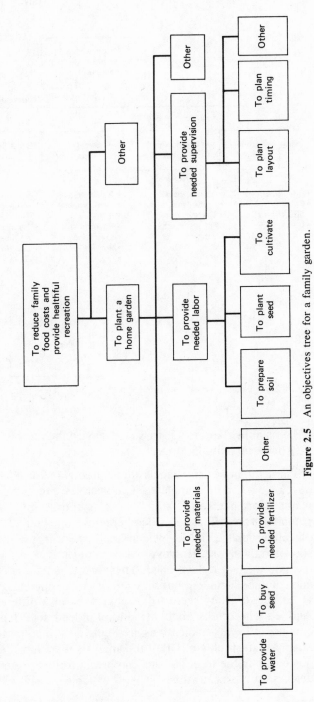

Figure 2.5 An objectives tree for a family garden.

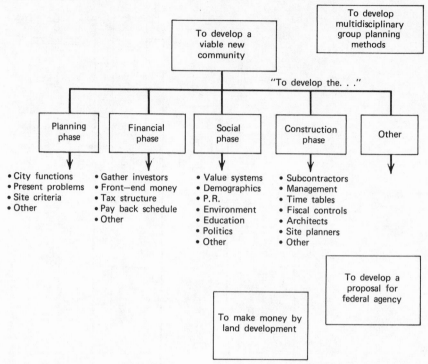

Figure 2.6 A partial objectives tree for the new city. See text for meaning of unconnected boxes.

To establish an attractive social environment.
(Approximately 45 more).

These might be arranged as shown in Figure 2.6. We will not emphasize developing a more complete NC objectives tree here, since this will be a major effort later on. Rather, we concentrate on a new difficulty. The planning group effort described here developed many specific and general objectives that could be placed somewhere in the main objectives tree shown in the figure. However, several objectives of the kind shown off to the side were also developed. These were general enough and important enough to be included, but they fail to satisfy one or more of the four tests given above. They seem to be objectives of a different *kind* somehow. And, as one thinks about it, this is indeed so. Thus far we have not emphasized *whose* objectives are being described by the tree. But this is an important problem. Often the analysis team includes its own personal objectives in the tree, but this can be controlled to some extent by group discussion; also, at a later stage this subjectivism will be rooted out by client discussions and in public presentations. On the other hand, some valid objectives do not find a place in the tree because of failure to keep firmly in mind whose objectives are being diagrammed. There are valid internal objectives for a new city planning team, such as making money and selling contract proposals, but these are hardly the objectives of a federal agency that might wish to build such a city. To make money in land development might not be an objective of a planning team, nor will it be an objective of a federal agency. However, it certainly would be an objective of a Rouse Company or Levitt or Boise-Cascade or Chase Manhattan Bank. Thus one must keep clear *whose* objectives a tree portrays and, at a minimum, develop separate trees for the planning group's internal objectives and those of the proposed client.

2.6   The Interaction Matrix

We have already noted that the objectives tree aids greatly in clarifying and organizing the goals of the project. But it does not illustrate in a systemic manner the *interrelations* between various goals and activities. Although an interaction analysis does not hold quite the same prime importance as establishing the goals of the effort, it is nevertheless of basic interest, since in considering the interactions among goals or activities one is forced to consider these objectives themselves from still another viewpoint. This provides another opportunity to reorganize or redefine the goals or activities if the need is revealed by the interaction analysis.

There is still another reason for the importance of the interaction matrix. The system team has a tendency to fragment itself as soon as the subtasks are assigned. Each subtask group will pursue its subgoal to the exclusion of all other considerations; thus certain subtasks may be developed well beyond the needed detail, while at the same time articulation with other groups will be ignored. The tendency to fragment and specialize has occurred in *all* system studies directed by, participated in, or observed by the author. This includes studies over a wide range of topics and with participation by almost every identifiable profession. It seems to be a general cultural trait to concentrate on specifics and to ignore interrelations. Yet in a general system study these interrelations are the central concern. Experts can usually be found with a deep and intimate knowledge of any specific activity one cares to name, but just as a group of skilled musicians cannot create great music without coordination and direction, knowledgeable specialists alone cannot provide a well-balanced system study. A properly conducted system study concentrates on goals and interactions. Specific topics are developed in sufficient detail only to permit the interactions, constraints, specifications, goals, and the like to be determined.

Here is another way of emphasizing the central importance of interactions among the elements of a system. We know from the mathematics of stability theory that it is possible for components which behave perfectly when separate to become violently unstable when allowed to interact as a system. Perhaps this is not too surprising, since we see the evidence all about us in the city. But what may be more surprising is that modifying the interactions of an unstable or unsatisfactory system without otherwise disturbing its components can lead to stable and effective performance of the modified system.

Figure 2.7 shows an interaction matrix of some of the important elements in a new city design. The shading scheme indicates a light, medium,

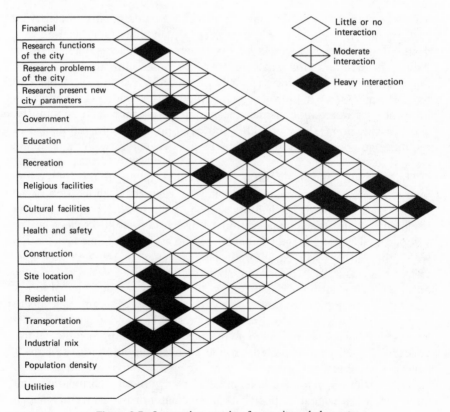

Figure 2.7 Interaction matrix of new city subelements.

or heavy interaction. This chart was the product of an initial system group meeting and thus provides an example of the team interaction process as well as the mechanics of building the matrix. Perhaps the most important use of the interaction matrix is to draw attention to the close coupling of certain pairs of elements, thus increasing the probability that decisions made concerning one element will take into consideration the effect of this coupling.

For example, Figure 2.7 shows that the design group expects "population density" to be heavily affected by "transportation" and "residential" design. It also interacts moderately with a number of other sectors. This indicates that one should not attempt to arrive at decisions on transport modes without knowledge of population density projections and the design of residential sectors. By analyzing the matrix, one can often find clusters of elements that seem tightly tied to one another, indicating that the design of the units in such a cluster must be very carefully integrated. Another insight may be gained by scoring the weighted interactions of each sector with all other sectors. This ranking will indicate quite clearly the most critical and sensitive sectors.

This particular matrix must not be taken too seriously. The product of only a few hours of discussion by an inexperienced team, it displays several rather important deficiencies that will be corrected in a later iteration.

One difficulty is implicit in the technique itself. We find that the reasoning behind a particular interaction weight is not apparent from the chart. Thus it is strongly recommended that a narrative discussion accompany the matrix when it is used for communication.

2.7   The DELTA Chart[14]

Network planning methods such as PERT and CPM have been in common use for a number of years. Such flow charts have been found useful in organizing the sequence of activities that must be carried out in order to complete a large-scale project. However, these network methods suffer from certain deficiencies when used in planning studies.

- Typical network methods such as PERT, although adequate for depicting and controlling a deterministic sequence of well-defined activities, do not conveniently allow the flexibility required for planning studies.
- Such methods have a limited and perhaps confusing vocabulary that tends to constrain thinking.

- Most network methods do not conveniently allow for alternatives, decisions, and logic, thus promoting a tendency to plan for only a single, most-likely approach.
- The lack of decision points in CPM and PERT fosters a tendency to total-package bidding of large projects and a loss of control during execution of the effort.

After pointing out these deficiencies, Warfield and Hill propose an improved network scheduling method, called the DELTA method, designed to correct them. The basic DELTA chart uses the five symbols in Figure 2.8. An additional feature of the DELTA chart is a precise syntax to aide in distinguishing "events" from "activities." An *event* is struc-

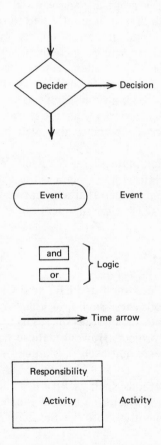

Figure 2.8   The five basic elements for a DELTA chart.

tured as a noun or object followed by a verb or action phrase followed by qualifiers. Table 2.1 gives some examples.

Table 2.1   *Proper Syntax for Expressing "Events"*

OBJECT +	ACTION PHRASE +	QUALIFIERS
Rats	Killed	In city
Seeds	Planted	In garden

The proper form for *activities* consists of a verb followed by an object followed by constraints or qualifiers. Table 2.2 gives some examples.

Table 2.2   *Proper Syntax for "Activities"*

ACTION VERB +	OBJECT +	CONSTRAINTS
Kill	Rats	In city
Plant	Seeds	In garden

The proper syntax for *objectives,* it will be recalled, is the infinitive form of a verb followed by the object followed by qualifiers. Warfield and Hill discuss more complex forms of the five basic elements of the DELTA chart and additional auxiliary elements are also added, but this basic form seems sufficient for our purposes. Rather than dealing in theoretical complexities, then, let us consider several examples.

In Figure 2.9 is shown two DELTA charts for the family garden. Two alternative diagrams for the same activities serve to demonstrate that a DELTA chart is not unique. Note also that the amount of detail shown is a matter of choice. For example, every activity box in Figure 2.9 could be preceded and followed by "start" and "finish" event ovals. We have chosen to show only a few events for simplicity.

Case 2.4   The Urban Rat Control Problem. Rats like cities as well as people do, and it has been estimated that in metropolitan areas such as New York City the rat population exceeds the human population. Almost a thousand rat bites of infants are reported annually in New York City, and these reported cases surely represent only a tiny proportion of the real total. Rats do millions of dollars damage annually and destroy crops, stored food, and other animals, as well as attacking human beings. Moreover, rats are known carriers of more than two dozen diseases and vermin.

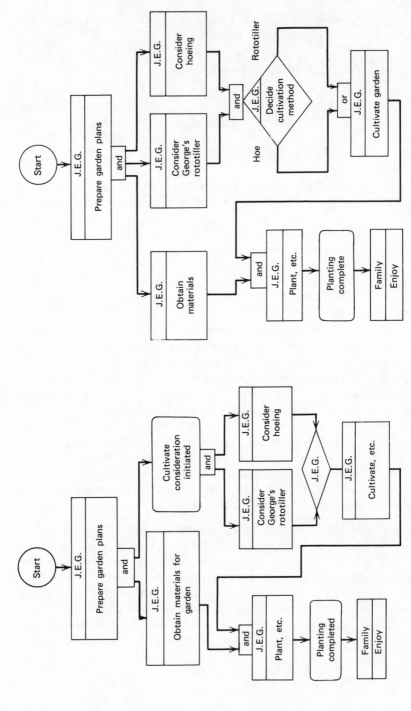

Figure 2.9 DELTA charts for developing a home garden. Two alternative diagrams for the same process are shown.

Millions have been spent on extermination programs, and there is no shortage of imaginative schemes for the elimination of rats. Suppose, however, that there is lacking a careful, scientific comparison of known rat control methods in regard to cost effectiveness, permanency, and lack of dangerous side effects. Let us construct a DELTA chart for such a project. A detailed comparison of *all* proposed extermination techniques, using the best operation research methods, should be made. This study should include dynamic simulation using computer models of these rat control methods. The prime candidates that emerge from this cross-comparison will be employed in a full field test using operational personnel from the city, which will be a full partner in this study. Use of city employees will ensure a practical, workable methodology as opposed to a theoretical, nonimplementable approach. Figure 2.10 shows a proposed DELTA chart for this activity.

2.8   The Gantt Chart

The Gantt scheduling chart illuminates still another vital facet of the overall planning effort.[15] Time sequencing and scheduling may be implicit in the other graphic aids we have developed, but they must now be fully articulated to ensure complete control of the effort.

In Figure 2.11 we return to our trivial home garden example. Note how well the prime objectives of time sequencing and scheduling are served by this chart. The basic sequencing of activities is obvious, but if more emphasis is needed on the required sequencing of certain activities, it is convenient to add a dotted vertical line called an *event marker* or *milepost*. This milepost indicates that certain activities must be complete before others can begin. Many other variations will occur to the practitioner as he adopts these charts to his own needs. For example, a moving marker can be added to represent present time. Then, should delay be experienced in completing certain activities, mileposts can be set back and later activities rescheduled. Readers having some experience with CPM will see echoes of that approach here. The concepts of a "milepost," "critical path," "slack time," and so on are latent in the Gantt chart, it should be clear.

One other variation of the basic diagram is the effort-intensive Gantt chart. In many planning activities it is essential to estimate the effort required by each activity well in advance in order to build up the needed pool of manpower and also to obtain a cost estimate. One can add several columns to the right of the basic Gantt diagram to summarize the needed effort in various categories. It may be also convenient to allow the

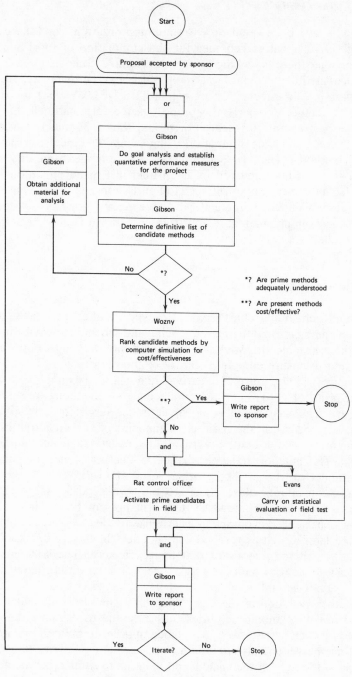

Figure 2.10 DELTA chart for rat control in urban areas. Team leaders for each activity are shown.

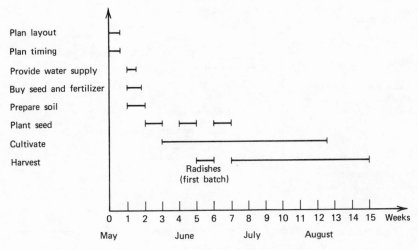

Figure 2.11 A GANTT chart for a garden.

thickness of each activity bar on the chart itself to reflect intensity of effort. In Figure 2.12 is shown an effort-intensive chart for the rat control project.

2.9 Analytic Tools in System Analysis

Analytic methods play a primary role in modern system analysis. Indeed, it could be argued that it is precisely the development of analytic techniques and electronic computers that has made modern system analysis practical and effective. Thus the absence of a complete discussion of such matters in this introduction to urban system analysis should not be viewed as lack of appreciation of this power. Such an omission may make this book less useful to the practitioner, since he must consult other sources for these vital analytic tools. At worst it may tend to convince the novice that analytic methods are not important and encourage him to omit, ignore, or even possibly disparage them. Such effects would be unfortunate. Rather, we hope that the reader already is familiar with some of the tools mentioned in this section and will find the time to learn about the others. Fortunately, there are many publications addressing each of these topics at whatever level and in as great depth as the reader desires. It seems superfluous, therefore, to reproduce readily available materials here simply for the sake of "completeness." This limited discussion is included only for the sense of symmetry implied in Figure 2.3.

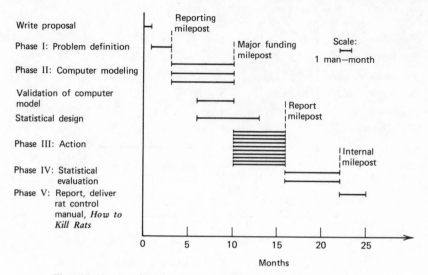

Figure 2.12 An effort-intensive GANTT chart for urban rat control.

Statistical Analysis. Probability and statistics form a basic mathematical foundation for much of system analysis. Often the best information to be obtained on a phenomenon of interest is of a limited statistical nature. Rarely, if ever, is an analytic functional relationship available in a large-scale system study. Proper experimental design, as would be utilized in the rat control study for which we have shown several diagrams, requires a competent statistician. The size of the rat population to be studied, the number of samples to be taken, the number of variables to be controlled, and other parameters must be established before field tests are initiated. Otherwise one runs the risk of an uncontrolled experiment, from which *no* meaningful results can be obtained. Unfortunately, such experiments seem to be the rule rather than the exception at the present time in urban fieldwork. Over and above this general, indeed universal, need for statistical control there are two specific aspects of statistical analysis that have a heavy impact on system analysis or operations research.

Queueing theory represents a specialized statistical analysis of waiting in line for service. We wait for our purchases to be checked out at the supermarket, and aircraft wait to be allowed to land and take off. Ships wait for docking space, and workers wait for parts and tools.

Decision theory involves selecting the correct choice at each of a number of decision nodes to arrive at a desired goal. Where the probability of success is less than unity, the risks differ and it costs time and money both to make mistakes and to gain the information required to assess the risk and thus reduce it.

Linear programming (LP) is concerned with the optimum allocation of limited resources to maximize a defined return when the costs and benefits are related to each other in a specific and simple (i.e., linear) fashion.

Dynamic programming is similar to LP in name only. It is useful in finding optimum solutions for much more complex sets of interrelations and thus is really more closely related to *optimization theory* than to LP.

Computer Simulation. Of course, all sorts of mathematics are found useful in system analysis, but we have mentioned here only the few that enjoy a special relationship. The differential equation description of the dynamic behavior of physical systems will be found valuable, and simulation of physical reality using such methods is essential. *Computer simulation* is one of the most important techniques of the system analyst.

2.10   Other Urban Planning Methodologies

The system approach is by no means the most commonly used method of urban planning. Thus it would be desirable to place systemic planning in context with the classic world view of the planner and other newer approaches for the purpose of comparison. The notion of a rational approach to urban design is not new, of course, but it is in opposition to the almost universally accepted pragmatic principle by which cities develop—incrementalism. With only a few exceptions (and, even in those, limited to the major thoroughfares and important public places), cities have always grown by accretion. As in a coral reef, thousands go about their daily business, and somehow, by individual, short-run, selfish purpose, the city is built up around them.

This essentially mindless and sloppy approach was not in keeping with the growth of rationalism in the late eighteenth and early nineteenth centuries. The great French rationalists—Laplace, Diderot, D'Alambert, Voltaire, and so on—accepted the notion, as expressed by Laplace, that "all effects of nature are only the mathematical consequences of a small number of immutable laws" (1796). And if this is so, why should not the future of man and his cities be planned? Thus the temper of the times was right when a rather unsuccessful dabbler in a number of abortive enterprises catalyzed the application of rationalism to city planning. Ebenezer Howard with his notion of the "garden city" (1894) was not the first to inject rationalism into urban planning, but he symbolizes the movement.

The factory process and rapid industrialization in the nineteenth century caused a rapid increase in the size and density of cities. Centers of industrial empires began to grow in Europe and America, and for the most part these new pressures toward urban growth were met with the same sort of incrementalism as in the past.[16] Nevertheless the concept of town planning gained adherents. One planned community in the Middle West which gained worldwide publicity doubtless provided inspiration for Howard, who brought forward his garden city plan 20 years later. Pullman, Illinois, was planned and developed by a very successful manufacturing enterprise of the day to provide convenient shelter for its work force. Many other "company towns" were also organized by industrialists of the middle and late 1800s to attract workers to their new factories. Pullman, however, was not just another company town.

George Pullman saw himself as more than a simple profit taker. He was, he thought, an industrial statesman, one of a handful of creators of the new rational, industrial American society. He was a man with a mission. Buder describes it well:[17]

In 1880 George M. Pullman hired an architect and landscape designer to lay out and construct a model town and factory eight miles south of Chicago. Pullman intended a community where the aesthetic and functional were equally emphasized and harmoniously related. He hoped that an "ordered and beautiful" environment complemented by public and community facilities would "uplift" its residents and solve the company's employment problem, while encouraging other businessmen to move their factories and workers to planned industrial suburbs. Attracting considerable attention, the model town of Pullman was generally hailed as a "model in the present, and a pattern for the future."

The failure of the community of Pullman may have been precipitated by the disastrous labor strike of 1894,[18] but other factors, which seem to be unlearned lessons for the present generation of planners, were also involved. Pullman, the garden city movement, and other planned communities of that period were designed by architects. These professionals and their sponsors seemed to feel that the goals of such developments were obvious. Indeed, to stop to discuss goals would have seemed frivolous to these men of action. It is true that the technical defects of the Pullman plan seem patently obvious to today's planner. To quote Buder again:[19]

Close-ended and self-contained, the Pullman [Illinois, 1880] plan is clearly of little practical interest. Ignoring its surroundings, the plan provided no direction for growth or flexibility for change. In many ways it was little more than a blueprint for instant town building according to the normative values of the times. As an early experiment in what the twentieth century would call social engineering, the town of Pullman was a disappointment.

Yet are not the present-day attempts at new community development "instant town building according to the normative values of the times"?

Despite the failure of Pullman and the ubiquitousness of incrementalism, the concept of rational planning continued to gain adherents. By 1916, Hancock says, the three major urban planning elements—physical planning, economic planning, and social planning—were included in major planning textbooks and in most comprehensive reports.[20] The notion of the "master plan" for developing American cities had gained currency; and, although honored more often in the breach than in the observance by practical local politicians, it still remains the dominant theme among planning practitioners, in spite of increasing denigration of late by theorists.

For a variety of reasons, "planning" and "planners" concentrated on the physical aspects of the city. Economic planning as viewed by planners was strictly work for cost estimators and accountants, who came in after the physical plan was produced to put the price tags on various items. The notion of normative urban economic planning was absent.[21]

Still less evident, if possible, was normative social planning. Politically sensitive and ideologically explosive, explicit social planning is almost totally absent from most master plans of American cities. "Providing jobs," "preserving green space," "protecting property values," "rational zoning policies," "building codes," "downtown parking," "the journey to work," "preserving the CBD," and the like are acceptable planning terms, but to attempt "social planning" is to risk one's job and perhaps the next election.

Continually in planners' minds from the 1880s through the 1960s ran the unarticulated principle that "the planner knows best." From Pullman almost to the present day the values of the planner remained unarticulated and unquestioned. But the social revolution into which many American planners perceived themselves to be thrust by the middle 1960s brought an end to the universal acceptance by planning theorists of the concept of classical planning, and an examination of the philosophical underpinning of urban planning began. Racial unrest, Viet Nam, "future shock," social permissiveness undreamed of a decade ago, the evident crumbling of the urban core—all have brought the planning theorist to an ideological crisis.

"Not till we are lost . . . do we begin to understand ourselves," Henry David Thoreau once observed. The American planning profession may be nearing that point today . . . . Yet we remain divided over which of our fundamental societal problems other than space allocation are "planning" problems, frustrated with our record to date, and uncertain about how to proceed.[22]

The planning profession (or at least its academic theorists) seems ready for careful examination of the philosophical underpinnings of their craft. For perhaps the first time, will that profession make an objective evaluation of its grammar of assent? It is to be expected that the majority of the work-a-day practitioners, trained as they were perhaps an average of 20 years ago, will at worst oppose or at best ignore this reevaluation.

R. S. Bolan, in a seminal article, has initiated this philosophical reassessment.[23] He points out that the classic world view of the planner starts with the understanding that as a staff professional he is not a decision maker. He[24] does assume that he is rational and objective. The classical planner's world view, according to Bolan, is as follows.

- He is a rational, objective, white, middle-class, staff professional.
- As a staff professional on a planning commission, he advises policy makers on comprehensive goals.
- He is capable of, and responsible for, establishing long-term goals for his planning region.
- His main task is to develop the regional "master plan," which is exclusively a physically or geographically oriented document plus some attempts at industrial site location studies.
- He measures proposed short-term tactics against the master plan and recommends approval or disapproval on the basis of concurrence or lack thereof.

Bolan reports, however, that this classical, simplistic viewpoint is now breaking down. Planners are beginning to feel that they have no universally accepted, circumscribed area of technical expertise. The classical approach is being modified in two specific ways.

- Planning is recognized as a process.
- The "master plan" is accepted as being flexible.

But others oppose master planning in principle. Banfield[25] and Braybrooke and Lindblom,[26] for example, claim that comprehensive planning is an impossible ideal. In practice, Braybrooke and Lindblom claim, planning is just the opposite of comprehensive. Rather, it is:

- Incremental—makes small changes of the status quo.
- Remedial—reactive against deficiencies.

- Serial—takes one problem at a time.
- Exploratory—without a known result in view.
- Fragmented—limited objectives.
- Disjointed—many decision points.

To some observers Banfield's world view seems a slightly more sophisticated and updated version of the Gospel according to Adam Smith. But Banfield's "disjointed incrementalism" viewpoint is not alone in opposing the classical position. Bolan cites the following positions as examples of the differing and possibly conflicting stances advocated by various modern planning theorists:

- Probabilistic programming.
- Informed coordinator–catalyst planning.
- Disjointed incremental planning (Banfield, Braybrooke and Lindblom, et al.).
- Advocacy planning.
- Multiple-scenario planning.
- Adaptive and contingency planning.
- Systems analysis and simulation.
- Cost effectiveness and program planning.
- Quasi-Keynesian or managed economy planning.
- Ad hoc opportunism.

Although these and other possible world views may be separate and distinct in the minds of their originators, it appears possible to classify them into five generalized groupings.

Classical World View

Rational comprehensive planning is possible. The master plan concept must be followed, and the planner knows best. Planning is a process, and the master plan should be modified when necessary, but only very gradually.

Disjointed Incrementalism

"Let's be practical. Comprehensive planning has had almost a hundred-year trial, and it has failed. In practice planning is remedial, serial, fragmented, disjointed, but we do the best we can." A variety of styles are possible within this viewpoint, including the informed coordinator catalyst, the honest broker, the ad hoc consultant, and adaptive and contingency planning.

Advocacy Planning

Inflamed, perhaps, by radical sociologists and younger activists, a few planners see themselves as the spokesmen of the downtrodden and oppressed. "Find out what the poor people want, and confront City Hall with it." It is difficult to maintain a condition of social detachment. Advocacy planners would argue that conventional planners have long since sold out to the power structure, if they ever were independent in the first place. Thus advocacy planning is a necessary reaction.

Quasi-Keynesian Planning

This economic world view holds that, if the economic incentives are properly managed, the physical environment will respond.

System Planning

System planning uses such analytic techniques as probabilistic programming, multiple scenarios, computer simulation, and cost effectiveness analysis. Just as disjointed incrementalism may be described loosely as an update of Adam Smith, system planning may possibly be viewed as a polished version, using slightly more modern mathematics, of the struggle by eighteenth century rationalists to impose reason upon an unreasoning and unreasonable world.

These five views seem together to complete the planning universe. The classical view emphasizes physical planning; advocacy planning places primacy on society or the individual; quasi-Keynesian planning is essentially an economic stance; disjointed incrementalism rejects the whole notion of comprehensive planning; and the systemic approach regards itself as perhaps the first truly comprehensive planning. This is probably not the place to continue a detailed exegesis of this multiplicity of planning stances. Let us leave it with this observation. The traditional world view of the planner has been badly shaken by the social revolution of urban America of the 1960s. Perhaps for the first time, planners are examining a variety of philosophical stances. The system viewpoint is one of these possibilities.

2.11   Three Urban Planning Styles

There appear to be three generic planning styles. They may be termed the incremental, the monumental, and the objective.

Incrementalism

Most American private developers opt for this strategy. It involves extensive reliance on the market mechanism and on "giving the customers
what they want." Since private developers are optimizing their own
short-run entrepreneurial gain, this is a perfectly valid strategy. Its only
possible disadvantage is that it replicates the status quo. The author has
heard a developer of one of the Title VII new towns damn the status quo
and the lack of foresight that resulted in Greenbelt, Maryland, in the
1930s, and yet at the same time maintain the imperative of the marketplace. Only his egotism prevents him from realizing that he is in the
same trap as the planners of Greenbelt.

Perhaps the most forthright advocates of "disjointed incrementalism"
are Braybrooke and Lindblom.[27] They boldly attempt to raise to the level
of virtue what others have defended as grim necessity. They argue that
the "synoptic" or systemic planner is deluding himself by following a
methodology doomed in principle to failure. Their careful and reasoned
arguments require response by those of us who argue for the synoptic
approach.

Monumentalism

An occasional star of the planning firmament is given the opportunity of
impressing his own personality on a whole community. Frank Lloyd
Wright was denied this ultimate accolade when his "Broad Acres City"
failed to advance beyond the project stage, as was Le Corbusier with his
compact high-rise "Radiant City" project. Yet Le Corbusier did succeed
with Chandigarh and influenced Niemeyer, who developed Brasilia.
Howard saw Letchworth developed by Parker and Urwin, and Rouse
developed Columbia.

Columbia is of particular interest because Rouse was not protected
from the market mechanism, as was the case, for example, with Brasilia.
It gains further importance from the fact that Rouse has made it part of his
mission to train a future generation of planners. Thus much of the thinking
of HUD and the planning of Title VII new towns, as well as other
ventures, are influenced by Rouse Company alumni.

Rouse began with an attempt at objective planning. He assembled a
number of academic sociologists, anthropologists, and social psychologists in seminar, and asked them to tell his planning team what social
values Americans wanted and should have for their own and the nation's
best interests in Columbia. The academics reacted variously to this challenge, but almost none of their thinking was productive. The Columbia
planning process continued, but the academics were dismissed because

they were unwilling or unable to respond in a goal-oriented way to the planners' needs.[28]

Led by Rouse's vision, the Columbia planners then designed what they felt citizens *should* want. The famous Columbia neighborhood concept emerged,[29] as did the Johns Hopkins preventive medicine complex, the open-air concert center, the minibus routing, the attempt to provide industrial job self-sufficiency, and the Columbia education experience. Much of this social planning was "good" in an abstract sense, and some of it has survived, in modified form, the rigors of the marketplace. But none of it was based on objective social planning.

Objectivism

Is it possible to develop, through objective principles and wide-ranging involvement by citizens' groups, a dialog on "Goals for Americans"? This is certainly visionary, but the very concept of explicit social planning is a recent phenomenon. By illustrating the results of various value choices, planners may be able to draw from the citizenry a commitment to a consistent set of social goals and then to use these goals in planning the new city.

Exercises

2.1. John Dewey[30] suggests "Five Phases of Reflective Thought" for systematic inquiry into the solution of a problem. List these steps, and compare them with the six phases in a system study given in this chapter. Discuss.

2.2 Polya gives four steps in problem solving.[31] Compare and contrast with the six phases of this chapter.

2.3. Draw an objectives tree for an urban rat control project similar to that described in the text.

2.4. Draw an interaction matrix for the sections of this chapter.

Notes and References

1. Ida R. Hoos, *Systems Analysis in Public Policy*, University of California Press, Berkeley, 1972, is an extremist critic who sees system analysis as evil incarnate. Hoos's book has been called overbearing, repetitious, and one-sided. It also subscribes to the conspiratorial theory of governance and is careless of facts. Nevertheless, Hoos has a valid point when she accuses system enthusiasts of sometimes setting up easily quantified but nonmeaningful performance criteria.

2. A. Koestler, *The Ghost in the Machine*, Ch. III (1967), Gateway Ed., Henry Regnery Co., Chicago, 1971.

3. S. Ramo, *Cure for Chaos*, David McKay Co., N.Y., 1969.

4. U.S. Department of Commerce, *Research and Development for High Speed Ground Transportation*, Clearinghouse for Federal Scientific and Technical Information, PB 1739, March 11, 1967.

5. G. R. Herbert, "High-Speed Ground Transportation—A Research Challenge," *Proceedings of the IEEE*, Vol. 56, No. 4 (April 1968), pp. 487–492.

6. In this book the word "client" is used synonymously with "decision maker" or "sponsor." The client may be a single person or an amorphous group. As we will see, the decision maker may not know that he is one, and the decision maker may change as the project progresses or as a result of the actions of the analyst.

7. D. N. Rothblatt, "Rational Planning Reexamined," *Journal of the American Institute of Planners*, Vol. 37 (January 1971), pp. 26–37.

8. Analyst bias is still a problem, of course, but group dynamics helps to reduce the bias of an individual member.

9. I am indebted to J. Warfield and J. D. Hill for stimulating discussions and useful suggestions concerning this material during a system workshop at the Battelle Seattle Research Center in February 1971.

10. No simplification can be completely true. One can provide executive summaries, abstracts, and the like, but these are modifications of pure narratives, and are necessary precisely because of the deficiencies of the pure narrative form.

11. R. Sommer, *Personal Space*, Prentice-Hall, Englewood Cliffs, N.J., 1969.

12. J. N. Warfield, "Intent Structures," Ch. 9 of *An Assault On Complexity*, Battelle Monograph No. 3, Columbus, Ohio, April 1973.

13. J. N. Warfield, "On Arranging Elements of a Hierarchy in Graphic Form," *IEEE Transactions on Systems, Man, and Cybernetics*, Vol. SMC-3 (March 1973), pp. 121–132.

14. J. N. Warfield and J. D. Hill, "The DELTA Chart: A Method for R & D Project Portrayal," *IEEE Transactions on Engineering Management*, Vol. E-18, No. 4 (November 1971), pp. 132–139.

15. Henry L. Gantt was one of the small group of pioneers who gathered around Frederick W. Taylor about the turn of the century to develop the principles of scientific work measurement, time and motion study, and industrial engineering.

16. Indeed, while rationalism provided a social atmosphere conducive to the encouragement of planning, it simultaneously supplied a "rational" justification for incrementalism. Adam Smith proclaimed in the *Wealth of Nations* (1776) that the invisible hand of the marketplace will guide matters to a logical and optimum conclusion. Thus "planning" is certainly unnecessary, probably unpatriotic, and possibly against the will of God. Vestiges of this position remain today.

17. S. Buder, "The Model Town of Pullman: Town Planning and Social Control in the Guilded Age," *Journal of the American Institute of Planners*, Vol. 33 (January 1967), pp. 2–10.

18. Indeed, some historians assign the coersive and paternalistic social control exercised at Pullman as one of the causes of the strike. See R. A. Mohl, N. Betten, "The Failure of Industrial City Planning: Gary, Indiana, 1906–1910," *Journal of the American Institute of Planners*, Vol. 38, No. 4 (July 1972), pp. 203–215.

19. S. Buder, *loc. cit.*, p. 9.

20. J. L. Hancock, "Planners in the Changing American City, 1900–1940," *Journal of the American Institute of Planners*, Vol. 33 (September 1967), pp. 290–304.

21. Economic geography and urban economics have never attracted the main stream of economic theory or leading economic theorists. This situation may be in the process of changing, however. See H. W. Richardson, "A Guide to Urban Economics Texts: A Review Article," *Urban Studies*, Vol. 10 (October 1973), pp. 399–405.

22. J. L. Hancock, "History and the American Planning Profession: Introduction to a New Biographical Series," *Journal of the American Institute of Planners*, Vol. 38 (September 1972), pp. 274–275.

23. R. S. Bolan, "Emerging Views of Planning," *Journal of the American Institute of Planners*, Vol. 33 (July 1967), pp. 233–245.

24. As used here, "he" is not merely the generic personal pronoun, since most American planners are white, middle-class, males.

25. E. C. Banfield, *The Unheavenly City Revisited*, Little Brown and Co., Boston, 1974.

26. D. Braybrooke, C. E. Lindblom, *A Strategy of Decision*, Free Press, Glencoe, Ill., 1963, 1970.

27. D. Braybrooke, C. E. Lindblom, *loc. cit.*

28. Contrary to Brooks, who seems unwilling to credit perhaps the most innovative planning initiative yet taken under private enterprise. See R. Brooks, "Social Planning in Columbia," *Journal of the American Institute of Planners*, Vol. 37 (November 1971), pp. 373–379.

29. Based on Perry's New York City studies of the late 1920s and Stein's planning for Radburn in the 1930s.

30. John Dewey, *How We Think*, D. C. Heath, Boston, 1933.

31. G. Polya, *How to Solve It*, Anchor Books, Doubleday and Co., Garden City, N.Y., 1957.

3

Managing a System Team

The shift at Bell Labs shows up most sharply in what has been happening lately to its team of systems engineers. Since 1955, these engineers—about 15% of the Labs 7,500 man graduate technical staff— . . . have worked largely as a single company-wide force of planners within the Labs and with Western [Electric]. Up to last year, their job has stressed long-range objectives in pulling together highly specialized new technology into new systems . . . .

During 1970, however, short range planning to put existing technology to use, which has taken second place through the years, became top priority. The single systems engineering force was split up to serve in each of the main areas at the Labs . . . . 'You need deep specialization when you have time to be creative,' explains J. A. (Jack) Morton, Vice President for electronics technology, 'but you need close coupling when either technology or the social system changes rapidly.'

Business Week,
January 23, 1971, p. 39

Our biographical information is uneven and incomplete, but it suggests that the key members of the post-1930 teams were not colorless cogs in an anonymous machine. Usually we find among them strong and highly individualistic personalities, with some of the strengths and weaknesses found in the personalities of artists. Often they have appeared to some of their contemporaries as "rude and overbearing men," impatient with disagreement and obtuseness and unwilling to suffer fools or critics gladly. The decisive difference from the past is that today these creative individuals nonetheless know how to work with other people, how to support others, and how to elicit their cooperation and support in turn. Indeed, a surprising number of them founded significant organizations or institutes to carry on their work.

K. W. DEUTSCH, J. R. PLATT, D. SENGHAAS,
"Conditions Favoring Major Advances in Social Science"
Science, February 5, 1971, p. 457

3.1 Introduction: Special Difficulties

A number of experts feel that an essential feature of the system approach is a team effort with a group made up of experts from different areas.[1] Not only engineers but also psychologists, sociologists, architects, political scientists, economists, lawyers, and representatives of other fields, are often included in the team. Such a diverse group will inevitably include people accustomed to various styles of work, and this provides a special source of difficulty.

To illustrate this problem, let us consider an example of how different the thought process of the engineeer is from that of the social scientist or humanist. Suppose that an engineer is called to a meeting or conference. He will feel he has been asked to participate in order to transmit and receive facts and decisions or to take part in making recommendations. Unless it is "his meeting," he will expect to follow the guidance of the person who called it, preferably working from a written agenda, previously prepared by the convener. In the process he expects to compromise his initial position and for others to do likewise in order to obtain a decision. He presents his view forcefully to his boss but accepts the latter's judgment in order to get the job done. He wants the meeting to be over quickly so that he can get back to work. None of these things is true for the humanist. He is in no hurry for the formal meeting to start or end because he feels that he is engaging in social interaction all the while. He expects to think out loud in the meeting and sees no need to stick religiously to an agenda or time table. Once he arrives at a position, he will not relinquish it to help the group reach a decision because his position is arrived at by the use of principles and thus becomes a matter of principle. The concern of the engineer for reaching a decision seems very rigid to the humanist or social scientist. He cannot understand why the engineer is so eager to get the meeting over with because he believes himself to be at his best in such a setting. To the social scientist the meeting is the center of the day's activity. Moreover, the academic social scientist does not accept the concept of the "boss." He sees himself as equal among peers. This, of course, is just one small example. Neither the engineer's style nor the social scientist's is objectively good or bad, but the two *are* different and the team leader who does not recognize this fact is in for some trying sessions.

This anecdote of the "conference," though drawn from life, may strike some readers as mildly interesting or wildly exaggerated but in either case only a triviality. But is it more than this? J. N. Warfield[2] conceives of the system analysis process as a succession of what he calls outscoping and inscoping activities, as shown in Figure 3.1. An *outscoping activity* is one in which the team bends its efforts at broadening its view and including factors that otherwise might be ignored in the analysis. Wide, sweeping speculation is encouraged, and critical analysis is postponed. Then, when the question has been broadened sufficiently to ensure that no viable

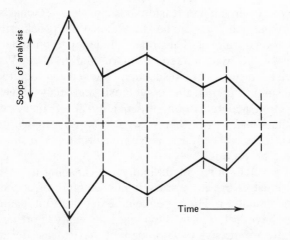

Figure 3.1 System analysis as a succession of outscoping and inscoping activities. (SOURCE: After J. N. Warfield, J. D. Hill, Battelle Seattle Research Center System Workshop, 1971.)

solution has been excluded, the attitude is reversed. A detailed analysis is carried through on all the ideas advanced in the preceding outscoping session. This *inscoping activity* may take longer than its outscoping counterpart, and it should result in a field of candidate solutions somewhat smaller than existed at the start of outscoping. Each of the remaining candidate solutions should then be supported with documentation. At this point the cycle is repeated. Each time the cycle of outscoping and inscoping is completed, the candidates are fewer and more completely analyzed.

Most professionals tend to feel more comfortable with either the more broad, speculative outscoping activity or the more detailed, analytic inscoping process, but not with both. Humanists and social scientists often are attracted toward outscoping activities, whereas statisticians, accountants, engineers, and so forth are more likely to enjoy inscoping. The outscoping mind is often bored with details and impatient with specific difficulties. It is interested in the philosophy of approach, the general concept, intriguing anomalies, unexpected interconnections. The inscoping mind, on the other hand, avoids vague speculations, since it sees nothing to relate to. It finds it difficult to suspend judgment and criticism. It enjoys getting to the bottom of things, laying bare the ultimate bedrock, specific concepts by rigorously peeling off the frills and ornamentalities. The outscoping mind resists closure and premature decision for fear of neglecting a long-shot winner. The inscoping mind has a low tolerance for ambiguity and needs to make choices.

If one has chosen his profession because his personal style seems adapted to its methodology, he has had his natural proclivities enhanced by his professional training. Thus one's tendency to outscope or inscope has been reinforced by extended education and practice. Very few professions have been successful in sustaining the tension required to contain both centralism and periphralism, synthesis and analysis, generalist and specialist, action and reflection, practicality and artistry within themselves simultaneously. Yet that is what we propose with the system method. That there will be tensions within a properly constituted systems team let there be no doubt.

A second special source of difficulty in managing a system analysis team is that most of the early work is in the nature of concept development and manipulation. These concepts exist in the minds of the team members but have little physical evidence of reality. Furthermore, there is little to show progressive development of these ideas. Because of these factors there exists a danger of misunderstanding and delay in the vital early phase of problem definition, as well as the possibility of failure to complete later crucial elements of the project on time, or at all.

3.2 Group Communication

It may be possible to do system studies with a hierarchical group structure in which participants report only upward and directions are dispatched downward, but this seems unlikely. A more open communication method in which each member of the team reports progress to all the others appears more logical. Documentation is especially important but will be resisted by some. The individualist will correctly argue that time taken to write a weekly progress report is time taken away from creative effort. But he is ignoring the communication function within the group which his memoranda serve, as well as the organization that his written reports will impart to his own thinking.

The critical path method and other network planning methods are popular in some planning circles as intrateam communications devices, but in a paper study such approaches must be used with care. The team effort should not consist of a number of separate efforts going on simultaneously. Rather, there should be an interlacing of concepts and a deepening of understanding as a field or totality experience. Moreover, CPM mileposts may be artificially contrived in a paper study. In an attempt to make the milepost a concrete event, such things as "conference held," "concept approved," or "report delivered" are chosen, yet these events may be more shadow than substance. One can achieve all these mileposts and still have the system study fail overall. I have no complete solution for this problem, but here are some suggestions.

- Staff meetings should occur weekly or more often.
- Each staff member should submit a weekly effort report and estimate percentage fulfillment of specific items. Encourage staff members to circulate concise working papers to their colleagues. Some joint working sessions are necessary.
- The tendency of individuals to carve out portions of the project in a personal effort to gain control should not be allowed.
- An interaction manager will be necessary. But even then interactions are often deemphasized in favor of detailed analysis of individual elements.
- DELTA charts may be used to organize staff effort but should not be permitted to substitute for reality.
- As candidate solutions are developed or discarded, they should be mentioned in client conferences.
- Client conferences should be held monthly. Engineers and architects seem to tend naturally toward underdisclosure. View interim reports and media publicity in public system studies, not as hindrances to your work, but rather as helping to build a consensus.

3.3 Hamilton's Experience[3]

Hamilton's report on a system study done on the Susquehanna River basin contains a number of interesting insights on the problems of managing a system group. Among these insights are the following:

- The planning staff should not be built to full strength before starting analysis. Several iterations should be made with a skeleton staff of key people. Often this analysis reveals that a considerable change in emphasis will be required. If the full staff has already been assembled, some will have to be let go.
- Assembling a group of people who are individually competent does not automatically serve to generate an efficient and competent research team. Some persons are unwilling or unable to put aside their own needs to help satisfy those of the group.
- An interesting insight is that "idle curiosity" is more difficult to control than the more obvious (to me) problem of lack of communication.
- A balanced study must be sought. This is one in which no more expense and detail is permitted than can be justified. One must combat

the academic tendency of elaboration and detail produced because an individual researcher has fallen in love with his work or feels the need to justify himself professionally to his peers in his guild.

3.4 Project versus Function Organization

A system team is often assembled initially to tackle a large new project. After the successful completion of the project the question is whether the team should be held together to tackle new projects or its members should be assigned to separate duties. This question does not arise, of course, if the group consists of outside consultants brought into the organization for a specific job. In other situations as well, the question is not open for discussion. Furthermore, it is apparent from a review of system engineering literature that some authors advocate one approach and others favor another, so apparently there is no universally accepted answer.

Naturally, managers of system analysis groups think their problems are unique, but an objective look at the situation will probably reveal similarities with managing any group of creative professionals. Computer groups, electronics groups, accountants, research groups, and so forth will argue, almost without exception, that they will better be able to serve the total organization if they are kept together and allowed to work for a boss who is one of themselves and thus understands their unique problems. Although this is true, the concomitant disadvantage is that there may be a lessening of pressure to serve the goals of the organization.

The experience of the systems group at Bell Telephone Labs may provide a case history of this problem. Bell Labs is generally acknowledged to be the finest industrial research laboratory organization in the world, and there is no university which can challenge it in its chosen fields either. Bell Labs is usually credited with a major role in the early development of the concepts of systems engineering, and the 1000 or more professional systems analysts working at the Labs in the late 1960s were among the leaders in the field. Yet we see from the quote at the head of this chapter that in 1970 the corporate systems group at the Labs was broken up and its people were distributed out to Western Electric and among the operating companies. Why?

John Brooks' recent book, *Telephone*[4], may have supplied the answer. AT&T committed itself to installation of electronic switching (ESS) in 1955, and in 1956, newly-elected President F. R. Kappel announced publicly a target date of 1959 and a target development cost of $4.5 million. In fact it was 1969 before ESS was in widespread use, and the total development cost was over $500 million. There is a widespread feeling at AT&T that the systems group at Bell Labs dropped the ball by failing to take sufficient interest in the practical difficulties of manufacturing, installing, and maintaining ESS once they had proved it in principle, in favor of blue-sky non-goal-oriented work. Thus the group was broken up.

The organization does not exist to serve the needs of a group of specialists. On the contrary, they are employed to help the organization meet its goals. Because of the difficult problem of harnessing a myriad of groups to meet performance requirements on time and within budget in a company or institution organized along functional lines, organization by project has been developed. Each project leader has as his goal successful accomplishment of a major project of the organization. In a project organization, system types and other specialists are assigned to project groups, and there is no system group as such. Since this is not a book on management theory, we will not develop these ideas any further. Suffice it to say that, on the surface at least, there appears to be nothing unique about a group of system analysts. They should fit into the structure of the organization, whatever its form, functional or project oriented, just as would any other specialists.[5]

3.5   The Final Report

A planning document produced as a final report is only the first step in bringing the proposed system into physical realization, but it is by the quality of this report that the system group will be judged. The report should be keyed, if possible, to the request that originated the study. This may seem like obvious advice, but experience teaches that it is not. When it comes time to write the final report, the study group will have progressed far beyond even a well-constructed request for proposal (RFP) or initial problem statement in its understanding of the problem. Thus the temptation will be very great to write the report from this more sophisticated and integrated point of view. Furthermore, many RFPs are poorly constructed, thus increasing the temptation to ignore them. Nevertheless, if the RFP has section headings and if specific items of work are listed, use exactly these headings in the final report. The young analyst is inclined to expect the client to modify his approach to conform to the one that the analyst has adopted. Try to keep in mind who pays the piper.

If a formal RFP does not exist, the final report can be organized around the steps in the system study. In this situation it may seem unnecessary to expend much effort in the final report on "goal development," but experience indicates its value. If the presentation moves directly to the proposed solution without placing it in context, the client is less likely to accept it. Do not assume that the client is fully familiar with the situation. Start at the beginning with a descriptive scenario.[6]

For example, it may seem foolish to begin an oral presentation to the "Mayor" of Detroit on the Woodward subway problem discussed in section 3.11 by showing him pictures of the city and of Woodward Avenue. But a well-done 5-minute descriptive scenario, possibly via a multimedia film-slide-nonsynchronized sound presentation, is vital. Doubtless it tells the client little or nothing he does not know about his city; but at the very least it convinces him that the analyst has been on the scene, and it seems to reassure him that the analyst takes this specific problem seriously.

Technicians generally make rather poor oral presentations. In most professionals there seems to exist a deep block against appearing to "act" or "sell." Thus their oral presentations are flat, dull, and uninspired, that is, "professional." Yet the final oral presentation may be all that the client has from which to judge the effectiveness of the entire effort. Keep in mind also that there is a great deal of latent hostility in the minds of members of the client organization at the audacity of an outside system group coming in to tell them how to solve *their* problem. Thus the initial mind set of the audience at a final oral presentation is quite negative, and a mind-blowing, multimedia descriptive scenario helps to turn them around. Without a descriptive scenario the audience may leap to the erroneous conclusion that the analyst does not understand the problem, especially if he is young. But even if the analyst is experienced, he will encounter initial latent hostility.

I was present recently when a famous regional analyst opened a presentation to a local government group that his company had as a client. He omitted the descriptive scenario, but with 40 years' experience, heavy with honors from presidents and princes, and massive regional and national developments to his credit, it was impossible for his listeners to think that the great man did not understand regional analysis. Hence they transferred their hostility to the young assistant analyst who followed his chief with the details. "Of course L is a master regional analyst," they said afterward, "but after all this is a small project and he couldn't give it his personal attention." And the proposal got shot down. Had L opened with a descriptive scenario instead of philosophy, the critics of his regional plan could not have circumvented him to attack his young assistant. As it was, L was finessed, his assistant was pounded to a bloody pulp, and the action phase was stalled.

Following the steps of the system approach for a final report format results in an effective presentation with one vital exception: a general system planning document without a description of the action phase is almost useless. Such omission implies that the system planners are uninterested in the client's needs and that the study is an end in itself. The minimum elements in the action section of the final report are as follows:

- *Suggested phasing.* Many large-scale systems can conveniently be designed, constructed, and brought on stream in distinct phases or increments. These phases should be delineated, and specific mileposts identified. A PERT or DELTA chart is indicated here.
- *Suggested management.* An organization chart should be provided for the action phase. Clearly show the relationship of the proposed action organization to the client. Bend every effort to eliminate ambiguities between the proposed action management team and the client, as well as between the management team and proposed subcontractors.
- *Time and cost budgets.* A Gantt chart showing the duration of major activities and the interrelations among them is suggested here. In addition, a cost estimate for each major activity should be inserted to the right of the Gantt chart. These costs can be broken down quite easily into four or five major subcategories.
- *Suggested sensors.* Specific indicators and sensors of progress along with interim success points must be defined for the action phase. This is especially difficult and uniquely critical when progress and success must be defined in terms of societal attitudes and actions, rather than in terms of a physical or structural goal.
- *Project payout.* The specific accomplishments and rewards for completing the plan must be identified along with the costs. Compute for the client the cost effectiveness of your proposal.

The oral and written final reports must give evidence that the system planning group has internalized the problem of the sponsor. Think of it in this way. The sponsor has a difficult problem. He has tried to solve it himself and failed, or he realizes initially that the problem is too complex for him. Thus he calls in the system team. Now, if the system team stands off and says, "Well, yes, you certainly do have a problem there," the sponsor will be alienated. Rather, the attitude to be engendered can be expressed as follows: "Yes, *we* do have a problem here, but *we* are going to solve it!"

3.6   Civil Systems and Military Systems

A rather common suggestion of a few years ago ran along the line that a nation which can put a man on the moon should be able to clean up its rivers and make its cities livable. The downturn in the aerospace industry of California after the end of the Korean conflict caused that state to attempt to implement such a redirection of talent with results that we will discuss below. In 1970, as the Viet Nam war moved into its closing phase for the United States, and the aerospace business again experienced a decline, the same concept was revived. Senator Kennedy called for an "urban NASA," and Mayor John Lindsay invited the RAND Corporation to New York to develop new solutions for the city's problems.

Although some useful results have been forthcoming from these and other, similar efforts,[7] a number of system analysts have been quite candid about the difficulty in making the apparently rather simple transfer of techniques from military and aerospace systems to civil systems.[8,9] Unfortunately a number of broad and far-reaching assertions have been made in the past about the ease with which such transfers could be made, without the slightest evidence upon which to rest such promises. Now, after several years of experience, analyst expertise has risen and clients' expectations have dropped, so that the gap is closing. Unfortunately, however, the systems method and its practitioners' credibility have been seriously and perhaps permanently damaged in the process. Among the major differences between civil and military and/or aerospace systems cited by Canty, Strasser, and Morse et al., as well as other serious students of the situation, which have prevented easy translation of success in the latter sphere to solutions in the former are the following:

- *Multiplicity of goals.* Military and aerospace missions are usually specific and clear cut. Occasionally a civil system has a simple goal, but typically it is a complex of interconnected objectives.
- *Multiplicity of decision makers.* To do a system study is not to have earned the right to make the final decision on system acceptance. The acceptance procedure for a military system is clear cut in principle. In a civil system, however, there may not be an isolated decision maker; multiple jurisdictions are the rule. By design or inadvertence the nominal political leaders may by their conduct cause the decision procedure to escalate to a more participatory level. Even if this does not occur, a massive civil system will be subject to numerous and possibly conflicting constituencies.
- *Economic constraints.* Cost, in a strictly economic sense, is an effective index of performance only in the idealized free marketplace, in which a number of competing products are available at various prices and meet given standards. It may be extended to competitive bidding on an object for future delivery only if extreme care is used in constructing a complete set of detailed specifications on required perfor-

mance. Unfortunately, complete specifications with guaranteed future performance clauses are impossible if the object in question is far in advance of the state of the art. Furthermore, cost may be quite inappropriate as a trade-off item against performance in a military system. This situation of cost being an inappropriate index of value also occurs on occasion in civil systems. But, more typically, economic competition in the marketplace does result in the buyer's welfare, especially since continued use of the system will reveal an unjustified performance claim or unsatisfactory first cost. Thus civil systems differ significantly from military systems in making cost rather than performance the primary consideration.[10]

- *Time constraints.* As Strasser points out, the length of service of many urban officials and military officers is too short for the planning, construction, and completion of a large-scale system to occur in one term. In the military, however, unlike urban administration, personnel will be given credit for successful completion of one phase of a major project. To show meaningful results in a 1-, 2-, or 3-year term, incremental implementation must be employed in a large-scale urban system, even though this often may reduce somewhat the overall cost effectiveness.

3.7   System Team Management: Four Examples

In the next several sections we will consider the team management problems that arose in four separate cases. Since each of these examples absorbed several man-years of effort and some involve considerable analysis and advanced technology, no attempt can be made here to give the substance of the problem analysis. The emphasis will be solely on the team management aspects of the question. Since we concentrate on the team management aspects of each case, the technological content becomes somewhat incidental. Therefore the fact that several of these cases range rather far afield from urban systems does not invalidate their usefulness to us insofar as team management is concerned.

3.8   The Urban-System Problem Environment: The California Aerospace Contracts Case

In November 1964 the state of California announced its intention to request aerospace firms to do system studies on certain socially relevant state problems. After the preliminary proposals were evaluated, a

6-month contract was negotiated early in 1965 in each of four areas: a statewide information system, waste management, crime and delinquency, and a transportation system. Walt's summary[11] of the state's experience with those system studies should prove useful for system managers of socially relevant studies.[12]

It soon becomes apparent to the reader of Walt's evaluation of this pioneering experiment that communication was a major problem for all concerned. Most offices of state government are not attuned to the system approach and lack the capability to respond in a meaningful way to the probing of system analysts. The analysts, on the other hand, were naive in their approach. They used system jargon to the uninitiated and failed to understand that they could be viewed as a threat to the job security of the civil servant. Moreover, the analysts failed to understand the political boundaries involved in their studies and generally ignored such boundaries in making their recommendations. The short-term job tenure of political appointees and elected officials was ignored in favor of recommendation of long-range programs. A recommendation of a multimillion dollar program which overrides political boundaries and whose benefits will not be felt for many years will not be received with enthusiasm by a politician whose term of office is 2 years and who must be concerned with financing the program and carrying it forward. In the installation of a large-scale system it would seem reasonable to provide for gradual introduction with balanced costs and some immediate results. There is no evidence that these sutdies included such considerations.

On the other hand, the broad sweep of the system approach (which, incidentally, a number of bidders could not define satisfactorily to the state procurement officers) provided public officials with a number of worthwhile insights. One general recommendation appears to mandate a broader approach to specific problems than is usally taken. In the transportation study, for example, the team suggested that one must consider changes in living habits and new technology. "Information about many aspects of the state, seemingly unrelated to the problems of transportation as such, were shown to have effect. What would be required [for a successful transportation study] is virtually a complete model of the state's economy."[13]

This system exercise cost $500,000 of state funds and probably an equal amount of matching funds from the companies involved. The total is a high price to pay to learn rather elemental lessons, of which the following seem to be typical.

- One must use tact and discretion in studying large organizations that include many persons of moderate to low education and income. It seems incredibly naive for system engineers to say they learned *after the fact* that their social study was different from dealing with a task-oriented federal government agency bent on procuring specific military hardware.

- One cannot ignore with impunity problem boundaries as defined by the customer. To recommend more time, more money, and more studies as a next step in the California exercise was hardly responsive to the needs of state officials for short-term results.
- One should include the possibility of incremental introduction of modifications to socially relevant systems so as to provide interim evaluation points, and certain short-term tangible pay outs. This is true even if overall costs are slightly higher as a result.
- One cannot substitute men and money for time. The California studies were done on a crash basis over a 6-month time period. A number of difficulties could have been avoided had a lower-cost and less frantic approach been adopted.

Even with the difficulties involved in this set of studies, however, a number of benefits were derived; in fact, one specific output was of very great importance. In discussing the system approach with those unfamiliar with it, one is often asked for specific practical examples of its successful application in socially relevant areas. One specific finding of the crime and delinquency study is a powerful argument in this case. More than a year before the civil violence in Los Angeles, this study isolated the Watts area as the *one* locality of Greater Los Angeles in which were present all four negative social characteristics likely to trigger riots.

3.9   Goal-Centered Planning: The Mars–Earth Television Link Case

During the late 1960s it appeared likely to NASA that its Apollo series of manned moon missions would be a success and that planning should be inaugurated to establish Apollo's successor. Hundreds of specific missions suggested themselves as possible candidates. To narrow and rank-order this list, NASA chose to apply a criterion for ranking called pacing technology. Missions or elements of missions that were expected to prove most challenging and that, if successful, would automatically ensure the success of less exacting possibilities, without carrying through detailed analyses of the latter, were to be designated as *pacing missions*, and the specific technology required for success, as *pacing technology*. From this narrowed list of candidates, final selections would be made, using still more elaborate criteria.

A group of mature engineers was assembled to do initial planning on one element of this large-scale project. The group contained no people with experience in aerospace design, nor were there any in the group with an electronics background. Moreover, the steps and phases of the "system method" proposed in this book were not available to them. That the project could be judged as marginally successful was a tribute to the native intelligence of the participants rather than a result of their experience or specific training.

The task was presented initially to the group in one sentence: "Do a preliminary design for a live TV link for a manned Mars mission in 1975 and report on the feasibility and the difficulties." The responses were edged with panic. "But I know nothing about communication theory or aerospace engineering." "How can you make such a complex assignment as that in one sentence?" "We don't have time to do a task as big as that!" Dozens of detailed questions were asked to which the group members felt that they needed answers before they could begin.

The group was told that a large-scale system study was, almost by definition, ill defined. Even if the sponsoring agency wrote a book on the subject rather than a single sentence, the team would not find in it all of the constraints and data it would need. The team was reminded that the sponsor did not know the answers, nor could he properly define the problem; this was to be the group's task. The group complaint that it did not contain the required specialists seems to be universal when attacking a new system task. How does one handle this complaint? It is obvious that, if the required specialists can be found, answers will be available immediately that otherwise may take months to obtain. Yet early requests for more specialists probably arise from the same source that seeks from the sponsor a well-defined problem and indicate an unwillingness to accept broad systems responsibility. The problem is not a lack of "experts." There are thousands of experts and hundreds of thousands of books and technical reports. *The problem is to formulate properly the critical questions to which one really needs answers.*

The group was temporarily mollified by this little lecture and began its work. It decided that it would be useful initially to outline all the steps needed to successfully execute the manned Mars mission. But this attempt created more problems than it seemed to solve. It was obvious immediately that the group did not have time to study thoroughly the entire space mission, nor was it clear exactly what steps in the overall manned Mars mission were crucial to the group's specific problem and which were not. Several hundred specific tasks were generated by the group, but one member commented that he felt he was being swallowed by the problem rather than him digesting it.

How does one overcome this difficulty, so common to what might be called a time-sequential or historical approach to problem solving? In Figure 3.2 is shown a small portion of the subtask activities in a large-scale system. Although a few of the branches may rejoin well before project completion, the overall tendency is for subtasks to be more and more finely divided as time goes on. In other words, in the early phases a few activities support many others, but as more detail is required, the bifurcation must continue. It is almost impossible, in a really complex problem, for one to predict in advance how one subsystem will interact with another. Thus it is difficult to identify and eliminate extraneous branches from consideration if one takes a time-sequential approach.

Consider, on the other hand, an inverse time, or goal-oriented, approach. By starting with the goal and working backward, one can place specifications on other interacting subsystems with some authority. The designer will also avoid excessively detailed concern with other subsystems that do not interact with his assignment, as shown in Figure 3.3. Take just one example. The TV system will consume electric energy that must be carried on board. The complete design of the energy system is not the TV group's assignment, however; it will be sufficient for the group to

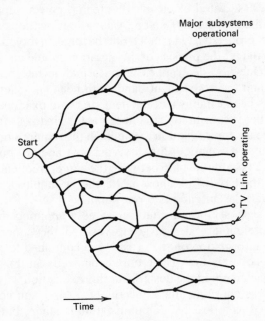

Figure 3.2 A portrayal of subsystem activities in a large-scale system, the Mars–Earth live TV link system.

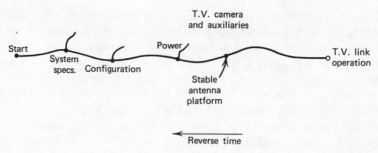

Figure 3.3 Goal-oriented or reverse-time traversal of relevant branches for one subsystem.

state its expected energy needs. Note also that these data are needed for the energy group to begin its task. Thus it would appear that a goal-oriented approach not only is a design convenience, but also is necessary to generate the requisite specifications for the various system design activities.

To follow the goal-oriented approach the TV group should ignore the maze of problems involved in establishing a suitable vehicle in Mars polar orbit. Rather, it would begin with the TV camera itself and work backward through associated electronics, antenna, power supply, space required inside the capsule, and so on, placing specifications on these other systems as it proceeds. One must not become involved initially with detailed technology; the physics of the situation should be the first technical concern. One first determines the information rate required for TV transmission and the consequent bandwidth needed. When the required bandwidth has been established, the next step is to examine the available electromagnetic spectrum to find acceptable windows. Then one can move on to the antenna equation to establish the required radiated power. With the antenna equation the first major trade-off point has been reached. There is a relationship between the center frequency chosen, the antenna size, the bandwidth chosen, the energy required, and the precision with which the antenna is to be pointed.

Even after discussion and after supposedly adopting the system approach, the preliminary design group resisted the concept. They demanded more information on the project and continued to generate time-sequential lists of activities. The group recognized that the antenna equation is one key element in the design, but this realization was buried under a number of less consequential concerns. The laser and coherent optics were mentioned as a possible communication medium, but coherent optics versus electromagnetic radiation was not recognized as perhaps the single most important technical trade-off of the project. The group of engineers assigned to this problem decided that, since communication is the central element of the problem, this should receive maximum subtask differentiation. The subtask grouping they chose is listed in Table 3.1.

Table 3.1 *Subtasks Chosen in Earth–Mars Wideband Communication Problem*

Microwave communication techniques
Optical communication techniques
Video and telemetering problems
Pointing problem
Power sources
Configuration
System integration

At this point one of the team began to question the purpose of the TV link and was able to conclude from his questioning that only a one-way link (Mars–Earth) was desired. There was no need of an Earth–Mars TV link. This reduced the required bandwidth almost in half and greatly simplified the system. This is the only example in this exercise, however, of the step we now call generalizing the question. Perhaps this vital activity was nascent in this perceptive team member's thinking, but it was never articulated as a principle.

The pointing problem became critical when one team member reported to the group that to hit Earth from Mars involves an antenna pointing accuracy of 0.1 arc second. But the system team never fully realized that this was "pacing technology," since no one in the group was an antenna design expert. The system study was successful in this regard, nevertheless, because the proper performance specification was established. A system team cannot be expected to supply all possible specialized technical details from its own knowledge; its job is to ask the right questions and identify the needed contributions of specialists.

This is a crucial point in developing the system viewpoint, and it produces unbearable tension in dedicated specialists. A technical specialist believes that a complete rigorous analysis of each element is required to produce a successful whole and that the alternative is careless and perhaps criminal neglect of professional requirements. He sometimes cannot accept the iterative, generalist system viewpoint that it is a waste of time and money to pursue further the antenna design, for example, at this point since many other gross performance characteristics remain to be established. In such cases he will either:

- Demand that an antenna specialist be added to the group.
- Attempt a detailed design himself.
- Reject the whole TV link system study as improperly defined in the first place.

Each of these "solutions" permits the specialist to retain his rigid self-image of professional integrity, but does not satisfy the needs of the group. Although the dedicated specialist is a valuable professional, he cannot remain on a system team, since if he does he will knowingly or unknowingly either subvert the effort or damage his own personality.

The system integration activity had begun to function about 4 weeks into the project. Its task was at first not clear, but soon the group decided that the system management task was threefold.

1. Programming by CPM and other management techniques the activities of other subgroups and establishing schedules.

2. Defining the cross coupling between and among subgroups and ensuring that interim subgroup studies were transmitted among subgroups. The team chose to illustrate these couplings with a form of interaction matrix chart which they developed. Here in nascent form is another rudiment of the system approach advocated in this book.

3. Organizing and editing the written and oral design-study reports. Some 3 weeks later the team had produced a report over 100 pages long. Since this activity occupied only 20 to 25 percent of each man's total work activity during this period, the whole study including documentation took about 2 man-months of effort.

The final report dwelt very heavily on the technical aspects of the problem, and in this respect it made a contribution. There was also a great amount of material on the operating characteristics of various types of lasers and of nuclear energy sources. This material could be useful but probably was inserted because it was easy to obtain. The trade-offs involved in each of these subsystems were not adequately considered. As a general-system planning document the report was a failure for the following reasons:

1. It did not give an estimate of the cost and time required to produce an operating device. This is an omission often made by engineers.

2. It recommended the use of a subsystem (laser) that was not then "space qualified" without detailing special preliminary tests to obtain this qualification. Furthermore, the proposal did not specify an alternative plan for use if the critical laser subunit did not become available at a defined milepost.

3. It did not give a careful step-by-step description of the phasing required to bring the project to completion; that is, the follow-on study was not organized.

4. The team never did understand the concept of pacing technology since it did not establish a goal-definition dialogue with the client. Thus the group never established for itself the real goal of the project. Instead, it saw the project as purely a technical problem.

In other words, the task force never fully accepted its role of leadership in goal definition. It left unarticulated the painful decision on whether or not to proceed with hardware design and testing. Another possible criticism is an inadequate goal development phase. The group resisted an attempt to delay closure and subtask breakout. This group, as many engineers, was ready to accept the problem statement as given.

Suppose that the problem definition phase had included an adequate analysis of the values implied by the problem statement. Then the discussion might begin with the following questions and comments. What technical or scientific value is satisfied by a TV link? Perhaps none. Is the axiological component primarily a human value then? A sense of presence or actuality perhaps? An attempt to involve the tax-paying public in an emotional way in an epoch-making achievement? A confirmation to the nontechnical mind that the event is really taking place? Then a Mars–Earth link will suffice; an Earth–Mars link is not needed. What about image reconstruction: if wide-bandwidth transmission over this path link is technically difficult and expensive, why not narrow the bandwidth and accept the consequent reduction in information rate? We could reconstruct the TV image after reception. Why is real-time transmission necessary? And so forth.

The group lost a great deal of time initially in attempting to understand the problem because it lacked a detailed procedure for goal definition. The group was unable to "get on top" of the problem; it felt that the problem was steering the group rather than vice versa. To be more specific:

- The group failed ever fully to understand the sponsor's motivation for assigning the problem.
- The group wasted a month in attempting to define unilaterally the goals.
- The group failed to control certain of its members who remained dedicated specialists to the end and insisted on overdeveloping certain details (on the energy subsystem and on the physical principles of laser operation, for example), whereas other, more important system elements were neglected.
- The group failed to produce an action-oriented final report.

3.10 Internalizing the Client's Problem: The Board of Education Case

The full-time professional staff of a state Board of Education in the north-central region of the nation was asked by the Board to recommend a general systemic approach to public higher education in the state. The Board is elected and consists of public-spirited citizens who give 2 days a month out of a commitment to representative democracy. The elected Board members are the representatives of the people in assuring a sound, efficient educational system for the state. Although the Board must be responsive to the changing needs of society, it must also live within the annual appropriations of the state legislature and the existing public educational system, built up over more than 100 years. Thus it would be inane for it to consider a plan for higher education in the state that ignored the status quo.

The full-time, salaried staff of the state Board is divided into sections; the section concerned with post-high-school education, that is, "higher education," was assigned to make this system study. The leader of this section of the staff was a university professor of economics on leave with the Board to do this study. In his final oral presentation, after 1 year of effort, he made the following points.

- We know you Board members have to be practical, and may have to make political compromises. We on the staff believe, however, that you should have a complete, detailed, normative plan for higher education in the state from which to work.
- We recommend a complete moratorium on all new programs in higher education in the state for 2 years while this staff completes its study on the educational needs of the state.
- In particular we urge that you reject all the proposals for new programs that have been stalled before you for the past year while the staff was preparing this proposal, so that the staff may complete its work.
- We feel that the present staff resources are inadequate for this purpose and must request a substantial increase in budget to accomplish it.

The Board sat helpless before this report. It was as though some outside group had come before it to recommend a systems study of higher education. But the Board already knew that it wanted such a study; indeed, that was exactly what it had asked of the staff a year before. Now here was its own staff refusing to internalize the Board's problem. By its report the staff refused to acknowledge the realistic limitations of the Board's jurisdiction, and it failed to achieve a contextural integrity in its assignment. By acknowledging the *Board's* need to be practical while

claiming the *staff's* right to do a normative study without realistic constraints, the staff in reality was refusing to come to grips with the problem. Suppose that the Board were to say, "OK, go ahead with your study.
In the meantime we'll stop the world for 2 years and wait for you." Then
the Board would still need *another* analysis of how the staff's theoretical
plan could be tailored to real-world exigencies. The staff claimed the right
to do an academic position paper on the pure theory of higher education
organization and then leave to the Board itself the reconciliation of theory
and reality. This could not be accepted. Although it disliked overruling its
own staff, the Board was forced by the staff's ineptitude to reject each of
the latter's recommendations. The Board knew that the staff was wrong,
although the Board itself was not a system planning organization. It
depended on its staff for this, and the staff had failed the Board.

What should the staff have done? Here are some suggestions.   *191197*

- At the beginning of the year-long study, the higher education staff
  should have iterated through one or two outscoping–inscoping sessions and then briefed the Board on its proposals. Thus the Board
  would have had the opportunity to direct the effort and to acquaint
  itself with the planning method.
- Since it is apparent that previous decisions and history have established the status quo, it should be apparent that planning can do little,
  if anything, to influence immediate conditions. In the past, by involv-
  ing itself in one immediate decision after another, the staff had lost all
  flexibility. Rather than choosing its own planning course, the staff was
  placed in the position of responding to whatever proposals colleges
  and universities chose to submit. It should have cut back to a
  minimum all efforts on immediate proposals and concentrated on the
  normative situation 3 to 5 years hence.
- By announcing as soon as possible state needs in higher education in
  the 3- to 5-year future, the staff would be encouraging the various
  schools to cooperate with it. Most university administrators would
  prefer to be allies rather than adversaries of the state Board.
- The staff could persuade the universities to help develop much of the
  background material needed for planning. Most of the university administrators in the state interact regularly with their opposite numbers
  from other institutions. The academic VPs have their group, and the
  academic deans in the various areas have their individual groups. The
  state Board staff could work with these groups to develop overall
  needs and plans, thus minimizing additional cost and utilizing all
  available expertise.
- All known constraints—money, past agreements, the status quo, em-

ployment in the state, limits on Board authority, and so on—should be considered.

- Certain schools may be more powerful than others and find it more difficult to cooperate. This is a political problem not to be handled unilaterally by the staff. If it occurs, it should be mentioned to the Board, but not given undue emphasis. By making extra .efforts to cooperate with the schools that do seem willing, one rewards cooperation and encourages positive action.

- All this and more could have been accomplished in the first year, and the report to the Board could have covered the general outline of these accomplishments and rough indications of any areas of special need for future programs that had already become apparent.

- In all its planning the staff should maintain some flexibility. All too often, planning in higher education seems to consist of rigid moratoriums, proscriptions, and limitations. It would seem that many state boards actually seek controversy rather than cooperation from the educational units over which they have jurisdiction. When this occurs, it may be taken as a signal of improper or nonexistent staff work on the part of the Board involved.

3.11   Generalizing the Problem: The Woodward Avenue Subway Case

In December 1969, on his last day in office, Mayor Jerome P. Cavanagh of Detroit recommended, via a press conference and formal presentation, that construction be initiated immediately on a $100 million, 4.5-mile subway along Woodward Avenue from downtown to the "new center" area. Detroit is a major industrial city of over 2 million population (about 4 million in the greater Detroit SMSA) and has no rail rapid transit.

Woodward Avenue is the main radial, connecting downtown with the fast-growing northern suburbs (see Figures 3.4 and 3.5). It has been the major target for transit proposals for over 40 years and presently supports the only money-making line of the city bus system, DSR. The Cavanagh proposal gave no evidence of intent to extend the subway to the state fairgrounds and city line, 8 miles from downtown, or to suburban centers such as Pontiac, 25 miles away, although this obviously would be the next step.

A system team was formed and asked to assume that the new mayor had given them the task of analyzing the problem and making a recommendation within 90 days. The four team members were graduate engineers, some with industrial experience, but all new to large-scale system analysis. This case study relates the experience of the team, called Omega

Figure 3.4   Photo of downtown Detroit, looking northward from Cobo Hall on the Detroit River along Woodward Avenue toward the new center area in the distance.

Engineering, Inc., in its early "client" interactions and then presents the first few iterations of the system analysis based in part on the Omega effort.[14] One can consider the mutual education of the Omega Engineering system team and its client, "the Mayor," in four phases. These phases correspond to the periods of work between milepost meetings of the team with the client.

Phase I: Problem Definition and First Client's Meeting

For the first several weeks of the project, the Omega team members familiarized themselves with the problem and their available resources. They found that TALUS Origin Destination (O/D) transportation demand study was available,[15] and they obtained material from the Doxiadis study of Greater Detroit.[16] The material was immensely useful in the system study, and the reader should be aware that such a data collection phase can be expensive and time consuming. Then the team organized itself for the task ahead. Various members took specific assignments, and organization charts, DELTA charts, and the like were constructed. Omega prepared for its first milepost meeting with the client 3 weeks into the project, and made, in the opinion of one interested observer, an excellent presentation.

The team presented the six essential phases in a system approach to the

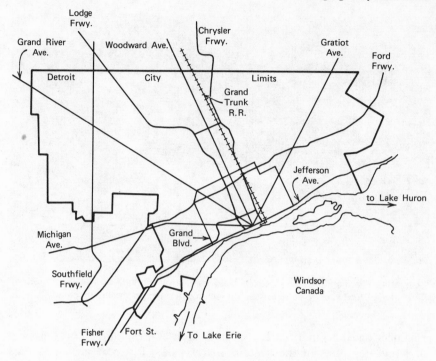

Figure 3.5 Street map of major Detroit arterials.

client's problem as the "Mayor" sat impassively smoking his cigar. The team then explained the necessity of embedding the client's specific question into the following series of five increasingly general questions:

1. Should the 4.5-mile Woodward subway be built? (The original question.)
2. What are the transport needs for this 4.5-mile section of Woodward?
3. What are the transport needs of Woodward as a whole?
4. What are the transport needs of Detroit (city)?
5. What are the regional transport needs of the Urban Detroit Area (UDA)?

Omega then presented an explanation of the meaning of an index of performance and its application to a system study of transportation. It was proposed that a computer simulation of the Detroit urban region would aid in placing specific transport choices in proper perspective. The "Mayor" was then asked to define and rank-order the elements of his chosen index so as to allow the team to proceed with its simulation and to evaluate the candidate systems.

At this point the meeting disintegrated into chaos. The "Mayor" opened his remarks by disclaiming any knowledge of an index of performance. He next declared his unwillingness to learn. He insisted that taxpayers' money should not be wasted on a computer model of the urban region. Finally, he stated that embedding the specific question in a more general one appeared to him to be a dodge to avoid the issue. He closed his remarks by demanding a "yes" or "no" answer to his specific question (1) above. He then sat back and relit the stump of his cigar.

After a hurried consultation the team assured the "Mayor" that he would have his answer, on time, and within budget. The team then attempted to approach the index of performance indirectly by suggesting four possible options for justifying an investment in transportation.

1. Improve transportation along the 4.5-mile corridor, that is, reduce travel time.
2. Reduce traffic congestion in the corridor.
3. Induce new commercial, residential, and industrial development along the corridor, as well as halting decay.
4. Increase the mobility of residents near the corridor.

The team asked the "Mayor" to rank these priorities. He replied that all were extremely important objectives and adjourned the meeting because of a previously scheduled appointment elsewhere.

Phase II: The Antisystem Phase

The team, chastened but wiser, assembled the following day to survey the situation. Several things were agreed upon:

● The "Mayor" did not "buy" the system approach, and any further effort at explanation would confirm his suspicion that it was an excuse for not solving his problem.

● Even if the "Mayor" accepted the system approach, it would be impossible to construct a computer simulation of the Detroit metropolitan region within the time and money constraints of the contract.

● Therefore the team decided to answer the "Mayor's" specific question, given the existing conditions in the 4.5-mile corridor. This could be called an antisystem approach. Omega correctly anticipated the "Mayor's" probable reaction to this and prepared itself as well to propose the next phase.

Two weeks later the second milepost meeting was held. The "Mayor" was seen to smile with satisfaction when the presentation skipped all talk of a general system approach and began immediately with an evaluation of transport in the 4.5-mile Woodward corridor. The presentation indicated that little new development could be expected along this corridor. It showed a maximum potential daily mass-transit ridership of less than 50,000 persons and revealed that a yearly operating subsidy of $3 to $5 million would be required for even minimum service. Thus this proposal could not be recommended as feasible.

The "Mayor's" reaction did not surprise the Omega group. He asked a few questions and then accepted the negative conclusion. After a few moments of thought he then asked what he *should* do. Omega pointed out that this was precisely why the system study had been proposed originally. For little more than the cost of answering one question, the system- or goal-centered approach answers hundreds of specific items. In highlighting the best option, one also answers "no" to all other alternatives. For the first time the "Mayor" seemed ready to accept the system approach. At this point he was informed that only 5 weeks remained and that, by insisting on a specific answer first, he had foreclosed the possibility of a complete study but that the team would do as much as it could in the time remaining. The concept of an index of performance was reviewed, and the "Mayor" agreed that his main purpose was to spark development and arrest urban decay. He commented that Detroit had constructed 50 miles of urban freeways in the past 20 years to decrease congestion but the city still decays.

Phase III: A System Approach

The Omega team decided that a logical procedure for the time remaining would be to take the following steps:

1. Identify the major transport corridors of Detroit.
2. Apply the "Mayor's" ranking of criteria to find the best corridor for development.
3. Consider technological alternatives to find the best mode for that best corridor. It was anticipated that this phase could not be completed in the time remaining.
4. Present recommendations.

Doxiadis' data are available for resident population, working population, commercial land use, industrial land use, and vacant land for 28 sectors of Detroit. A computer program was written that utilizes the data to analyze and compare various corridors. Unfortunately the Doxiadis data base does not include traffic studies. Therefore a second computer program was written to utilize TALUS O/D data for 64 survey districts in Detroit. This second program permits one to analyze trips between defined areas or along defined corridors. The six major radial corridors and an important circumferential corridor, Grand Boulevard, were included in this analysis.

The results of the analysis indicated the Grand Boulevard corridor to be the prime candidate for development. This was rather surprising, since no previous study had ever included Grand Boulevard. Not only was the result surprising; it was also "robust." If the weighting of the elements in the performance index were varied over a significant range (more than 10 to 1), Grand Boulevard remained the best choice.

At the third milepost meeting these results were reviewed with the "Mayor." He expressed increased confidence in the system approach and, although surprised at the recommendation of Grand Boulevard, seemed to approve the results. The team felt that they would be allowed to write up these interim findings and terminate the study. To the team's surprise, however, the "Mayor" then announced a formal public hearing on the study and stated that the oral presentation of the team would be evaluated by a panel of outside transportation experts hired for this purpose. He also requested results of the intermodal study and delivery of the written report before the oral presentation. When the team protested that this formal presentation was not in the original contract, the "Mayor" replied that the exercise was completely voluntary but that he would soon be awarding a contract for a follow-on system study. The meeting adjourned.[17]

Phase IV: Formal Presentation

Multicolored flip charts were the order of the day. The panel of transportation experts was impressed in general, but pointed out a number of specific items that could have been better covered in the presentation. The arguments against Woodward Avenue and for Grand Boulevard as the "best corridor" were accepted. However, the tentative results of the intermodal study were declared unconvincing. The Omega report was accepted, and the panel of experts recommended to the "Mayor" that Omega Engineering be placed on the list of qualified bidders for the follow-on study.[18]

3.12   The System Analyst's Decalogue

1. Your client does not understand his problem. You must help him to gain this understanding.

2. The problem as posed by the client is too specific. You must embed the specific problem in the next more general question.

3. Your client does not understand the concept of an index of performance. You must help him to weigh the several desired attributes of the problem solution.

4. You are the system analyst, not the decision maker. You present weighted evaluations of options. The client makes decisions.

5. You must present your recommendations to fit the agreed-upon time scale and level of generality. Generalization of the client's problem is a technique for finding and solving the correct specific problem, not for avoiding the issue.

6. A goal-centered approach, rather than a technology-centered, time-sequential approach, is essential.

7. The disadvantage to the nonuser must be included in your weighted evaluation of each proposed candidate system.

8. A universal computer simulation model of a complex system cannot exist. You must postulate a priori the specific questions that you wish the model to simulate.

9. The role of the "decision maker" in a socially relevant, large-scale system is generally unclear. You must expect to engage in building a political consensus if your recommendations are to move to an action phase.

10. A system study that begs the question and has as its major recommendation another study more costly in time and money is a failure. Answer the client's real question.

Exercises

3.1 Prepare a tree of client objectives in the Earth–Mars TV system analysis.

3.2 Prepare a tree of system team objectives in the Earth–Mars TV system analysis.

3.3 Prepare an interaction matrix for major subsystems of the Earth–Mars manned probe. Show how the TV link interacts with other subsystems of probe.

3.4 Prepare an interaction matrix for subsystems of the TV system.

3.5 Prepare a DELTA chart for a system study of the TV project.

3.6 Prepare a Gantt chart for the Earth–Mars mission. Emphasize mileposts important to the TV project.

3.7 Prepare a Gantt chart for the TV feasibility system study.

Notes and References

1. For a contrary view cogently expressed see W. Alonso, "Beyond the Interdisciplinary Approach to Planning," *Journal of the American Institute of Planners*, Vol. 37, No. 2 (March 1971), pp. 169–173.

2. J. N. Warfield and J. D. Hill, "Notes for Systems Workshop," Battelle Seattle Research Center, February 1971.

3. H. R. Hamilton et al., *Systems Simulation for Regional Analysis,* M.I.T. Press, Cambridge, 1969.

4. John Brooks, *Telephone*, Harper and Row, New York, 1976, pp. 278, 279 and 288–295.

5. There are many textbooks on management organization theory. See, for example, R. Carzo, Jr., J. N. Yanonzas, *Formal Organization, A Systems Approach,* Irwin-Dorsey Press, Homewood, Ill., 1967.

6. This is *not* to say, of course, that one should use a chronological description of one's process! Always orient the report to the client's objectives, *not* to the team's subjective concerns.

7. For a survey of a number of such efforts see A. W. Drake, R. L. Keeney, P. M. Morse (Eds.), *Analysis of Public Systems*, M.I.T. Press, Cambridge, 1972.

8. E. Canty, "Civil Systems," Adaptive Control Symposium, Pennsylvania State University, November 1969.

9. G. Strasser, "Urban, Military and Aerospace Systems: A Comparison from the Analyst's Viewpoint," Ch. 21 in A. Blumstein, M. Kamress, A. B. Weiss (Eds.), *Systems Analysis for Social Problems*, Washington Operations Research Council, Washington, D. C., 1970.

10. On the other hand, cost cannot be ignored in military systems. "Gold plating" of several weapons systems in recent years has resulted in poor cost/effectiveness ratios. See "A Tight Limit on Army Costs," *Business Week*, June 10, 1972, p. 40, in which a new cost consciousness is said to be influencing military procurement.

11. H. R. Walt, *The Four Aerospace Contracts: A Review of the California Experience*, Appendix Vol. 5, pp. 43–73, Report of the National Commission on Technology, Automation, and Economic Progress, U. S. Government Printing Office, Washington, D. C., February 1966.

12. See also H. D. Watkins, "Socio-Economic Aerospace Market," *Aviation Week*, January 31, pp. 52–61; February 7, 1966, pp. 79–87.

13. H. R. Walt, *loc. cit.*

14. The material presented here is based on work done within a 10-week period in a

graduate course on large-scale systems at Oakland University. The role of "Mayor" in this system project was played by a university faculty member (not myself), skilled in practical politics and experienced in local government procedures. He was not "primed," nor was he familiar with the approach favored by the team. The transportation experts mentioned in the report on the oral presentation were experienced analysts from consulting firms and the transportation industry. For a discussion of this exercise from the participants' point of view see A. W. Turski, R. A. White, "A System Approach to Urban Transportation in Detroit," *IEEE Transactions on Aerospace and Electronic Systems*, Vol. AES-7, No. 3 (May, 1971), pp. 438–442.

15. *Growth, Change and a Choice for 1990,* Preliminary Plan for Southeast Michigan, Detroit Regional Transportation and Land Use Study (TALUS), 3 Vols., 1969.

16. C. A. Doxiadis, *Emergence and Growth of an Urban Region*, 3rd Vol., Detroit Edison Co., 1966.

17. In an off-the-record conference with his advisers, which followed, the "Mayor" blasted naive engineers who expected him to "take the rap" at the polls for an expensive gadget. He argued that it was good politics for a group of experts to make the first presentation of a controversial idea. He then could claim to be "evaluating the proposal" while he sensed public reaction.

18. Although this study received some publicity on local television in Detroit and the full report was made available to city officials, no use of it was made. Subsequently the choice of the Woodward corridor was confirmed officially for further planning purposes.

Part II
STEPS IN A SYSTEM ANALYSIS

4

Goals for American Society

It is difficult to speak adequately or justly of London. It is not a pleasant place; it is not agreeable or cheerful or easy, or exempt from reproach . . . . The fogs, the smoke, the dirt, the darkness, the wet, the distances, the ugliness, the brutal size of the place, the horrible numerosity of society, the manner in which this senseless bigness is fatal to amenity, to convenience, to conversation, to good manners—this and much more you may expiate upon.

Henry James's Journals
1881

For the problems of the central cities are beginning to penetrate the suburbs . . . . We have been throwing billions of dollars into these problem areas without making a dent upon them. It is now foolish to say that if we will only spend a little more money we will resolve these difficult issues . . . . The truth is—none of us are now sure what are the right things to do.

GEORGE ROMNEY
Secretary of Housing and Urban Development
March 6, 1972

Over the objections of proponents of "disjointed incrementalism," I argue that the social-action analogue for developing and marketing products in the private sector is by formulating, debating, and getting consensus on goals that express the community's aspirations for itself. Goals provide the sense of direction essential in a purposeful, dynamic society.

L. C. FITCH
"Eight Goals for an Urbanizing America"
Dáedalus, Fall 1968, p. 1142

4.1   The Status Quo

America is predominantly an urban society with a strong residuum of agrarian values. Thus, although it seems appropriate to concentrate on urban America to revitalize our nation, this psychic tension cannot be ignored. In Chapter 1 of this text we attempted to place the urban problem into context. Now we wish to apply the system approach described in Chapters 2 and 3 to the solution of the massive problem indicated in the final sections of the first chapter.

An obvious alternative to this systemic approach is the present piecemeal attempt to address bits of the problem. Yet it is obvious that disjointed incrementalism has resulted in a number of significant and expensive failures. Among its marginal successes and outright failures must be included the following:

- Federal public low-cost housing efforts.
- Operation Breakthrough (a specific federal low-cost housing effort).
- Aid to Dependent Children program.
- Extension of interstate highway system into major cities.

It seems beyond controverting to most observers that American cities are steadily growing poorer, more segregated, dirtier, less safe, more expensive, and less satisfying places in which to live. But there are those who try to advance the opposing view. Banfield, for example, argues that cities are really getting better and better. It is only, he says, that our expectations rise even more rapidly than the great improvements in urban performance.[1]

4.2 The Future of the American City

Some observers would argue that the large city does not have a future. Arguments for this position include the following:

- The rising crime rate and failure of law and order in all large American cities indicate an obvious trend toward decay that cannot be reversed.
- People want privacy and are willing to pay for it. Thus the trend toward suburban single-family dwelling units will continue. The core of the city will continue to decay.
- Cities are an expensive drain on the economy. All the unemployables and ne'er-do-wells are attracted there for a free ride on social welfare.
- The development of ubiquitous transportation has removed a constraint on industry. It is no longer forced to pay high urban land costs and city taxes in order to gain access to transport connections, nor need it be concerned with transporting its labor force. Thus industry will continue to migrate from the city.
- Videophones and other devices such as cable television and computers will permit the dispersal of commerce; hence the "center of communication" will not require physical centralization.

- People will not go downtown to shop. Why fight for a parking place when one can go to an enclosed shopping mall in the suburbs?

Let us see whether these arguments can stand the test of analysis.

Crime Rates Are Rising

Crime has been rising in large cities during the past several decades. This is true even after corrections are made for the more accurate collection and reporting of crime statistics. However, it is not clear that the cause is large agglomerations of people, although some statistical correlation is apparent. One statistical artifact that, although real enough, must be discounted, is the result of the rise of affluence and the inflation that has occurred in the past several decades. Thus a theft of $50 in 1940 or 1950 had more impact than it should now be given. In 1977 $50 is not worth as much to the thief, nor does its loss hurt the owner as much, as would have been the case 25 years ago. Yet crime statistics do not take this into consideration. For a cool and expert appraisal of the "rising wave of crime," see Biderman.[2]

Next, we must recognize that the city has been the focus of the social revolution which has been carried out during the past several decades and is still under way in the United States. Poor and uneducated people of predominantly rural backgrounds have flooded the major cities of the nation since World War II to find a better life; and as incredibly bad as are our urban ghettos, *they have found it*. Let us say this is another way, focusing on a given deteriorating neighborhood. Those who migrate from the neighborhood to the suburbs improve their lot. But those who come into the area from rural backwaters or still worse urban areas may also improve their living conditions. In a sense the neighborhood deteriorates, but both former residents, landlords, and newcomers may benefit. The flood of rural–urban migration is now slackening off, it for no other reason than that rural areas have been depopulated. Thus it is to be expected that urban social service agencies will be better able to cope with their assignments.

Finally it should be remembered that major cities have always seemed to some observers as pestholes on the verge of collapse. This is not meant to excuse the condition of our cities, but merely to point out that doomsayers have been consistently wrong about the death of the city.

People Are Willing to Pay for Suburban Privacy

This is really not true. The flight of the urban middle class has been subsidized in large part by the very cities that are being deserted. As John

Lindsay[3] has pointed out, two federal laws have subsidized this migration. The National Defense Highways Act encouraged the construction of the interstate highway system into the city via urban freeways, thus opening up the suburbs for 30 miles or more in all directions. City taxes helped to finance the flight, via these freeways, of persons earning their livings in the city, thus permitting these jobholders to avoid city taxes. Moreover, the establishment of FHA low-cost mortgages permitted many city wage earners with little or no equity to buy their own suburban homes; thus again the city financed its own economic destruction. The purpose here is *not* to condemn the construction of highways and low-cost suburban housing, but merely to point out that through drawing artificial political boundaries certain classes of citizens, predominantly white and middle class, profit by association with the city through jobs without bearing a fair share of the city's costs.

It should be apparent that almost all services and utilities can be provided more economically to a given number of people in a moderate-density configuration than in low-density suburbs. Police and fire protection cost more in the suburbs, as do roads, gas, water, and telephone and sewer lines, as the distance between houses increases. Yet many utility rate structures fail to reflect these factors. Even if the city extends its boundaries to include the entire metropolitan region, new schools, libraries, and other public facilities must be supplied to the suburbs while similar, fully amortized facilities are underutilized nearer the center. Yet central city residents may subsidize such new construction.

Cities Are an Economic Drain

This is a common misunderstanding, and the larger the city the stronger this fallacy seems to become. New York City is the extreme example. The city receives a largesse of approximately $1.5 billion annually from the state legislature, but what is not as obvious is the approximately $3 billion in tax revenues that the state extracts from the city![4] If each of the major cities of this nation were able to organize itself into a separate state within the union, its financial problems would be solved overnight!

Ubiquitous Transport Permits the Dispersal of Industry

This is true. The city as a center of industry appears doomed.

People Will Not Go Downtown to Shop

This may or may not be true. Retail trade must orient itself to the customer's demand to use his automobile, but a balance is in the process of being struck. Suburban shopping malls are growing larger. Retail merchandising theory has undergone a major change recently. When early suburban shopping malls were constructed, major food stores and department store chains insisted on exclusive occupancy. Now the reverse is true. Just as auto dealers learned empirically of the advantages to them of assembling in an "automobile row," so Sears, A & P, and other major retailers now insist on a mall large enough to provide space for their major rivals. Thus we see a familiar agglomeration effect in action. We note also that the peripheral land outside the perimeter parking lot surrounding large, enclosed shopping malls is rising in value. Finally we note that new large malls are located near major freeway interchanges. Thus we ask, "What's the difference from downtown?" The answer appears to be convenient access and free parking. The gridiron city street pattern may be inadequate for full downtown shopping malls, but free parking plus moving belt transport between buildings plus an equitable tax burden over the metropolitan region would seem to be all that is holding back the downtown "shopping mall," provided that urban freeways permit rapid access.

Communication Centers Will Not Require Physical Centralization

Technically speaking, this is true, but psychologically it is probably false. Although in principle a commercial enterprise (excluding retail trade and manufacturing) could be held together with an electronic web if face-to-face interactions were extremely rare, this eventuality appears unlikely within this century. Since managers, clerks, banks, insurance companies, educational institutions, and so on seem to deal almost exclusively with symbols rather than artifacts, whole organizations could operate with no central workplace. Even the computers that would activate the symbol transfer and manipulation could be remotely programmed. Each knowledge worker in principle could perform his "work" in a special area of his home, communicating with his coworkers, subordinates, boss, teachers, customers, and other persons via telecommunications.

All this is possible in principle today, no additional technical breakthrough being needed. Yet we say that this scenario appears unlikely for this century. Why? Since this is a matter of values and societal mores, it is not one in which an untrained person can risk dogmatism. We badly need value system research in the social sciences. This research should be directed, not at what is *possible*, but rather at what is *likely*. The work should include social indicators so that movement toward the predicted value structure can be measured. I base my present guess on the permanence of the "value bundle" that surrounds and supports the world of work. Here are my indicators.

- There is no present evidence of work week reduction. As Peter Drucker says,[5] "Work is growing faster than the work force and is likely to continue to grow faster." A few unions were able to reduce their work week to 36 hours, but some of these have already had to go back to 40 hours; Akron rubber workers and General Motors Frigidaire workers are examples. The movement to the four-day work week should be watched as an indicator of change in this value. A possible sequence would be as follows: move to four 10-hour days and show that productivity remains steady or increases; then after a few years begin agitation for the 9-hour day.
- A permissive management environment would be required to carry out work dispersal to the home. Although MacGregor's theory Y has been tried in scattered instances,[6] a reaction appears to be setting in.
- Permissive management and worker participation in the planning of effort are effective only if there is an internal dedication to the effort by the workers. Alienation from the value of work may cause the worker to reduce his productivity if permitted. Union doctrine opposes the principle of incentive pay and piecework; thus the natural reinforcement of reward for increased productivity is cut. Alienation and increased polarization between worker and management are indicators that the environment for work dispersal is not general. One might expect a few small companies to be successful at it without this being an indicator of a general trend.
- Work dispersal to the home requires a "professional" attitude on the part of those involved. Self-motivation and self-discipline are needed. Indications are quite to the contrary in the American work force. Even such highly skilled and highly paid "professional" as airline pilots, registered nurses, physicians, and college professors are unionizing. This must lead to an increase in an adversary attitude which seems contrary to that needed for successful work dispersal.
- Fear and insecurity of managers will inhibit work dispersal. Symbol manipulation is difficult to quantify. One finds it difficult to measure the output of "paper shufflers" in any objective manner. "Management by objective" is a current catch phrase, but is easier to say than to translate into action. One must fall back on evaluation by relative measures and often by appearances. Over a long period (several years) it is possible to form a more objective evaluation, but on a daily, weekly, or monthly basis subjectivity is paramount. Thus the manager will insist that his workers be in the office where he can keep his eye on them.

Thus I would argue that the world of work will continue to dominate our lives and that this work will take place in or near large cities in the 10- to 20-year future.

4.3   The American City of the Future

Does the city have a future? And, if so, what kind? It seems unlikely that in the 20- to 30-year future society will move away from the mutual exchange of goods and services among its members for their mutual convenience. Moreover, it appears likely that money in some form will continue to be needed as a medium of exchange and will be as avidly sought as ever, and that specialization of labor will become increasingly sharp. Agglomerations of people will continue to be needed to accomplish these ends. These agglomerations or cities should take on a form convenient to modern life and to the provision of amenities not now universally available. It is not apparent from this, of course, how large or how dense these urban agglomerations will be, or what physical form they will take.

It goes without saying, perhaps, that the basic needs of the individual must first be met by the city. Rarely, if ever, however, has urban development been concerned with a broad spectrum of human needs. Usually, conventional cities of the past and present have attempted to satisfy only a few selected human needs such as safety and economic needs.

On the most basic physiological level the future city must help us meet our needs for food, water, light, and air. Clean water and clean air mandate careful control of industrial pollution. It hardly seems correct for this reason, however, simply to bar heavy industry; rather, the full spectrum of work should be permitted. The need for food must be met by clean markets selling reasonably priced goods. But in addition there must be accessible job opprurtunities that enable one to earn the basic necessities. The proper spectrum of work opportunities deserves careful consideration. Present cities meet most of these physiological needs with the possible exception of pollution control and accessibility.

But present cities are deficient in meeting safety needs. Man needs protection from the weather by adequate housing. We will see that the cost of providing this housing is the largest single cost in the city. Thus, to permit expenditures to meet higher-order needs in the future city, design of lower-cost housing must become a critical short-term goal. Also, safety in transportation is deficient in existing cities. Congestion and failure to control traffic flow result in an unacceptably high accident rate on urban roadways. If the automobile is to be allowed into high-density sectors of future cities, entirely new means of controlling these vehicles must be found.

But the safety need found most wanting in present-day American cities is protection from crime. A debate presently rages on what to do about urban crime. The liberal position, represented perhaps by the American Civil Liberties Union, argues that crime increase is an inevitable result of the rapid shift in social values and increased mobility of our citizens. In effect, it argues that crime is a symptom rather than the disease itself. It implies that crime will dissipate when injustice and poverty are removed. The more conservative position, represented by many law enforcement officials, holds that the judiciary's increased absorption with procedural defects in law enforcement and its emphasis on the rights of the accused to the neglect of those of the injured and of the general public have made prosecution of criminals difficult. Drug-related crime has multiplied, and the fear of assault has increased the sales of hand guns manyfold in the past decade. In all probability, neither the short-term, purely defensive conservative position nor the long-term, liberal sociological approach is sufficient. Each is excessively doctrinaire and seems more concerned with winning arguments than with providing for safety needs. Social support mechanisms, the physical structure of the city, police protection, the legal and criminal justice system, the schools, and the family—all must contribute to the solution. This appears to be a critical study area.

The need to belong to a group—at the minimum a nuclear family and, almost as important, an extended family group—must be met in the future city. Such matters as provisions for the aged, the opportunity for parental supervision of children's play area, and the opportunity to walk to church, school, shopping, and recreation are not adequately addressed in present-day cities. Some regulations of social agencies presently militate against the basic human need to belong. In the past, the Aid to Dependent Children (ADC) program provided help to mothers only if there was no male head of the household. Not only did this regulation break up families, but also it led to flying raids on ADC mothers by social workers to ensure that no male was secretly in residence. Such aberrations are the result of a failure fully to think through social legislation, and to provide for modifications if a program goes off course. The emotionalism with which this problem is presently addressed is a clear signal to the observer of a marked dissonance in social values. To ignore this dissonance is to court difficulty.

The need for esteem is present in all normal human beings. Indeed, a lack of self-esteem or of concern for gaining the respect and esteem of others is taken as a symptom of degeneration of the subject's personality. This seems to say that in the new city a social–political power hierarchy will exist, that it must be open, and that it must reward behavior which contributes to the overall good of society. A closed power structure is to be discouraged, just as is the perversion of esteem needs in the form of street gangs and organized crime. All of these provide a twisted satisfaction of the need for esteem in ways incompatible with the well-being of society. On the positive side, an increase in participative, public political deliberations seems to be indicated. With modern telecommunications and the shortened work week, it seems entirely practicable that all citizens be permitted to vote on all issues, and there will be less need for the interim compromise of representative democracy.

The four needs discussed thus far—the physiological need, the need for safety, the need to belong, and the need for esteem—are basic but in a sense are less than human, if by the word "human" we wish to distinguish ourselves from other animals. Many mammals exhibit some or all of the above needs. Herds and flocks contribute to more than safety; from these, individuals satisfy their need to belong. Also, individuals thrust themselves into leadership positions, even at some personal danger, to gain esteem.

The new city certainly must satisfy these basic needs in a fashion superior to that characteristic of existing cities. Indeed, it will be judged initially on the way it satisfies these basic needs. In effect, these are necessary conditions for success, but they are not sufficient. The city that satisfies only the four basic needs will be flat, insipid, and vaguely unsatisfying to its residents in the long run.

Once these basic human needs are satisfied, and essentially in the order in which we have described them, other, higher needs will become apparent. These higher-order human needs are difficult to rank even in approximate order. Not all people experience all the higher needs all the time, even if the basic needs are satisfied. Some people appear willing or able to exist on a lower level than others, although it seems probable that all these higher needs are at least latent in most of us. By now, too, the schema of this discussion is becoming apparent to some readers. We are following the general organization of Maslow and his list of human needs.[7] But Maslow should not be held responsible for the interpretation placed on his categories. Furthermore, we will add one additional category that appears to set up a mental block in some social thinkers.

Among the higher-order needs is the impulse to cognition. This is a way of saying that we seek knowledge for its own sake. Perhaps man's need to know or his so-called idle curiosity has long-run racial survival value. Be that as it may, the impulse exists. We should not take cognitive need, however, as the rationale for universal higher education. The vast majority of students in American colleges are there for more basic reasons, such as finding a mate and/or learning a job-related skill. Some adults and the occasional college student are fulfilling cognitive needs. It is fashionable to disparage job-related training in American colleges, but that is not our purpose. In fact, since this is a more basic need, it is not surprising that it is met first. But as society organizes itself more effectively to meet the basic needs, the higher-order needs will be uncovered. It is to be expected that in an advanced society such as ours and especially in the new city the cognitive need will be stronger than it presently seems to be among the general population. Thus one would expect to see a demand for more organized adult learning. Programs directed at skills and hobbies, travelogues, and courses in literature, history, astronomy, ecology, political science, psychology, sociology, anthropology, language skills, and other areas would be in demand. A more participative mode than the lecture seems desirable, perhaps one utilizing telecommunications in the home. No doubt spectator sports and entertainment will continue to be popular, but a more participative component will probably become increasingly important and perhaps utimately replace spectatorship.

Aesthetic needs provide another component in the higher category, and the desire to see beauty and order in one's surroundings will grow as leisure time becomes more common. This will increase the demand for art galleries and museums, art appreciation programs, the theater, and concerts, but it will also do more. The citizens of the new city will extend their critical aesthetic judgments to their everyday surroundings. Public and private architecture will be affected, as will transport networks, landscaping, and the general community ambience. Nor will the workplace escape the demand for aesthetic satisfactions; the new city resident will not be satisfied with the twentieth century equivalent of the "dark satanic mills" of the 1800s. Indeed, demands for improvements in the workplace have already begun to be heard.

One of Maslow's major contributions to psychology was this organization of needs and, in particular, his articulation of the need for self-actualization. Maslow calls this, rather vaguely, the need to become everything one is capable of becoming. He discusses it in terms of peak experiences or the moments of exultation occasionally felt when one seems to transcend his daily limitations and all goes right. The most common examples of peak experiences are drawn from love and sport. But concentration on peak experiences to illustrate self-actualization distorts this admittedly imprecise concept. A self-actualized person is achieving, rather than questing, and is self-fulfilled, confident, at peace with himself, assured that he is giving the best of himself to the task at hand, and satisfied with the reward of this knowledge. Exactly what, if anything, is required by the new city to encourage self-actualization beyond meeting man's other needs is not clear at this time.

Finally, we will add the transcendental need to Maslow's list. It is interesting that such a widespread and long-existing need should be ignored by Maslow. This need is usually approached through organized religion, and perhaps the struggle of many intellectuals to free themselves from childhood rituals is so intense that they become unable to discuss this need with dispassion. In any case, the likelihood of religion entering into an urban planning discussion spontaneously is extremely remote, and any proposal to discuss the subject will usually be ignored.[8] Organized religion is only one way, however, of satisfying the transcendental need. This need can be defined as the drive to understand mankind's place and destiny in the cosmos. The militant atheist is surely seeking, in his own way, to satisfy the transcendental need. Other than providing the normal tax exemptions for nonprofit organizations and practicing the new disestablishmentarianism, what can urban design do to help satisfy transcendental needs? I do not know. This subject uncovers deep dissonances, and most suggestions are met with highly emotional arguments. It may be impossible to integrate religion, whatever its form, into the life of the new city. Perhaps transcendental needs may have to be left entirely separate, as they are now, but if this proves true it seems an important loss.

Although this commentary on the city of the future is based on Maslow's list of human needs, other approaches to predicting the future are possible. In a series of RAND reports O. Helmer developed an approach that he calls the DELPHI method, which he has applied to studies of future values.[9] T. J. Gordon has also utilized this approach to predict the future.[10] Since both of these studies were done 10 years ago, one may begin to measure the accuracy of the DELPHI approach by direct comparison with reality. The method consists of soliciting the opinions of "experts" in their areas of competence. It is not a popularity contest. The participants do not interact in person, thus reducing the effect of persuasion. Reasons for predictions are circulated in writing, and special attention is given to experts whose estimates differ significantly from the norm, under the assumption that they may have access to special insights. Several rounds of prediction are conducted, and convergence is usually noted.

4.4 A Value System of American Society

The sociologist considers "values" to be the internalized concepts or ideals held by a person that are the criteria by which goals are chosen.[11] As might be expected, there is room for considerable discussion concerning the range and full implications of such a philosophical construct.[12] Nevertheless, the concept of "value" seems to have considerable operational efficacy. It is generally understood that values do not stand as isolated elements but rather form sets or groupings; hence it is common to speak of a "value system." Although individuals generally hold many values in common with their fellows, complete uniformity is lacking. Certain individuals hold more strongly or weakly to various elements of a set. Many individuals will declare for a bundle of values that when examined may be found to be internally inconsistent or nonoperative in practice.

Williams lists and discusses the following elements, which, he is persuaded, make up a common set of values for American society:[13]

- Achievement and success.
- Activity and work.
- Moral orientation.
- Humanitarianism.
- Efficiency and practicality.
- Progress.
- Material comfort.
- Equality.
- Freedom.
- External conformity.
- Science and secular rationality.
- Nationalism–patriotism.
- Democracy.
- Individual personality.
- Racism and group superiority.

One can see the internal conflicts, and we repeat that no specific American can be said to hold any particular one (material comfort, say) or several of these values in strength or at all. Moreover, some observers claim to see a gradual though emphatic shift in this value system. A start has been made at tracking these value shifts and projecting forward several decades in time.[14] The methodology is inadequate as yet, and results to date are of doubtful validity. Nevertheless, it appears possible in principle to predict with reasonable certainty prospective global shifts in American values if any such are in prospect over the next several decades. This will greatly aid in the design and redesign of our cities. Furthermore, the difficulty, if not the impossibility, of precision[15] can be turned into a design principle itself.

Because of the rapid shift in society's needs and the rising demand for participation and personal control, good urban design must be minimal design. Maximum flexibility must be retained, variety and free choice must be available, continuous change and renewal must be provided for, and authoritive dogmatism must be avoided in favor of participative determinations. Maslow's basic needs are presumed to remain stable for humanity over a long period of time, but the value structure of a particular group of people can vary in some important details in the course of a decade or so. Thus we should not presume that present values in American society will remain fixed throughout the remainder of this century.

We have listed above the general values apparently now operative in urban America. Next let us attempt to predict the values that promise to have an important influence on the structure of the new city for the remainder of this century.

- It is presumed that the world of work will continue to have a strong influence on urban America. Less than half the total jobs will be industrial, however, with the remainder in commercial, government, service, and administrative sectors.
- Work will continue to be carried out in specialized places, rather than in the home, for example, as some have proposed, and working hours will continue to be regulated. Thus the journey to work will continue to be the major stress in transport links.
- Personal privacy will be increasingly valued. In transport and housing this trend will be important.
- The 4-day work week will become increasingly common, resulting in a greater exodus to weekend retreats and recreational facilities.
- Living arrangements will continue to become more casual; and although the nuclear family living together will remain the chief mode, other arrangements will become more common than they now are.
- Participative rather than representative democracy will be more common, and all segments of society will increasingly demand self-determination not only in politics but also in the workplace.
- Complete social protection from all concerns will increase. Poverty grants, free medical service of all sorts, free legal aid, complete job protection through a guaranteed annual wage, old age security, and so forth, will steadily become more common.
- Leisure time activities—recreation, hobbies, adult education, and participative sports will all grow in importance.
- Increased centralization of governance will continue at all levels. Cities will merge into metropolitan government, states will take over local school systems, and the federal government will assume functions now filled by the states. Government will grow at all levels and become less personal, and this will be actively resented by the people, who may succeed in reversing the trend.
- Racial, sexual, and religious equality will be complete, but immigration will increasingly be restricted as the income gap between the United States and the rest of the world continues to widen.
- In the near future, political neoisolationism will grow in popularity,

and the U. S. political "presence" on all continents will decrease with
the exception, perhaps, of South America. This will be countered by a
distinct trend by large corporations to become increasingly multina-
tional.

- Individualism, progress, and achievement will be less valued, while
  greater emphasis will be placed on getting along with others, immediate
  gratification, hedonism, and the like.

To add that to predict is not necessarily to approve is, it is hoped,
redundant.

4.5 Citizen Participation in Goal Development

From the basic human needs and the value structure that may be presumed to be operative it should be possible to develop the specific objectives of the new society. In Figures 4.1, 4.2, and 4.3 are shown
objectives trees proposed by three different groups. Figure 4.1 shows the
objectives of a group of college students; Figure 4.2, those developed by
some system analysts; and Figure 4.3, those of a church discussion group.
In the nature of the system process more trees should be gathered from
various segments of the target population. By meeting with a group of
citizens for several hours an analyst can explain the issue and obtain from
them a draft of an objectives tree. We find that, although most citizens are
inarticulate and wish neither to give nor to hear lectures, they quickly
become absorbed in constructing a tree. It would be difficult to explain
the concept of a "value structure," for example, to a group of citizens,
but by encouraging them to build an objectives tree they project or act out
their values. The students, for example, were less interested in police
protection than in being protected from the police. They were young and
beginning to exert their independence, so perhaps this is not too surprising. But the church group, consisting of middle-aged, middle-class types,
was also concerned with an educated police force. The system analysts
emphasized organizational structure, as might be expected, but they also
showed a sense of political awareness. Although the objectives of the
groups illustrated in Figures 4.1, 4.2, and 4.3 vary in detail, it seems
possible to extract objective statements for the top one or two levels that
would meet with widespread if not universal support. These are shown in
Figure 4.4.

Naturally this is not the end of the process in developing objectives for
revitalizing American society. However, following the iterative philoso-

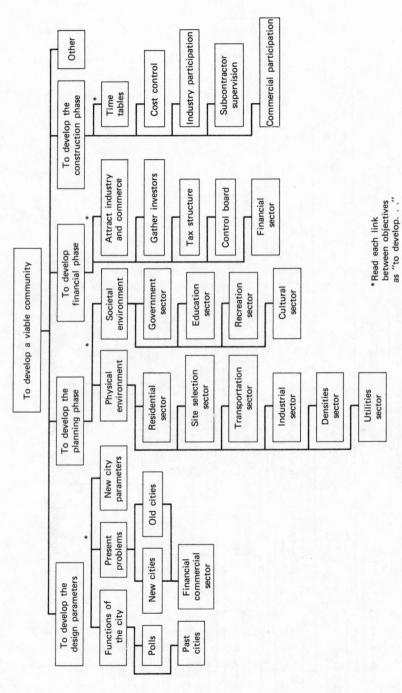

Figure 4.1 A new city objectives tree developed by a group of college students.

*Read each link
between objectives
as "to develop. . ."

125

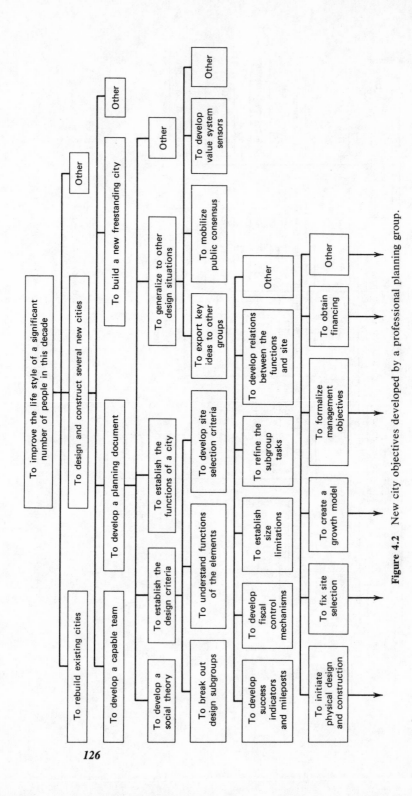

Figure 4.2 New city objectives developed by a professional planning group.

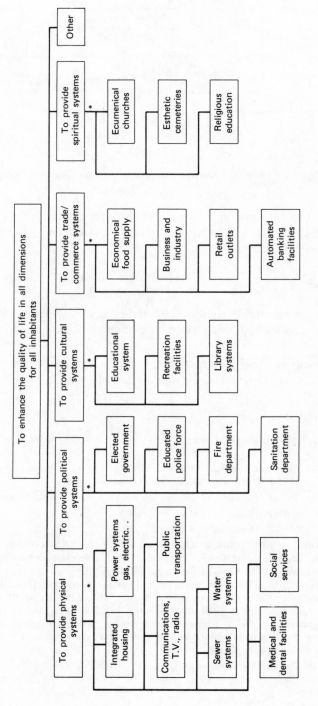

Figure 4.3 A new city objectives tree developed by a church discussion group.

*Read each link as "to develop . . ."

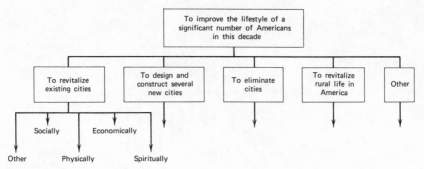

Figure 4.4 A widely acceptable objectives tree for societal revitalization.

phy of the system analysis process, it appears proper to continue on through the analysis to gain perspective before returning to a more intensive goal articulation.

Exercises

4.1. Examine Fitch's eight goals[16] and comment on them in the light of the approach in this chapter. Develop an objectives tree for Fitch's goals.

4.2. Compare, and contrast with Fitch's approach, the position of Banfield, as given in the same issue of *Dáedalus*.[17]

Notes and References

1. E. C. Banfield, *The Unheavenly City Revisited*, Little, Brown and Co., Boston, 1974, p. 22.

2. A. D. Biderman, "Social Indicators and Goals," in R. A. Bauer (Ed.), *Social Indicators*, M.I.T. Press, Cambridge, 1966, pp. 68–153.

3. J. V. Lindsay, *The City*, W. W. Norton and Co., N. Y., 1968, 1970.

4. J. V. Lindsay, *loc. cit.*, p. 186.

5. P. F. Drucker, *Dáedalus*, Fall 1968, p. 1243.

6. Examples of participative management usually cited are Alcan's Oswego, N.Y., rolling mill, Eaton Yale and Towne's Kearney, Neb., valve plant, and some IBM, Texas Instrument, and Motorola plants, along with R. G. Barry, a footwear maker. Failures such as Control Data and others are not so well publicized. See, for example, "Where Being Nice to Workers Didn't Work," *Business Week*, January 20, 1973, pp. 99, 100. The total number of workers involved is very small, however, and does not appear to be growing. In cases where participation has been tried, management often admits a desire to avoid unionization, and the threat of return to authoritarian measures is always in the background.

7. A. H. Maslow, *Motivation and Personality*, Harper & Row, N. Y., 1954.

8. The fervent dedication to a principle that will save the world, remake society, raise up the individual, and enlighten our communal living patterns no longer finds its focus in religion for most intellectuals. Rather, all the old hopes are now centered on "education." When the word "education" comes up in planning discussions, make the silent substitution "religion" in your mind in order to see the analogy and to realize the extravagance of the claims made for education by its prophets.

9. O. Helmer, "Simulating the Values of the Future," in K. Baier and N. Rescher (Eds.), *Values and the Future*, The Free Press, N. Y., 1969, pp. 193–214.

10. T. J. Gordon, *The Future*, St. Martin's Press, N. Y., 1965.

11. E. M. Williams, Jr., *American Society*, 2nd ed., Alfred A. Knopf, N. Y., 1960, Ch. 11.

12. K. Baier, "What Is Value?" in K. Baier and N. Rescher (Eds.), *loc. cit.*, pp. 33–67.

13. Sociologists appear to some observers to be almost psychopathic in their determination to avoid definitive statements and goal-oriented activity. Thus Williams specifically denies that this list is a value set and then proceeds to operate with it as exactly that.

14. See, for example, N. Rescher, in K. Baier and N. Rescher (Eds.), *loc. cit.*, pp. 133–147.

15. It is obviously impossible in principle to predict precisely what people will want in the future, since no measuring scheme can determine something that people themselves do not know. Yet good approximations are possible. After all, bankers, a group not known for their faith in omens, do grant 30-year mortgages.

16. L. C. Fitch, "Eight Goals for an Urbanizing America," *Dáedalus*, Vol. 97, No. 4 (Fall 1968), pp. 1141–1165.

17. E. C. Banfield, "Why Government Cannot Solve the Urban Problem," *Dáedalus,* Vol. 97, No. 4 (Fall 1968), pp. 1231–1241.

5

Criteria for Selecting from among the Alternatives for Urban Revitalization

. . . almost nobody thought that the [government] management of [Ciudad Guayana, Venezuela] would welcome sustained and systematic efforts to clarify and make explicit the most important goals, values, and assumptions. Exposing markedly different values—which were roughly understood—might only encourage misleading generalities, cause embarrassment, and perhaps even sharpen differences.

L. RODWIN
Planning Urban Growth and Regional Development
M.I.T. Press, Cambridge, 1969, p. 474

Even if we supposed that people could be brought to agree to definite rules for applying evaluative themes to the ranking of policies, it would be difficult to deduce from among the multiple possibilities precisely which rules would suit their intentions—and their intentions are liable to shift as they combine one formulation with another.

D. BRAYBROOKE, C. E. LINDBLOM
A Strategy of Decision
Macmillan Co., N. Y., 1970, p. 26

5.1 Introduction

There are at least eight different scenarios for carrying through urban revitalization. With this number of basic strategies plus the large number of possible combinations among them, it is important that there be established a set of selection criteria with which to judge success. It seems unlikely that any one option for urban revitalization will be completely superior to all others. This is so because it is unlikely that a single set of selection criteria will be the universal choice of all the people. In fact it is not at all unlikely that many of the possible options will be in operation simultaneously in different places, a situation that is not necessarily bad. Parallel pursuit of several options will present the following opportunities:

- Multiple life-style choices will be provided.
- Rapid testing of theoretical scenarios will be accomplished.
- Experimental testing of aspirational selection criteria will be carried through.
- Other.

At least one danger exists, however, in encouraging a multiple approach. The temptation will be strong to postpone the definition of success criteria until after the option testing is complete. "After all," one could argue, "what's so important about defining, before we begin, the criteria upon which we will judge success? We will have the various projects in operation. We will know what each cost. Why can't we then just look around at what we have accomplished and the price tag for each and decide what's best? Why waste time setting up the criteria beforehand with those 40 million people waiting who are ill-housed and more coming along all the time? Let's get going!"

As appealing as is this argument, I believe that it must be rejected. Here are some reasons for establishing a priori the criteria upon which success is to be judged.

- Most social experiments are uncontrolled, that is, statistical validation is impossible after the fact because norms and controls are absent. Thus it is difficult to extract general principles from a single unique event.
- If vital process variables are not defined a priori, there is no assurance that they will be tracked properly during the process. Data gathering is expensive, and it is impossible to measure everything. Many examples can be cited of uncontrolled social experiments in which vital data were discovered, after the fact, to be missing.
- Human nature being what it is, there is a strong probability that the backers of a failing option will consciously shift their criteria for judgment and declare a success. Pruitt-Igoe, it will be recalled, was given a gold medal by the American Institute of Architects when it opened.
- Without goals and defined success criteria, those pursuing a given option will lack means of making day-by-day decisions.

- Without criteria, partial successes and progress toward goals will be difficult to detect and substantiate.
- Other.

5.2 Nine Sample Criteria

The system analyst does not select or rank the criteria for choice; this is the task of the decision makers. Nevertheless, it is the analyst's obligation to aid the client in clarifying these choices. An almost unlimited number of criteria are conceivable, but only a few will capture sufficient support to be viable. Among these will be the following:

- *Minimize risk.* Some clients may be convinced that American society needs to be revitalized, but they may wish to minimize the political and/or financial risk in doing so.
- *Maximize entrepreneurial return.* This is a very popular criterion— certainly the single most widely used of all.
- *Maximize immediate social impact.* This would be a satisfactory guideline for a politician running for office or one seriously concerned with unrest in his city.
- *Maximize long-run national impact.* This is a rather theoretical and vague goal that needs to be made more explicit if it is to be operational.
- *Correct past and present social inequities.* This worthy though vague goal accepts the status quo and aims to bring minorities up to the median.
- *Increase the gross national product (GNP).*
- *Solve the energy crisis.*
- *Reduce environmental insult.*
- *Other.*

5.3 Cost

Whatever selection criteria are chosen, it will be desirable to minimize cost. For this reason detailed cost estimates on the most promising candidates will be essential. Such estimates may require an intensive study effort, but rough estimates are easy to make.

The first question that will be asked concerns the financial balance of the new city. When a potential source of funds is approached, whether public or private, the source will ask to be shown in detail the process for recovering the funds to be invested. Thus criteria must be established on spending rates, payback rates, and return on investment. These must be based on current conservative practice and supported by detailed data; guesses will not suffice.

Although a detailed cost study of each candidate solution is beyond the scope of this initial study, we can take one such candidate and provide a rough estimate of the cost of construction. We will attempt to calculate all capital costs for a new city of conventional form for 1 million persons. To begin, we list the major capital investment sectors and then obtain their costs from a variety of sources. The results will be indicative on an aggregated basis, even though they are not precise in detail. These estimates will be based on replacement costs for a conventional city. By "conventional" we mean to include urban form, function, building materials, and construction methods. Thus this will be an upper-bound estimate of the capital investment required with one exception: the cost will be given in 1970 dollars, and inflation is not included.

Let us take one or two specific sectors and indicate how the estimates were obtained. All the estimates are for replacement costs of capital items in the Detroit metropolitan region in 1970. Consider the cost of electric utilities as an example. We can find the number of megawatts of installed capacity required for a given number of people by consulting the records of any electric utility that serves a large metropolitan area, in our case the Detroit Edison Company. Next we can find the replacement costs from the same source by examining the testimony of the utility to the state rate-governing unit. Detroit Edison must project growth well into the future, and it has hard cost estimates available. Street and highway costs are available from city governments, highway contractors, and state highway bureaus, and the other costs are similarly available. We will consider the investments required in the following eight major sectors. These costs are assignable to a variety of different groups and thus would not all be due simultaneously.

Land

From 5000 to 10,000 persons per square mile is a relatively low urban density. Use of this figure indicates a total requirement of 200 square miles for the city. At $250 per acre, $16 million would be needed, whereas over $60 million would be needed if the price were $1000 per acre. Thus $70 million would seem to be quite a conservative estimate for the total cost of land, in the absence of speculation.

Housing

If housing costs are about $5000 per person, as seems to be the national average, $5 billion would be needed.

Utilities

Capital investments for various utilities based on typical costs seem to be as follows:

Electric	$1000 (million)
Sewage	700
Water	400
Gas	000
Communications	000

These figures assume that there is no city gas supply and also that communications capital costs are negligible. The assumption of zero cost for gas is not as radical as might be first supposed. A report[1] prepared for HUD shows that various forms of energy supplied to the home are entirely competitive. Thus an investment in gas reduces dollar for dollar the investment required for electricity to a first-order approximation.

Transport

The cost of local and arterial streets, assuming a conventional form and density, is approximately $750 million. This does not include urban expressways, which cost $10 million per mile provided that site acquisition costs are minimal. Let us allow 50 miles of urban expressways, which seems to be a minimum if any noticeable effect is to be achieved. Perhaps 100 miles of expressway would be needed, but let us also include 100 miles of high-speed transit, although not both would be required. An airport would cost about $100 million. Thus we have:

Arterial and local streets	$750 (million)
Urban expressway	500
HSGT	1000
Airport	100

Health

Hospital capital costs are well known because of extensive studies under the Hill–Burton facilities act. Approximately $40 million is a first order estimate.

Recreation

For these costs we have:

Athletics	$65 (million)
Cultural	25
Libraries	60

Work

The costs per square foot and the number of square feet per worker combined with the number of workers (see below) yields:

| Industrial construction | $1800 (million) |
| Commerce and government | 2600 |

Education

Education capital costs average about $5000 per student, and in a city of 1 million persons perhaps 200,000 are students. Thus we arrive at capital costs of about $1 billion.

These figures are tabulated in Table 5.1. More detailed work has gone into the estimates than is shown here, but it is omitted deliberately. We do not wish to permit any great confidence to be placed in these first-order approximations.

This calculation results in a surprisingly low figure. A $16 billion to $18 billion program is important but not large with respect to either the gross national product or the federal budget. When it is realized, moreover, that most if not all of these funds are self-liquidating and need not cause a net drain on the taxpayers, the project becomes still more attractive. The total investment is about $16,000 per person in the city and about $60 per capita for the nation. Figure 5.1 shows an approximate investment schedule over the 10-year construction period. The maximum annual investment is less than $2 billion and after the first few years is still less. Furthermore, this is input cash required; it does not show the return on the investment which would begin to be realized at about year 3. For typical annual interest charges and reasonable rates of return on investment after taxes, it would be some years after construction was completed before a net positive cash return could be expected, as we shall see.

Let us consider a simplified cash flow calculation simply as an example. We make the following assumptions:

1. That K dollars are needed to finance construction of the physical infrastructure of the city for each year of the 10-year construction cycle.

2. That dollars have a constant value; that is, there is no inflation.

3. That the money may be borrowed at an annual interest charge of m percent. Let $m = 5.5, 6, 6.5$.

4. That an n percent annual return on investment after taxes begins on each increment 1 year after it is invested. This simulates construction time and other lags before money begins to earn its return. This return is

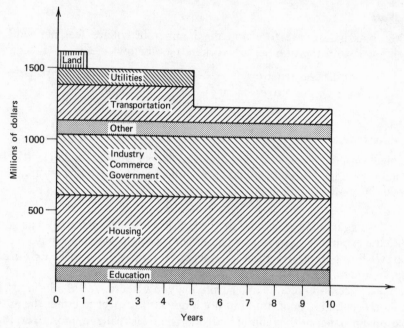

Figure 5.1 Approximate 10-year investment schedule. Public and private costs are lumped. Cash return is not shown.

reinvested if needed to reduce the annual increment of new money required. Let $n = 10, 15, 20$.

4. That after 20 years the rate of return on each increment invested is reduced by 0.5 percent per year until it goes to zero in order to simulate the deterioration of the physical structure which generates the return.

In Figure 5.2 is shown the plot of cash flow for the various interest changes m and rates of return n.

5.4 Location

It is difficult for people to interest themselves in reorganizing the city if it remains in a theoretical vacuum. They wish to see candidates individualized and related to reality. Perhaps this is why the location question is pressed. In theory a major portion of an urban design is not site sensitive, yet the site question is primary in many persons' thoughts. Some of the general criteria for site selection of a large free-standing new city are as follows.

Table 5.1 *Approximate Total Cost of City for 1 Million Persons in 1970 Dollars, Using Conventional Forms and Structures Throughout.*

Item	Cost ($ million)	
	Private	Public
Land		70
Housing	5,000	
Utilities		
Electric	1,000	
Sewage		700
Water		400
Gas	000	
Communications	000	
Transport		
Arterial and local streets		750
Urban expressways		500
HSGT		1,000
Airport		100
Health		
Hospital	20	20
Recreation		
Athletics	65	
Cultural	25	
Libraries	60	
Work		
Industry	1,800	
Commercial and government	1,300	1,300
Education		1,000
Subtotals	10,270	5,840
Total	16,110	

Continuing Economic Viability

Economic viability will be assured by providing a mix of industrial and commercial jobs, sufficient in size, variety, and growth potential to guarantee challenging opportunities to the residents. Industrial site location studies must be undertaken for all preliminary site candidates to determine what industries could locate in or near the site while enhancing their profits.

Minimization of Environmental Insult

National forest and park lands will be included in preliminary lists of candidate sites for new developments because such national lands are

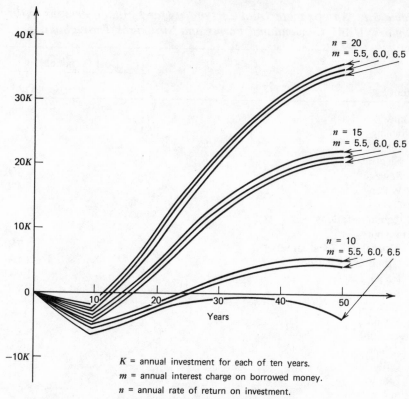

Figure 5.2 Cash flow for simplified investment model of the new city.

available at much reduced front-end costs. Although automatic rejection of such proposals is unwise, it would be equally unwise to destroy unique national treasures.

Minimum Site Preparation Costs

Reasonable climate requirements should be imposed on the selection process. The site should not require abnormal preparation costs, nor should construction costs due to unusually difficult location and terrain be ignored.

Sufficient Natural Resources

The site selected should not require abnormal efforts to supply adequate water, as does Los Angeles, for example.

Consistency with National Growth Policy

Certain small regions of the United States appear to be overpopulated, whereas most of the remainder is underpopulated. As mentioned in Chapter 1, Doxiadis has identified three existing or developing megalopolises, namely, the Boston–Washington corridor, the San Francisco-San Diego corridor, and the corridor below the Great Lakes, which includes Milwaukee, Chicago, Toledo, Detroit, Windsor, Cleveland–Pittsburgh, and Buffalo. These three major concentrations should be avoided.

Social Impact

If site selection criteria are limited to those resting on conventional economic factors, the result will be consistent with conventional economics. Some students of present urban problems argue that this is precisely what is wrong with past corrective actions, yet others maintain with equal vigor that to ignore economic viability is to ensure failure as soon as artificial supports are withdrawn. Is there a middle ground? Suppose it is shown that a particular urban candidate would have a major social impact and would be economically viable ultimately but not in the short run. Such a candidate would be rejected by conventional economic criteria, such as those given above, in favor of candidates of lesser ultimate promise. Although it could be argued that this is an error, to sustain this point would require a major goal-oriented effort by social scientists. The burden of developing a persuasive case must be carried by professional sociologists and social psychologists if a social impact criterion is to be included.

Other

5.5 Human Needs Criteria

The immigrants to the site will not expect an explicit set of performance indices before moving into an urban revitalization project, but the indices exist nevertheless. Each person will place a subjective evaluation on the human needs met by the city and will measure it against his own implicit value structure. He may not even be able to tell himself why he likes or dislikes the city, but he will know that he does or does not enjoy living there. Initially the prospect of employment opportunities will attract the new resident. We can measure the numbers and kinds of jobs, the salary and wage levels, and the unemployment rate; thus this matter submits easily to analysis. The satisfaction of certain other human needs that we have discussed above can be measured with equal ease. We can determine the pollution level and ensure that residential densities are within the desired range. We can count traffic deaths and church attendance. But other values prove more difficult. How can self-actualization be measured? How can we demonstrate that neighborhood town halls and police stations provide a better balance between personal service and economy than would the more conventional centralized organization? These and dozens of other elements will be considered by the citizens in their evaluation. Some may permanently elude quantification, but a concentrated effort must be made at developing sensors and indices for the values and needs of the residents.

We are not completely without resources in developing the scenario for meeting human needs or the indices by which we may judge the success of this scenario in action. However, the available resources are not of a normative nature. Rather they are and must be based on the experience developed to date in the New Town movement both here and abroad.

Very little if any conscious preplanning of cities to meet higher-order human needs is to be found in the records of historians, anthropologists, or archaeologists. A major milepost in this regard, therefore, is Ebenezer Howard's *Garden Cities of Tomorrow*, published in 1895, Da Vinci's effort for the Duke of Sforza during the fifteenth century in Milan and similar instances being only marginal exceptions. Greenbelt, Maryland, of the 1930s is a more recent antecedent of the present-day activity. The Greenbelt designers were imaginative and progressive architects, nevertheless they were prisoners of their professional training, and therefore devoted themselves primarily to physical and to a lesser degree to financial planning, but not at all in an objective and explicit way to social planning. This is not to say that these planners and later new town enthusiasts down to the present lack a vision of the social environment they desire. But such visions are almost entirely emotional and grow out of each architect–planner's fantasy. This is true of Le Corbusier's "Radiant City," Frank Lloyd Wright's "Broad Acres City," and Oscar Niemeyer's Brasilia, as well as almost all other recent projects. Even Howard must be included in this indictment, if it is such. Letchworth (1900s) and Welwyn (1920s) failed productive because Howard and his successors refused to accept the desire of British citizens after World War I to adopt the automobile[2] as a basic mode of transport. Howard had decided in advance that the residents of his garden cities "should" want to use mass transit. When this turned out not to be the case, the planners could not surmount this ideological impasse. More recently British new town planners have repeated this error. The first series of six British new towns designed after World War II (the so-called Mark I) allowed parking space for only one family in eight. The resulting auto congestion has been significant. More recent designs, as represented by Milton Keynes, for example, quadruple this allowance to space for one car for every two families.

Planners familiar with the British experience report that no objective social planning is evident in either the Mark I or the Mark II series of new towns. This is equally true of the American Title VII experience. Indeed, the concept of objective social planning is so new and untried that it must be advocated with care.

Exercises

5.1. Elaborate upon the nine sample criteria for urban choices given in Section 5.2, and compare and contrast them.

5.2. Choose one of the human needs criteria, and consider the indices required to measure its satisfaction. Then describe the process required to measure and document the satisfaction of this need.

Notes and References

1. *Developing New Communities*, Department of Housing and Urban Development, U. S. Government Printing Office, Washington, D. C., December 1968, p. 193.

2. F. J. Osborn, A. Whittick, *The New Town: The Answer to Megalopolis*, M.I.T. Press, Cambridge, 1969.

6

Eight Scenarios
for Urban Revitalization[1]

The eightfold way
. . . It is also called the middle path, as it steers a course between the sensual pleasures of the materialists and the self-mortification of the ascetics. Those who follow the eightfold path are freed from the suffering that is an essential part of human existence and are led ultimately to Nirvana or Enlightenment.

Encyclopedia Britannica
Micropaedia, Vol. III, 15th ed.,
1974

6.1 The Eightfold Way

Given the goal of revitalization of American society and translating this to the more specific objective of revitalizing American cities in this century, we come to the point of developing a variety of options to which to apply the chosen criteria. It appears that there are approximately eight options from which to choose. We will list these eight possibilities here and discuss the strengths and weaknesses of each option in separate sections that follow. See Figure 6.1.

- *Eliminate the problem.* One obvious way of eliminating the problems of cities is to eliminate the cities themselves. Many upper-middle-class Americans have chosen this as a personal solution. Is it viable as a major solution scenario?
- *The transcendental solution.* The transcendental solution requires a basic change in the mind set and behavior patterns of all members of society. After all, one sometimes hears, it is not the bricks and mortar, the steel and concrete, that go into cities that cause the problems. It is the people who live in them.
- *The status quo.* A nonintervention strategy is possible and has been called "benign neglect" in a similar context. If present urban condi-

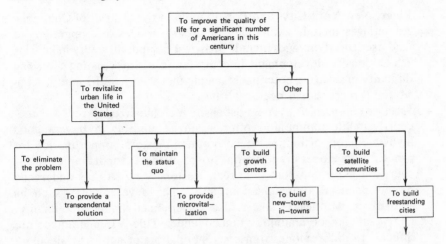

Figure 6.1 The eightfold way.

tions seem unsatisfactory, but appear also to be improving rapidly, this policy may be acceptable.

- *Revitalization on the small.* A microstrategy that supplies help to single dwellings or neighborhoods is possible. This scenario might include developing better individual components for the physical infrastructure, say, and urging adoption of these devices by designers. Individual FHA loans would fall into this category. No upset of current marketing methods or political structure would be required. In fact, the program could be so subtle that its existence would be difficult to detect.

- *Growth centers.* In accord with a yet-to-be-developed national growth policy as called for by the Housing Act of 1970, certain healthy small towns could be selected for controlled but rapid growth to provide suitable shelter to meet needs. Advantages of this scenario include utilization of existing political infrastructure and financial facilities, as well as existing job markets, residential and commercial facilities, and so on, as a base for expansion. Disadvantages include possible resistance to expansion by the existing population. No growth centers have been funded under Title VII, although Johnathan outside Minneapolis is claimed by HUD to meet its criteria for growth centers.

- *New-towns-in-town.* Rather than isolated housing projects located in slum clearance land, the new-town-in-town concept includes a more or less complete living environment in a relatively high-density urban environment. Examples under Title VII include Cedar–Riverside in Minneapolis, Roosevelt Island (formerly Welfare Island) in the East

River, New York City, and Fort Lincoln in the District of Columbia. Advantages include availability of urban services and upgrading of land use. Disadvantages include high cost of land, difficulty in knitting a high-density development into the fabric of the existing city, and difficulty in assuring potential residents that their health, safety, security, and recreational needs will be met.

- *Satellite communities.* The most easily merchandized of renewal concepts, satellite communities offer organized suburbias to buyers, good investment opportunities to corporate investors, opportunities for profit by developers, and so on. Some of these opportunities, however, are more apparent than real. Reston, Virginia, has undergone forced financial reorganization, and other developments such as Johnathan, Minnesota, have also experienced financial difficulty. Other satellite communities funded under Title VII guarantees are difficult to differentiate from conventional major suburban developments (e.g., Flower Mound in Texas, Park Forest South in Illinois, Audubon in New York). A major hidden disadvantage to the host city from a parasite development is that the suburban community depends on the host for urban services and jobs, but avoids the urban tax structure.

- *Freestanding new city.* Major advantages of this concept include the opportunity to achieve major cost savings by integrated, innovative design and modern technology. The major disadvantages lie in the need for major long-term, initial low-return, front-end investment, as well as difficulty in site acquisition. Soul City, North Carolina, is the single freestanding community presently projected with the Title VII structure, and Soul City appears to be too small (projected population 44,000) to be truly freestanding, although it may have a sufficient hinterland to be stable in a central place theory sense.

6.2 Eliminate the Problem

It might be thought that this could not be a serious option, yet one should not prejudge the case. One must ask first what the functions of a city are and then whether these functions could not be served, given modern technology, without the high-density core presumably implied by "city." In the 1920s Frank Lloyd Wright proposed in his "Broad Acres City" project a low-density city organized around the automobile and with plenty of green space. Wright anticipated by several decades the flight of upper-middle-class Americans to the suburbs. Some modern suburban dwellers count the intervals between their occasional visits "downtown" in terms of months. Given ubiquitous truck transport and the vast land requirements for straight-through mass production, suburban locations for industry seem not out of the question. Given the telephone, the videophone, the remote control terminal, cable television with talk-back, and other conceivable communication devices, why could not knowledge workers and students work in their own homes?

In all probability, it is possible in theory for a large suburb to exist without an urban center; after all, the affluent few are already able to afford country living. But this is precisely the problem of living without an urban center: most of us could not afford it. Living in a dispersed sheet city with no center precludes the possibility of mass transport. Two cars per family become a minimum necessity, and reliable auto transport cannot be had for less than $2000 annually per vehicle. To allot $4000 annually from one's gross take-home pay for transportation is so distasteful a thought that most people reject the amount as unrealistic.

All utilities and services are more expensive in a dispersed sheet environment than in a denser environment. Roughly speaking, utility distribution costs vary inversely with population density or directly with the area over which a given population is distributed. Of course suburbanites do not know this, since utility rates are not usually computed in this way. Given the usual rate structure, the high-density-city dweller pays the same rates for gas, water, electricity, sewers, telephones, garbage collection, milk delivery, mail, and the like as does his suburban counterpart. For this reason he is subsidizing to a measure the suburban life-style. But suppose an extra $1000 were added to each suburban home to pay for all services and utilities plus an additional $1000 in taxes. This would not be far from the extra cost of providing these services. Thus the total marginal cost of suburban living is $6000 annually, not to mention the cost of housing.

As former Mayor John Lindsay of New York has pointed out,[2] FHA low-cost mortgages funded by urban taxes permitted many city dwellers with little or no equity to move out of the city, thus reducing its tax base and causing it to finance its own destruction. It is a common misapprehension that cities cost the state money. In fact, the reverse is true.

Suppose that the average income of suburbanite families lies between $10,000 and $15,000 annually. Suppose also that a minimum figure of 20 percent is extracted annually for income taxes, leaving between $8000 and $12,000 gross take-home pay. Does it seem likely that such families could afford an extra burden of $6000 for suburban living? Of course not. Then either we are not talking about paying full costs for suburban living, or else we are talking about families with annual incomes of $20,000 to $25,000. Either possibility seems unsupportable; thus, as a rough estimate, the eliminate-the-city option does not seem viable. Careful and detailed analysis plus imaginative new cost-reduction technology might change this first approximation, but it seems unlikely.

6.3 The Transcendental Solution

This label may be too bold, but it does appear that the proponents of this solution are asking for a change in human nature. Perhaps not, though; perhaps they are asking merely for a change in the reward and penalty structure. Human behavior changes and changes radically in as little as a decade, though we like to think of values as relatively constant. In 1955 President Eisenhower stated that it was inconceivable for the U. S. government to advocate birth control as an official policy. Yet by 1965 President Johnson was doing just that. Similar examples can be multiplied. Thus it is not out of the question for the urban population, aroused and frightened by trends and supported by changes in the laws, to alter basically its style of existence. Here are a few simple changes in the penalty and reward structure that might radically alter urban life-styles in a matter of a few years, indeed some of these are already in effect in certain localities.

- Legalized prostitution in licensed houses in a designated district, coupled with harsh penalties for street walking.
- Free methadone and drug clinics, coupled with the death penalty for dealing in narcotics.
- "Good Samaritan" laws and complete protection for going to the aid of those in distress.
- "No fault" insurance. "No fault" divorce laws.
- Complete removal of penalties for victimless crimes.
- Legalized gambling.
- Doubling police salaries.
- Other.

By removing the sources of corruption or reducing its profits plus substantially rewarding good behavior, much crime could be eliminated. Then, by reducing or eliminating the usual adversary process and institutionalizing plea bargaining, the criminal justice process could be speeded up. Next, by rewarding good landlord behavior with tax benefits and eliminating the profit in slum lording as well as windfall profits in urban land, positive land-use policies could be stimulated. Finally, by reducing the school-leaving age and requiring 2 years' service in an urban youth corps, followed by free practical job training and permanently reduced taxes for successful service, one might encourage useful social enterprise in young people.

The point of this illustration is not whether any or all of these specific suggestions would or would not help. Rather, the point is that the reward and punishment system could be arranged so as to encourage desirable behavior. Then, perhaps, the ills of the city would cure themselves. This view may seem idealistic since it is projected into the future. Thus a look into the recent past to see the effects of some lesser changes may be useful.

- The Pill has reduced the birth rate to less than the steady-state replacement rate in advanced countries such as the United States and Sweden. In Japan, population is actually declining. All this is a reversal of the situation 10 years ago.
- Seat belts, lower speed limits and better highway design have slowed the climb in traffic death rates, so that tens of thousands of persons are alive today in the United States who would have died had the trends of a decade ago continued.
- Television has changed the entertainment habits of a nation. Among other side effects is the fact that people read less. The verbal aptitude of college applicants in the United States has declined 25 points (SAT) in the past decade, perhaps as a consequence.
- The U.S. drug epidemic has exploded, leveled off, and begun to recede, and may again be revived, all in a decade.
- College students have gone from innocent enthusiasm for the New Frontier through violent anarchy to withdrawn cynicism, all in a decade.
- Other.

Nevertheless it does not seem prudential to assume the existence of the quality of leadership that would be necessary to develop and carry through such a far-reaching social revolution as is pictured above. Perhaps "transcendental" is the name for such leadership, after all.

6.4 Benign Neglect

To refuse to make a decision for change, it must be realized, may be the most far-reaching decision of all. "No change" must be viewed as a positive decision for retaining the status quo. This is the third option we have discussed, and the third that would be rejected out of hand by many reasonable people. Yet, as for the first two, a meaningful case can be argued for it. Daniel Maynihan has argued, as he served under three presidents, for a policy of deescalation of social intervention.[3] He did not mean, it seems to me, as was commonly thought or claimed, that all is well in American cities, nor was he advocating callous disregard. Rather, his argument has three parts.

First, Moynihan argues, much of the unrest in the recent past in American cities was due to the wave of rural poor, attracted by welfare and jobs after World War II, who engulfed the cities in the following several decades. This class, rather than race, problem is subsiding simply because the number of potential urban immigrants is no longer very large.[4] In other words, the problem is solving itself. The newcomers are adjusting, and no further significant numbers are to be expected. The problem was severe, but transitory.

Second, we now know that many past attempts at social intervention have been failures. They have had totally unexpected, counterintuitive results.[5] One reason for this is the lack of control in the experiments, but another reason is that the time constant of the system is greater than the rate at which major changes have been made. In other words, we have not waited long enough to see the final result of a new policy before reversing it or substituting for it something unrelated.

Finally, since things have begun, in the past few years, to improve in rather specific and demonstrable ways, all we need do now is to let events continue, and soon we will begin to enjoy the benefits.

The counterarguments to a policy of benign neglect are that, although the tide of rural immigration may have slackened, things are not improving, or if they are, progress is too slow. The Douglas Commission reported in 1968 that 40,000,000 Americans were ill housed,[6] and the situation has deteriorated further since then. Twenty-five percent of the housing units in the central portion of St. Louis are abandoned, and this is simply one example. Urban crime continues to rise even after statistical artifacts are eliminated. Moreover, the taxation inequities that require the cities to subsidize their own destruction cannot continue; the flight to the suburbs requires too much of the nation's income and energy to be allowed to continue.

6.5 Microrevitalization

A program of refurbishing single dwellings or small neighborhoods is the fourth option we will consider. A major advantage of this option is that the existing economic and political establishment remains completely in control. A second important advantage is that no focus of opposition develops; no one can claim that federal agencies are acting as outside agitators. The third advantage is that the program is completely voluntary. Only persons who wish to participate need do so.

There are a number of possibilities as to the precise form that microrevitalization could take.

- A government-guaranteed, low-cost program for refurbishing existing urban dwellings according to carefully established guidelines is one possibility. Unfortunately a program similar to this, operated by HUD, has recently been reported to have been ridden with corruption. HUD officials have admitted conniving with builders to approve loans for shoddy or nonexistent repairs to dwellings to be sold to poor people who remain liable for repayments. Over 12,000 of these homes were repossessed recently by the federal government in Detroit alone, one of the centers of the scandal. Of course a scandal does not prove that the idea itself was bad, but at the very least its administration must be changed.

- Rather than focusing on urban renewal projects in a concentrated area, this option would locate single freestanding houses and apartments in a scattered pattern throughout otherwise unsubsidized housing areas. This idea would be further strengthened if it were to be combined with innovative building technology that would lower the cost or increase the quality of the houses constructed. This is almost exactly the description of Operation Breakthrough, sponsored by HUD in the early 1970s. Unfortunately Operation Breakthrough failed for several reasons. First, the contractors for the innovative housing failed to produce reliable homes within their original price estimates. Second, there was an intense negative reaction by lower-middle-class and working-class residents against locating Operation Breakthrough in their neighborhoods. Undoubtedly some of this opposition was due to racial prejudice. In addition, however, there existed the concern that home occupants who did not sweat enough to gain their homes would be less likely to maintain them. Since a home is the single major investment made by most families, it is clear that this threat is a powerful one. The third reason for failure of the experiment was HUD's incompetence and inexperience. It seems apparent that government bureaucrats are incapable of operating any entrepreneurial program such as would be required in Operation Breakthrough or other microrevitalization efforts; thus a necessary condition for success is the inclusion of for-profit operators. Part of their risk must be shared by a federal agency to make the program attractive. Some risk must remain, however, along with a reasonable expectation of a fair profit.

- A low-risk form of microrevitalization would be one of indirect action.

A research and development program for developing new, cheaper, and more reliable materials and methods for shelter construction seems attractive. Moreover, successful opposition to such an idea appears unlikely. Architects, construction material manufacturers, and contractors should unite behind such a plan to stamp out any selfish opposition that might develop from construction labor unions. This would occur, perhaps, if the world were logical and susceptible to system analysis. In point of fact, exactly this plan was developed by system analysis in the Department of Commerce under President Johnson and pushed vigorously with the direct leadership of Dr. J. Herbert Hollomon, the Assistant Secretary for Science and Technology.[7] The concept failed to receive the support of Congress. Perhaps Hollomon, as a "system type," felt the concept to be so obviously correct that he neglected to mend his political fences, as Nelkin alleges. Nevertheless the opposition came from precisely the persons listed above as putative supporters; surprisingly, perhaps, the construction union leadership was moderately supportive. Life is complex.

• Undoubtedly other options could be developed, and a careful analysis of the failure mode of the three proposals described could be helpful in increasing the probability of success in the future.

6.6   The Housing and Urban Development Act of 1970

Since the final four options for urban revitalization are closely related to specific legislation, and the development of any of these options will be heavily influenced by the procedures developed by HUD for administering this legislation, it seems advisable to discuss it here. Spurred by the rising social consciousness of the 1960s, the Kennedy and Johnson administrations developed an imaginative domestic social program. Buttressed by such excellent studies as those of the Douglas Commission[8] (1968) and the Rains Commission[9] (1969), Congress passed the Housing and Urban Development Act of 1970.

Title VII of this Act was specifically directed at developing new communities within a national growth policy. The Act itself is well written and needs no specialized interpreters. It reveals a rather surprising depth of understanding of the national picture, and it is apparent that its drafters expended considerable effort and were familiar with the recent studies commissioned by Congress. The Housing Act of 1970 visualized much more than a mere patchwork palliative. It set down as the law of the land a far-reaching national goal for urban revitalization, and Congress subsequently appropriated funds to move at least part way toward this goal. Section 702 of the Act makes clear the intent of Congress to promote "a consistent national urban growth policy which shall incorporate social, economic, and other appropriate factors." Sections 719 and 735 further strengthen the Congress's intent to organize urban development in an integrated, rational, national pattern rather than placing minor local patches on the failing status quo. Under Title VII, Congress authorized a program of loan guarantees for new community ventures with plans that could meet administrative guidelines. A total of $500 million of loan guarantees was permitted, with a maximum of $50 million for any one venture. A variety of types of new communities were to be encouraged by the Act, and all were to provide a full range of urban facilities, not merely housing.

The Act provides under Title V, "Research and Development," that HUD "undertake such programs of research, studies, testing, and demonstration . . . determin(ed) to be necessary and appropriate." Large-scale experimentation in the use of new technologies, methods, and materials, with a view toward the ultimate mass production of housing and related facilities, was encouraged under Section 502(b). All in all, the Act must be considered a milestone in foresight and encouragement for total urban revitalization.

The administration of the Housing Act of 1970, however, has not been spectacularly successful. Despite the direct wording of the Act, HUD has argued until very recently that no research in new community planning is necessary, thus committing builders who are on extremely tight time schedules to utilize conventional technology exclusively.[10]

Under Title VII, the "New Communities" title, the Office of New Communities Development (ONCD) was set up to deal with the expected flood of loan guarantee applications. The Housing Act of 1970 did not have the support of the Nixon administration, however, and the rate of approvals has been very low. Moreover, because of understaffing and perhaps a lack of understanding of the far-reaching implications of the Act, HUD has moved very cautiously. The guarantees approved have been not only few but, generally speaking, unimaginative. By mid-1971 only 6 guarantees had been approved, and up to early 1974 a total of 16 guarantees under Title VII had been made since the Act became law. These "sweet sixteen" are named in Table 6.1.

Although HUD defines Johnathan, Minnesota, as a growth center, this is an obvious subterfuge; it is indistinguishable from the other satellite bedroom communities on the list. Soul City is to be freestanding, while Cedar–Riverside, Roosevelt Island, and Fort Lincoln are new towns-in-town. Soul City can be a success without proving the concept of a

Table 6.1 *The 16 New Communities Approved for Loan Guarantees Under Title VII, Housing Act of 1970, by Early 1974*

Name and Location	HUD Title VII Loan Guarantee ($ million)	Projected Total Population (thousands)	Total Acreage	People per Acre	People per Square Mile
Johnathan, Minn. (near Twin Cities)	21	50*	5,800* (see note 4)	8.6	5,520
St. Charles, Md. (near Washington, D. C.)	24	80 (see note 3)	7,900	10.1	6,480
Park Forest South, Ill. (near Chicago)	30	110	8,290	13.3	8,490
Flower Mound, Tex. (Dallas–Fort Worth)	18	64*	6,156*	10.4	6,654
Mammelle, Ark. (Little Rock)	7.5	45	4,945	9.1	5,824
Cedar–Riverside, Minn. (in Minneapolis)	24	30	336	89.3	57,143
Lysander, N. Y. (Syracuse)	(see note 1)	18.3	2,700	6.8	4,340
Riverton, N. Y. (near Rochester)	12	35§	2,650§	13.2	8,450
Woodlands, Tex. (near Houston)	50	150	17,000	8.8	5,670
Soul City, N. C. (freestanding)	14	44	5,200	8.5	5,420
Roosevelt Island, N.Y.C.	(see note 1)	18	143§	126	80,600
Fort Lincoln, D. C. (in Washington)	28	15	335	44.8	28,660

San Antonio Ranch, Tex. (near San Antonio)	18 (see note 2)	88	9,318	9.45	6,040
Shenandoah, Ga. (near Atlanta)	40	70	7,200§	10	6,200
Harbison, S.C. (near Columbia)	13 (see note 2)	23§	1,740§	13.2	8,460
New Fields, Ohio (near Dayton)	32	40†	4,000†	10	6,400

Note 1: N. Y. State Urban Development Corporation received grant assistance rather than land-acquisition loan guarantees.

Note 2: Final approval pending.

Note 3: Population of 80,000 cited by Mields, while Environmental League gives 30,000.

Note 4: Land area under development. Total area is 8192; see Wilburn and Gladstone.

Unless otherwise noted, data are from H. Mields, Jr., "Federally Assisted New Communities; New Dimensions in Urban Development," Urban Land Institute Report, 1971.

* M. D. Wilburn, R. M. Gladstone, "Optimizing Development Profits in Large Scale Real Estate Projects," *Urban Land Institute Technical Bulletin*, No. 67, 1974.

† G. Golany (Ed.), *Strategy for New Community Development in the United States*, Dowden, Hutchinson and Russ, 1975.

‡ W. T. Watterson, R. S. Watterson, *The Politics of New Communities*, F. A. Praeger, N. Y., 1975.

§ *The Environmental Monthly*, Environmental League, November 1973.

freestanding new town, since its population and hinterland fit it as a regional center in the central place theory sense. It remains to be seen how the three new towns-in-town will differ, when complete, from conventional high-rise, high-density public housing projects.

Perhaps it is not surprising that most of the projects guaranteed thus far are relatively conventional, since HUD has precluded itself from involvement in sponsoring attempts to develop new and innovative approaches for developers to employ. Present projects are patterned after Columbia, Reston, Irvine, and the like, which are entirely privately funded. Thus it seems fair to ask why late-coming "entrepreneurs" need to have loan guarantees to follow in the footsteps of independent, self-funded entrepreneurs such as Rouse.

We will now discuss the four options that HUD has defined as permissible under Title VII. These categories are implicit in the language of the Act, although they are not spelled out under it in so many words.

6.7 Growth Centers

Perhaps the least well-defined of the four options qualifiable under Title VII is the urban unit defined as a "growth center." Presumably this is an urban unit that wishes to organize and control its own growth. There are a number of problems with this concept. First, it would be necessary for a significant majority of the voters of the town or city to agree with the concept. Whether growth would take place on a scattered basis within the interstices of existing structures, in a concentrated way in existing space, or in a combination of the two would depend on the situation, of course. But in either case difficulties arise. Much of the profit available to Title VII developers comes not from the construction and sale of individual buildings; this construction takes a huge investment and a large organization. Most developers prefer to allow individual contractors to undertake the construction of homes and to earn their own profits. The developer gets his return from three other sources.

- Profit from the sale of land which has appreciated in value because of development activity. This is the major source of return, provided that the developer had sufficient "patient money" or "front-end money" to gain control of most of the land due for appreciation.
- Retention of key sites within the development and acting as landlord for commercial–industrial activities. The Rouse Company, which developed Columbia, Maryland, expects to realize a main portion of its

return from the major enclosed shopping mall which it controls and which has exclusive rights to provide commercial services in Columbia.

- Operation of ancillary businesses. The developer may choose to retain the exclusive right to engage in certain commercial activities. He may operate the only gasoline stations or food stores or banks permitted, or what have you. Rouse, for example, constructed and controls the high-rise office building at Columbia Center.

We can see that all three of these profit sources are threatened by a "growth center" operation. Presumably all of these opportunities would be preempted in some measure by local citizenry, who would wish to realize additional profits from their businesses as the price of agreement to the concept. Thus an urban development corporation of some sort would have to be formed whereby a fair sharing of the returns between the existing town fathers and the developer would be accomplished. This does not strike me as a particularly simple thing to do.

Why should the existing citizenry of a town encourage the entrance of a "growth center" operation? The motives of the local chamber of commerce are clear. But our first point above shows that the profits anticipated by the members of the local chamber are precisely the same ones that are anticipated by the developer. On the other hand, it may be that the town expects to experience growth in any case because several new industrial concerns have located there or for a similar reason. Thus the problem is how to control the growth in a rational fashion for everybody's benefit. Title VII funds might permit the installation of an adequate utilities network, for example, without which the proposed industry might not come or environmental standards could not be met. The improved service would be paid for by user charges. This seems to be a rational use of Title VII funds, yet it is apparent that here we are talking of funding normal indigenous growth, not a rapid expansion to solve a pressing national problem.

Perhaps this difficulty of identifying the precise mechanism of profit making is why no "growth center" has been initiated. Although, as mentioned earlier, HUD has chosen to identify Johnathan as a "growth center," presumably with respect to the nearby village of Chaska, the land for Johnathan was held in single hands before the development, and the plans for Johnathan are not oriented to Chaska. Rather, they ignore the village entirely. Johnathan is a suburb of Minneapolis. Its designers have profited from the experience of Columbia, to which there are a number of obvious resemblances, but other than the presence of a small enclosed shopping arcade it would be difficult to distinguish Johnathan from thousands of other suburban developments scattered across the nation near large cities.

6.8   New-Towns-in-Town

The "new-town-in-town" (NTIT) concept is an obvious counterargument to those who claim that all federal funds follow the white upper-middle class to the suburbs. It also recognizes that much of the physical infrastructure in slum neighborhoods is solid and reclaimable. Finally, it recognizes that many of the basic values of an in-town location are superior to those of remote suburban locations.

A major strength of the concept is the complete service infrastructure that is in place and operating. Police, fire, sewer, water, electricity, telephone, garbage collection, and other services can be extended into the NTIT with minimum cost and effort. This will be little appreciated by residents, since they will take such services for granted; nevertheless the advantage is real. The ambience of the surrounding city is real, as well. If it is positive, this will add greatly to the success of the NTIT. The concentrated market for commercial activity in the NTIT will permit developers to include a shopping center and other retail trade and service outlets in their plans, thus providing extra financial return.

The cost of land for the NTIT may not be excessive. Present federal regulations permit condemnation proceedings of a deteriorating neighborhood, followed by conveyance of title to a developer. The developer is permitted to realize a profit on this transaction, provided he can show that the resulting development will be beneficial and of higher use than was present before condemnation. This legal procedure, however, has been used sparingly.[11]

The few NTITs initiated thus far do not form a clear pattern. Roosevelt Island on the East River was controlled by the city of New York, and Fort Lincoln in the District of Columbia by the federal government, but the site at Cedar–Riverside was assembled piecemeal out of small parcels widely held in a long-time slum.

One NTIT that has escaped widespread notice may hold greater promise than massive projects such as Roosevelt Island and Fort Lincoln. It is a project that has been accomplished entirely by self-help and without any federal funds at all. There has been no single all-powerful entrepreneur behind it, and, to top it all off, it would not be recognized as a "new town" by a first-time visitor. German Village is a 10-by-10 block area within walking distance of central downtown Columbus, Ohio. An area of small, solidly constructed one- and two-story, freestanding brick houses and narrow streets sandwiched in between an industrial district, a freeway, and the formerly deteriorating downtown, it was originally established by immigrants and grew to its present dimensions around the turn of the century. Over the years the area became more and more run down as its original residents grew old and their children moved to the suburbs. The tax base deteriorated, and a slum was in the process of being born. Thus far, the story is depressingly familiar.

Concurrently with a modernization of downtown, however, a small group of young professional people, architects, and businessmen recognized German Village's possibilities. They bought a handful of rundown houses for the proverbial song, moved in, and began restoring them. The sturdy brick construction had withstood the stress of time and provided a patina of warmth and comfort. The early group often spent more on interior restoration than on the original purchase, but soon the idea caught on, and prices began to rise. After the first few difficult years, the concept snowballed. Fine restaurants moved in, and bric-a-brac shops opened. Now tourists enjoy parking their cars and strolling along the tree-shaded streets to look at well-kept houses, wrought iron, and flowers in planters. Real estate prices have stabilized at about 10 times their levels before restoration began, and the area has become a showplace. Perhaps, if we could capture the essence of the German Village experience, it would be more viable than the high-density, high rises seemingly dictated by current economics.

The difficulties of the NTIT concept arise from the same source as its advantages: the surrounding city. Crime in the streets, vandalism, rape, drugs, and the like will be imported from the surrounding slums. How can the city justify providing extra protection to the NTIT in order to make it attractive if it cannot do so for other areas? On the other hand, if adequate protection is not provided, the NTIT will not survive.

6.9 Satellite Community

Webster defines a satellite as a secondary planet revolving around the primary one. A parasite, on the other hand, is defined as an organism subsisting at the expense of another (or host) organism. The "satellite community" depends on the host city for jobs and financial viability. It also depends on the host city for the attractions that are available in a large city but could not be supported by the satellite population. A satellite of 20,000 to 50,000 people cannot provide major medical facilities, professional sports, a university, art galleries, theaters, and museums; for these and other urban amenities it must depend on the host city. Nor can the satellite provide a variety of jobs or financial stability without the host city. Some jobs will be available, but most workers will continue to commute to the host city. Furthermore, the jobs available in the satellite are made attractive by the fact that, should a layoff occur, a large employment market exists in the host city.

Yet the satellite can be an attractive proposition to the developer. Doubtless this is why all but a few Title VII loan guarantees have been made to satellite developers. All the sources of income for the developer pointed out above are under his exclusive control in the satellite new community. Even so, such a major venture is not without risk. Front-end money is expensive. Reston, for example, did not succeed with its financial plans. It was reorganized, and a number of the features that made it initially such an exciting and innovative venture were dropped. More recent developments have not been as creative as the original Reston, but they have provided a more satisfactory return on investment.

It should be recognized that satellites which succeed financially do so by virtue of a special situation that cannot long be allowed to exist. The satellite developer is permitted, indeed encouraged, to treat all factors, except those he wishes to include in his development, as external diseconomies. He cannot be denied the advantages of the host city; yet he need not bear any but marginal-use cost. For urban services, such as entertainment, that operate on user charges the presence of the satellite is welcome as an increased market. But for many urban services paid for by taxes or voluntary contributions over the years (e.g., hospitals and municipal museums) additional users from outside the city limits are an expensive burden. Thus the satellite (or parasite) is not an unalloyed pleasure to its host (or victim).

6.10   Freestanding New City

The cleanest and simplest solution to urban revitalization and the one that appeals to the frontier spirit of Americans is a new start and a clean slate. Critics of the new city sense something of this vain desire in the freestanding new city (FSNC) advocates, and they have a valid point. The new city concept must demonstrate that it is relevant to today's problems if it is to be taken seriously.[12] The FSNC seems to promise the following advantages:

- It does not externalize diseconomies and will be responsible for all its own costs. Thus it will not be a burden on the surrounding region.
- It may provide a market for innovative building techniques. A concen-

trated market for industrialized housing has not been available, and transport costs have crippled several such ventures. The FSNC could provide such a market.

- By careful and economic design of the physical infrastructure, significant cost savings may be possible in the FSNC. Thus it would provide direct benefits to its citizens.

- Carefully controlled experimentation with urban form and structures in the FSNC could provide a baseline for judging the components of existing cities most susceptible to cost-effective improvement. Further experimentation with existing cities is unfair because their populations are captive. This is not the case in the FSNC.

The major disadvantage of the FSNC is the high-level, long-range economic risk involved, which is well beyond the level of investment possible for even the largest corporations. Thus the FSNC would have to be handled by a quasigovernmental corporation, which might be called "NUCOM" for "new community organization." Such a corporation would not be unprecedented, of course. COMSAT is an excellent example. The difference between COMSAT and NUCOM, however, is that the corporations which pushed COMSAT were anxious for government help and willing to cooperate in order to get it. There is no evidence that the housing and construction industry, fragmented, old-fashioned, craft-oriented, and underfinanced as it is, will cooperate. Indeed, as we have seen above, the evidence points the other way.

To pursue the FSNC concept would require commitment to a new national goal of the same size, cost, and duration as the manned space flight program. The national bicentennial would have been an appropriate time to declare for such a goal.

6.11   Summary

The option chosen as optimum depends almost totally on the criteria of choice. Pastoral reactionaries, throwbacks to the preindustrial revolution, and visionaries may unite in deciding to eliminate the city. Almost no one else agrees, however, although few are particularly pleased with the present product. Some few hope for the transcendental solution. Moynihan and the Nixon-Ford administrations seem to advocate benign neglect. Revitalization on the small is a practical and low-risk solution; at the same time, its payoff appears to be limited. The concept of a growth center is apparently vacuous and has no operational definition. The NTIT, on the other hand, can work. It is a somewhat higher-risk and higher-investment option than revitalization in the small, but its payoff seems more than proportionally higher. The satellite community is the best solution for the entrepreneurial investor interested in optimizing his short-run gain by externalizing his diseconomies. Finally, the FSNC provides the greatest risk and perhaps the greatest potential return.

Let us rank the solutions on four different criteria. To minimize risk, my ranking would be as follows:

1. Microrevitalization.
2. Satellite town.
3. NTIT.
4. FSNC.

To optimize return to the entrepreneurial developer, my ranking is:

1. Satellite town.
2. NTIT.
3. FSNC.
4. Microrevitalization.

To maximize immediate positive impact on existing cities, my ranking is:

1. NTIT.
2. Microrevitalization.

To maximize long-run positive impact on the nation, my ranking is:

1. FSNC.
2. NTIT.

A system analysis concept developed by NASA to help it decide among the myriad of possible follow-ons to the Apollo project is the "pacing mission," discussed in Chapter 3. The pacing mission is defined as the mission that is barely within existing capability and that will return the maximum benefits. The pacing mission by definition will result in the development of pacing methodology, that is, technology with which to solve less-demanding and less-rewarding problems. In exactly this sense, the freestanding new city appears to be the pacing mission for the urban revitalization of the nation. Freestanding new cities have been constructed in other lands. Examples include Chandigarh, the new capital of Punjab State in northern India; Brasilia, the new capital of Brazil; and Ciudad Gauyana, Venezuela. But the concept is not currently under active advocacy in the United States.

The Minnesota experimental city ("MXC," projected population

250,000) advocated by Athelstan Spilhaus and Otto Silha[13] would have been freestanding. It attracted the attention of futurists in the late 1960s, but those invited to participate in early planning used "MXC" as a vehicle for their personal pet ideas. No systemic, organized plans were developed in the early days of the project, and this may have contributed to the faltering progress. Soul City is one of the new community projects funded under the "New Community Development" title of the Housing and Urban Development Act of 1970, but Soul City is too small to be freestanding in any but a central place sense, serving a special purpose and a rather limited hinterland.

In Figure 6.2 is shown an objectives tree for a freestanding new city. Not all of the objectives shown here are developed in this book, nor, of the topics discussed, are all presented in the same depth.[14] The financial and economic sector is almost entirely ignored in this book, for example, and treatment of the social sector is weaker than that of the physical and methodology sectors. Nevertheless this is the closest approach to a completely systemic process available, and with what has been given here the

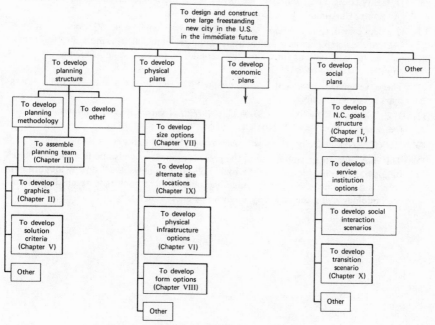

Figure 6.2 Objectives tree for a freestanding new city.

next step in each sector should be clear. The final four chapters of the text focus exclusively on the freestanding option among the eightfold possibilities.

Notes and References

1. J. E. Gibson, "Eight Scenarios for Urban Revitalization," *Proceedings of the IEEE*, Vol. 63, No. 3 (1975), pp. 444–451.

2. J. V. Lindsay, *The City*, W. W. Norton and Co., N. Y., 1968.

3. D. P. Moynihan, "The Schism in Black America," *The Public Interest*, Spring 1972, No. 27, pp. 3–24.

4. See also E. C. Banfield, *The Unheavenly City*, Little, Brown and Co., Boston, 1970.

5. See also J. Forrester, *Urban Dynamics*, M.I.T. Press, Cambridge, 1969.

6. Douglas Commission, *Building the American City*, Report of the National Committee on Urban Problems, U. S. House Doc. No. 91–34, U. S. Government Printing Office, Washington, D. C., 1968.

7. D. Nelkin, *The Politics of Housing Innovation*, Cornell University Press, Ithaca, N. Y., 1971.

8. Douglas Commission, *loc. cit.*

9. D. Canty (Ed.), *The New City*, Report of the National Committee on Urban Growth (A. Rains, Chairman), F. A. Praeger, N. Y., 1969.

10. G. Breckenfeld, *Columbia and the New Cities*, Ives Washburn, 1971, points out on p. 187 that the first $23 million Rouse borrowed from Connecticut General to allow him to pick up his land options for Columbia carried interest charges of $5000 per day. Thus any delay is quite painful.

11. The development now under way in San Francisco at the site of the old farmers' market is one example.

12. J. E. Gibson, "Why Build the New City?" *IEEE Transactions on Systems, Man, and Cybernetics*, Vol. SMC-3, No. 1 (January 1973).

13. "MXC," *University of Minnesota Experimental City Reports*, 5 vols., 1969.

14. This may indicate an imbalance in the presentation. It may also be that the objectives of this book are not identical to the goal of designing a new city. Probably the former is true, and certainly the latter is, since one object of the book is to teach the systems methodology using the new city analysis as an example.

Part III

THE NEW CITY

7

Optimum Size
of a Freestanding
New City

Others argue in terms of optimum numbers of people and of organizational and, more specifically, municipal efficiency, but they are not able to produce any convincing proof.

C. A. DOXIADIS
"Ekistics"
Science, Vol. 170 (October 23, 1970), pp. 394–404

However, it will be shown that even from a theoretical viewpoint the search for *the* optimal city size is unsound.

H. W. RICHARDSON
"Optimality in City Size, Etc."
Urban Studies, Vol. 9, No. 1 (February 1972), pp. 29–48

This all seems to suggest that middle-size urban areas of a couple of hundred thousand population, on up to perhaps a million or so, have the advantage of remaining relatively whole governmentally while becoming moderately stable economically.

W. R. THOMPSON
"The National System of Cities as an Object of Public Policy"
Urban Studies, Vol. 9, No. 1 (February 1972), pp. 99–116

. . . No city can regulate its population growth numerically so as to preclude residents of any other area from traveling into the region and establishing residence therein.

JUSTICE L. H. BURKE
Petaluma Decision
U. S. District Court of Northern California
January 1974

I see no solution for urban problems until cities develop the courage to plan in terms of maximum population, a maximum number of housing units, a maximum permissible building height, and a maximum number of jobs. A city must also choose the type of city it wants to become. To become and remain a city that is all things to all people is impossible.

JAY W. FORRESTER
The Washington Post, June 8, 1975, p. C4

7.1 Is the Question Meaningful?

Although optimum urban size is a popular subject of controversy among regional analysts, there is a school of thought that declares the whole question meaningless. The argument has two parts. First, it is said, the question is meaningless because no one optimum urban population number can be right for all persons and for all purposes. Second, the concept's opponents say, "Why argue about a particular number when the city will grow right on through that goal if it is healthy, and, if not, growth will eventually halt of its own accord?" At least one recent court decision declares growth restrictions by a community to be illegal. United States Federal District Judge L. H. Burke ruled in San Francisco that a Petaluma, California, ordinance limiting new residential construction to 500 dwellings per year is illegal.[1] While declaring himself in favor of orderly growth, Burke ruled that the ordinance interfered with the constitutional right to travel. He stated that, if many communities set population limits, the effect would be to immobilize the population. Perhaps this decision neglects the difference between a limit on growth rate and one on total population, yet it indicates, at the very least, that controls are politically sensitive.

Of course it is true that, when one speaks of an optimum size, this concept is meaningful only with respect to a specific criterion. Therefore, if the criterion changes, so probably will the optimum size. Thus to seek a single, fixed number as the unique urban population that would be optimum for all purposes and for all time is a useless quest. However, to seek a *range* of optimal solutions based on various criteria is not necessarily a vain hope. In fact, we will find in this chapter that various optima arrived at in a variety of ways seem to indicate rather strongly a definite population range within which most urban functions can be most efficiently provided. This efficient population range extends from approximately 200,000 to about 2 million persons. While a 10-to-1 range is by no means a single point, it does provide significant guidance. Furthermore, in the next chapter we will seek urban forms that will allow us to gain the various benefits available throughout this optimum range in a single integrated urban complex.

7.2   Natural City Size: Historical and Societal Aspects

We know quite well how to design a city for 30,000 to 50,000 people. For several thousand years students of urban design have known that this is the city of human scale. Plato, Aristotle, Da Vinci, Sir Thomas More, and Ebenezer Howard, along with the ancient Egyptians, Chinese, Indians, and Romans, can lend us wisdom on the organization of the city of human scale if we will listen. But we do not know how to build a livable large city, and, whether we like it or not, people will live in large cities.

The idea that a city should have a definite and limited size is not new at all. Ebenezer Howard made this a key element of his garden city plan at the turn of the century.[2] Sir Thomas More mentioned a size limit in his early sixteenth century book, *Utopia,* and Leonardo da Vinci about the same time reached a similar conclusion about Milan. Aristotle firmly maintained that there is a natural size for a city. All these and other savants have argued that city size be limited to what we have called a regional trading center with a population maximum of about 30,000 persons.[3] They seem to arrive independently at this estimate by observation of successful cities known to them personally. Some modern planners would argue that a city of 30,000 to 50,000 persons can meet most normal needs, without being so large as to promote a strong sensory overload. Such overloads seem to require the individual to construct a mental shell outside of which he consigns most of the population as nonpersons in order to maintain his psychological equilibrium. Others, however, would find such a small city lacking in variety and a sense of unexpectedness, which many require for a stimulating environment.

The Class A regional center as defined by Doxiadis appears to be the natural-size city of human scale. It requires little special treatment by its citizens to become and remain a desirable environment for many of its residents. Such is not the case for the metropolis. Urban regions often grow to 10 times the scale of regional trading centers. Such centers, called Class B by Doxiadis, require special care and insight in their design and maintenance if they are not to undergo rapid and possibly violent degeneration. The large city acting as the center of an industrial empire, as we have seen, is in all probability obsolescent. Nevertheless, large cities exist and grow in size day by day. Thus to ignore the large city is to ignore reality.

Beyond the human-scale city of 30,000 to 50,000, one begins to incur interpersonal social disadvantages not found in smaller cities, and new disadvantages continue to be initiated up to a population 10 times this number. This is not to say that at a population of 300,000 to 500,000 interpersonal problems begin to disappear. They do not. However, such a city begins to acquire compensatory benefits; more and more metropolitan advantages accompany increasing size. Then, beyond a population of 1 million or so, new disadvantages of scale become dominant. This concept is represented roughly in Figure 7.1.

Can we be more precise about these so-called interpersonal advantages and metropolitan advantages? The former vary from person to person, of course, but interpersonal benefits in a human-scale city of 30,000 might include the following:

- One would feel that he "knows everyone in town" yet has privacy and some variety. One does not interact daily with the same restricted group, as he must in a village, yet he "spans the space."
- There are sufficient churches, recreational opportunities, and stores for variety, but a small enough number of schools to give parents a feeling of control over their children's activities.
- One knows the power structure. It is numerically too small to be able to withdraw behind a wall of assistants and to find its own social life. The mayor, the banker, the superintendent of schools, and other public officials must be part of the mainstream of the city if they are to

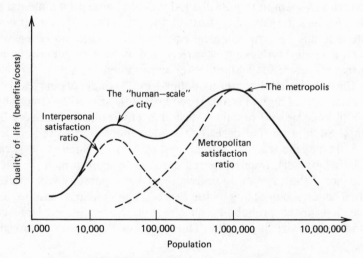

Figure 7.1 Satisfaction level as a function of urban scale.

have any social life at all. Thus they are part of the social fabric of the town.

This feeling of "control" begins to disappear, however, as the city grows beyond 50,000. There appear larger factories with absentee ownership and managers who are oriented toward faraway home offices. Unskilled workers are needed, and class and social stratification takes place. On the other hand, there are more jobs, more money, and more variety. When the population reaches about 250,000, specific new metropolitan benefits begin to be available.

- Large department stores and small specialty shops can exist.
- A symphony orchestra, an art museum, and at least occasional live theater are possible.
- A medium-size university is feasible.
- More important than these social and educational opportunities, however, is the new kind of job climate that develops in a city as it approaches a population of 1 million. Then there are multiple job opportunities for unskilled and semiskilled persons. A small city acts like a company town to semiskilled people. They have one, or at most a few, job opportunities, and they lack security through diversity. In a metropolitan regime, on the other hand, multiple job opportunities develop.

These arguments for metropolitan advantages might seem to be strengthened as the city continues to grow. This is not so beyond a certain point, however. Furthermore, specific new drawbacks develop one by one with increasing size.

7.3 Natural Size: Current British Experience

The reconstruction of Europe after World War II provided the impetus for planning a number of new towns[4] in England, France, Poland, Hungary, the Netherlands, and Scandinavia.

The 14 new towns founded in Britain between 1946 and 1950, stimulated by the Reith Royal Commission report and the New Town Act of August 1946, are currently referred to as the Mark I group. The Reith Commission recommended certain design characteristics as guides to planners. For example, the report called for a definite spacing between a new town location and the nearest metropolitan center in order to promote truly independent economic, social, and cultural communities. The planning called for high-density communities located on virgin sites and surrounded by green space, totally self contained with respect to employment and limited in population to the range of 20,000 to 60,000 persons.

None of these parameters worked out as planned. Another factor in the Mark I plan that failed the test of livability was the almost total dependence on public transportation with the consequent neglect of the private automobile. As pointed out in Chapter 5, parking was provided for one automobile per each eight families, and the streets in the new town centers were too narrow to permit on-street parking. The planning unit was the neighborhood of 5000 to 12,000 persons, which was to have its own shops, primary school, community center, church, and so forth. But in practice the neighborhood has failed to be a cohesive unit, and the shops are not financially successful because of their small size and limited clientele.

In the second wave of planning for the Mark II series, which was initiated by the publication in 1958 of the plan for Cumbernauld, Scotland, many of the observed deficiencies of the earlier Mark I towns were remedied. For example, the neighborhood as the basic planning unit was rejected for economic and social reasons.[5] It was also recognized by the Mark II planners that the size limits on Mark I towns seriously impeded their effectiveness. Hence Mark II town populations were generally set in the 80,000 to 100,000 range, and the populations in Mark III town plans were revised upward still further. Current Mark III projects call for planned populations in the 150,000 to 250,000 range.

The Mark I planners perhaps were influenced by the massive weight of the opinion of the classical philosophers as to the "natural size" of the ideal city in their initial choice of target populations. It is to the credit of British planners that, as evidence accumulated concerning the inability of a post-industrial-revolution new town to stand alone without burdening a neighboring metropolitan center unless its size is 5 to 10 times the so-called natural size as derived from consideration of pre-industrial-revolution concepts, these planners acted upon this knowledge.

7.4 Pragmatic Population Ranges under Various Criteria

It now seems certain from the British experience that a proposed freestanding new city with a population much below 250,000 cannot be successful as a modern general-purpose development. This provides a practical lower-bound design parameter. It is also possible to arrive at practical bounds by other means.

Various urban activities have limited population ranges over which they are effective. Depending on the specific activity, this effective range may be limited at the lower end of the population range, the upper end, or both. Urban governance is an example of an activity that is limited at the upper end. Smaller towns and medium-sized cities appear to be governable, but evidence is available which indicates that the largest cities cannot be governed by using conventional forms. John Lindsay's book, *The City*,[6] indicates that, even for a person of courage, will, knowledge, and apparently inexhaustible energy, the position of mayor of New York City is untenable. Greer argues that beyond a few million persons conventional urban governance forms break down.[7]

Many specialized commercial activities are limited at the lower end of the population range. And, of course, this is what central place theory is all about. By various methods the efficient population ranges of many urban activities can be found. A number of these ranges will be discussed below.

As an example of the process of computing the effective population range of a given activity, let us calculate the upper population bound as determined by transportation. Suppose that the supply of transportation increases with population. This is a reasonable assumption and is not disfunctional economically. Suppose that the city is roughly round and has the conventional street grid, either rectangular or radial. Then, for a constant population density, the radius (or travel time) is roughly proportional to the square root of the area (or population). It is apparent, therefore, that an incremental increase in population appeals to decision makers because, for no increase in per capita costs and a less than proportional increase in travel time, one gains a larger tax base, labor force, customer base, and so on. Thus, although in the abstract one can see that the city can grow too large, in practice incremental growth appears good. There will never appear an externally and self-evident "logical" population level at which to stop the growth of the city.

Gradually, as travel time continues to increase, the benefits supposedly obtained from the growing city become more difficult for any one person to realize in practice. It is unlikely, given the above reasoning, however, that proposals to limit the growth of the city will be accepted initially. Rather, attempts will be made to buy time with money.

The building of limited-access freeways through the heart of the city is an example of an attempt to buy time with money.[8] We should be able to compute the point in population growth of a city at which such freeway proposals will develop. To begin such a calculation, one needs an estimate of various travel times that appear acceptable to most citizens. The results of an informal survey that I conducted are given in Table 7.1.

In normal driving on typical U.S. city streets during rush hour traffic, it is difficult to see how one could average more than 10 miles per hour.

Table 7.1 *Estimated Travel Times (minutes) (Sample of Approximately 100)*

Travel Time	Minimum (Ideal)	Average (Don't Care)	Maximum (Barely Tolerable)
To work	10	25	45
To shop	10	20	35
To play	10	30	85

Thus we argue, from Table 7.1, that, if the average trip to work is greater than 10 miles, there will be agitation for superhighways through the city. If the city has a radius of 10 miles and we assume a density equal to that of the New York–New Jersey SMSA, it will contain about 1 million people.[9] Beyond this population point, pressure for urban freeways will mount. At least 40 miles of such highways will be needed to affect significantly the average travel time in a city of this size, and 100 miles would be better. At a typical capital cost of 25×10^6 per mile, we can therefore estimate the cost of this "improvement" at about $1000 per capita. Thus to say that we buy time with money is no idle phrase.

The urban freeway is an identifiable diseconomy that may be associated with unregulated growth of the city. If the population of an entire urban region were limited to somewhat less than 1 million persons, most, if not all, such diseconomies of scale could be avoided by careful design, while most of the desirable urban amenities would be economically feasible. A general plan could be drawn up that could balance industry, recreation, and public services with an absolute minimum of capital cost to all concerned.

Although transport is among the most highly interactive elements in the physical infrastructure of the city, there are many other activities that have limited effective population ranges. Following a suggestion by Cobb,[10] Wentz[11] has surveyed the literature and obtained the estimates of various authors as to the population ranges over which various urban services can be delivered efficiently; these estimates are shown in Figure 7.2. Of course these various estimates have been made using entirely incompatible indices, and care should be exercised in drawing detailed conclusions. Nevertheless it can be seen that, regardless of how one weighs the importance of the various measures, the cost effectiveness of this bundle of urban services grows larger until a population of 500,000 is reached, then holds more or less constant till 1 million is passed, and thereafter declines rapidly.

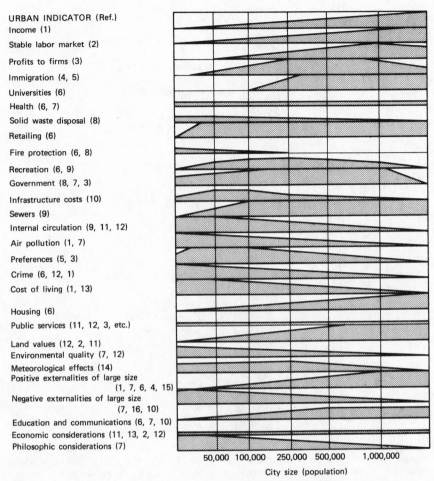

Figure 7.2 The population range over which specific urban facilities and services may be obtained in a cost effective fashion. Wentz rates the reliability of these estimates using a three-level scale and represents this by the thickness of the shaded bands. (SOURCE: D. N. Wentz, *loc. cit.*, Table 16, p. 32.)

It is interesting to note that the recent growth pattern in the United States reproduces this analysis of the availability of urban services to a remarkable degree. In Figure 7.3 is shown the percentage growth of SMSA regions in the United States from 1960 to 1970 as a function of size. We note that the percentage growth is greater in larger SMSA regions up to the maximum growth in regions of 1 to 2 million persons. These regions have grown at twice the rate of the smallest regions. Note also the

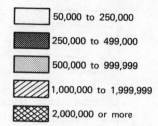

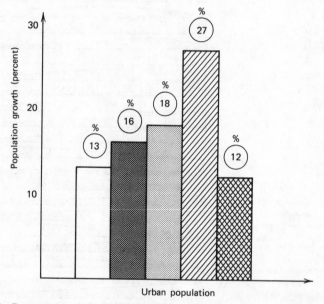

Figure 7.3 Percent growth in SMSA areas from 1960 to 1970. (SOURCE: U.S. Census data from *National Growth and Development,* HUD-386-CPD, December 1974.)

dramatic decrease in the growth rate for the largest SMSA regions. Regions of greater than 2 million show the smallest growth rate of all.

From these surveys it would seem safe to place a pragmatic upper bound on the effective population range at about 2 million persons.

The concept of optimality seems to hold a certain fascination for urban theorists. Three major aspects seem to attract the most consideration. First, there are size problems pure and simple. Second is the interrelated question of size ordering of the totality of cities in a region or nation. This question alone has a literature of over 100 entries. Finally there is the density question. If one proposes to arrive at an optimum total urban population by one measure and a total geographical area of development by another, then the average density is determined. And urban density is perhaps of more direct concern to residents than is total population. Thus density perhaps should be considered as a causative parameter in planning, rather than merely an outcome of other independent decisions. We consider the question of ideal density in Chapter 8.

7.5   Size Distribution Theories for Cities of a Region

Suppose that there is a "natural law" ordering the cities of a region by population. Then "artificially" to prescribe the population of a given city would disturb this natural order and perhaps anger the gods. This seems to be the metaphysical thrust of one implied argument against controlling the size of a given city within a region. Thus let us look into this question of the distribution of city sizes.

G. K. Zipf was fascinated by the readily observable fact that there is regularity in almost all human transactions in the bulk. He attempted to derive these results from basic physical laws.[12] One of the regularities Zipf studied was the distribution of city sizes in a nation. He argued that a plot of population versus rank for the cities of a region forms a straight line of unit slope on log-log coordinates, that is,

$$(\text{Rank}) \times (\text{population size})^q = \text{constant}$$

or

$$RP^q = K$$

Originally Zipf's theory encouraged him to believe that the slope should be unity, that is, $q = 1$, but he was forced by facts to generalize the coefficient. Later theorists have been critical of Zipf's derivation of his rank–size law, and examination of the actual statistics shows wide discrepancies from a straight line. Nevertheless the rank–size rule is a point of departure for many controversies.

The rank–size rule is classified as nonhierarchical by theorists[13] in that it examines the gross question and attempts to account for the observed statistics by inductive arguments. Central place theory, on the other hand, is representative of a deductive theory based on simple economics. Christaller[14] considered the smallest-viable-size village and its rural surroundings or hinterland as the basic unit. The size of the village and its hinterland are determined by the distance farmers will travel to trade at retail for certain basic goods, on the one hand, and the minimum population required to form a market for the retail tradesmen of these goods, on the other. On a smooth plane in equilibrium these villages would be evenly spaced, and their hinterlands form hexagonal trading regions. Centered among these hexagonals are second-order towns that trade in goods requiring a larger market than first-order necessities. Nested within second-order towns are third-order cities, and so forth, argues Christaller. In addition to a market-oriented central place theory, Christaller suggested other motivating forces such as a government-oriented hierarchy. Later theorists have elaborated both the hierarchical[15] and the nonhierarchical[16] approach, while others occupy themselves with reconciling the differences between the two.[17] Present mature judgment, if Richardson,[13] Rapoport,[18] and Mills,[19] and so on are reliable guides, is that there is no single, widely acceptable theory.[20]

Since the size distribution of a galaxy of cities per se is not our problem, we need only ask what the relevance of this question is to the question of optimality in size of a single city. Insofar as the nonhierarchical theory is concerned, the answer is "none." Adding or subtracting a single entry from a statistical ensemble should influence the gross statistics slightly, if at all. As it is, the rank–size rules must contend with rather gross deviations of actual data from any of the several proposed functions, and the microscopic examination of a trend line that holds on the macroscopic, if at all, has no theoretical justification.

But what of the hierarchical distributions? Perhaps plunking a large city down into an ideal central place distribution of cities would have a seriously disruptive effect on the delicately tuned web of commercial transactions that produced the hierarchy. As plausible as this argument may appear at first glance, it has little merit. One must recall the very special conditions to which central place theory is claimed to apply. Most, if not all, of the major cities of the world fall outside the category of central places of their regions. Only a small proportion of their commercial activity is concerned with supplying goods to their rural hinterlands. Most large cities are national capitals, world financial centers, seaports, manufacturing centers with worldwide markets, and the like. Central place theory, although a brave effort, attempts to explain the existence of a special class of not-very-important cities—and does that only in part. Naturally a new city will be related to its region, and indeed a major reason for a particular location might be to provide jobs that will not be available if only the central place function of supplying a rural hinterland is permitted. But the new city, if it is to be freestanding, must direct a major portion of its economic planning to exporting goods and services outside its regional boundaries.[21] Thus central place theory or any other hierarchical theory will have no inhibiting influence and is really irrelevant to our planning. Richardson[22] understands all this. He is explicit that a stable size distribution may result from short-run optimizing choices by individuals in a competitive economy. "It would be foolish," says he, therefore, "to treat the rank–size distribution as an ideal state and to adopt an urban policy aimed at correcting deviations from it."

7.6 Theories of Optimum Urban Size: Axiological Basis

Two axioms may be stated in regard to the question of optimum size. First, the concept of optimality carries with it the necessary condition of establishing the agreed-upon criteria. One must ask, whenever the term "optimal" or "optimum" is raised, "With respect to what?" It must also be understood that the criteria chosen for the judgment of optimality are value sensitive. Thus one should initiate the discussion with the axiological component. If these two simple propositions are accepted, much of the controversy is eliminated from the question of optimum urban size.

Next, we can state certain corollaries of these two axioms.

- *There is no one single optimum size.* Since various value structures and various criteria are possible, a single optimum size could not result.
- *Optimality is time variant.* As values change, the criteria produced by these values will also change. Moreover, as technology changes, the same criterion may produce a different optimum. For example, suppose the criterion is the time for the journey to work. This is obviously a technology-dependent calculation.

It follows, therefore, that the arguments of those who worship the past must be viewed critically. One properly studies the past if he wishes to perceive more clearly the lasting values of a civilization. It is a misperception of the meaning of history, however, to use the consequences of value-based and technology-dependent decisions of the past as operative guidelines for the present.

- *Optimality is culturally based.* The meaning of the word "culture" relates to the value bundle accepted by the given population group. If values vary from culture to culture, as they must by the very definition of the term, it follows that the criteria for optimality and the resulting calculations will differ.

Thus we will restrict ourselves to the consideration of possible criteria applicable in modern-day America. Here are some possible sample criteria. Of course it need not be pointed out that such lists as these are themselves culturally bound and value-laden.

- *Economic man.* Many regional analysts appear to give axiological allegiance to the concept of the individual's optimizing his private short-run economic self-interest.[23] It is one thing, of course, to say that the economic man thesis seems to explain mass behavior as well as any other social theory, but quite another to say that this is the way things *ought* to be.

- *Laissez-faire incrementalism.* This criterion is close to, if not identical with, the previous one. They differ, if at all, in only one respect. One could compute the optimum urban size, given various technical constraints and subgoals, using the principle of the economic man. The pragmatic incrementalist, on the other hand, would say the whole question of optimum urban size is meaningless and ignore it.

- *Architectural egocentricism and nationalistic monumentalism.* These criteria sometimes cooperate to produce a city unrelated in form and size to social needs. Brasilia and Chandigarh seem to be two modern examples of these criteria.

- *Social activism and pragmatic realism.* These two might combine as follows. It could be agreed that present American cities are perceived by sectors of our society as destructive to the aims and goals of many Americans. This results in social unrest, continued inequality, and a loss in national resolve. Therefore let us build at least one new city as a model. It must be as large as possible in order to benefit the maximum number of people, but not so large as to be destructive of the goals that cause it to be built. It must be freestanding, so that the process of its construction will not in itself cause deterioration of a neighboring metropolis. It must be located geographically so as to have an important national impact, and it must be carried forward, based on the principles of social justice. It must provide for improving existing cities by virtue of the experience gained in its design and construction, and it must be accomplished quickly because people are in need.

- *Other.*

7.7 Optimum Size: Economic Considerations

As we have seen, considerable attention has been given to the stability of the size distribution of cities, the rank–size rule and central place theory being two examples. Some economists have ventured to explain *why* this regularity exists. Hoch[24] states, "Large cities have become large because they have had 'natural' competitive advantages," which seems to be a circular argument. Hoch goes on to document the intuitively reasonable fact that money income of workers is proportional to urban size. He further cites evidence that the cost of living, as well as rent, transportation costs, pollution, and crime, is also directly proportional to urban size, so that the higher income received compensates for additional costs. This results in equilibrium, since real income must be equal in cities of different size if they are to maintain an existing size differential. Various conclusions can be drawn from these data. One could say, for example, that the stability of size distributions proves the economic equilibrium theory, or, one could argue, the observed economic data working through the theory prove the stability of size distribution.

We are left with the problem of answering why, if the cost of doing business is greater in the large city, as it clearly is, concerns knowingly settle there. Evans[25] answers this by advancing two main reasons. First, as Vernon has said and we have previously discussed, certain firms subject to marketing instability and uncertainty find that they can reduce these problems to manageable levels by locating close to a center of communication. Second, Evans discusses another rather interesting external economy based on the classic concept of division of labor. Think, says Evans, quoting other scholars, of a firm as consisting of a bundle of activities. The individual cost of each activity in the bundle is presumed to depend only on the rate of use of that activity. Not all activities have the same rate of use when a firm provides a certain product or specialized service. Therefore certain elements of the bundle of activities needed to produce that product or specialized service will be used at an inefficiently low rate. Thus it is more efficient to buy these elements of the bundle from an outside vendor than to maintain that activity in house, and such specialized vendors are more readily available in a large city than in a small one.

From this argument, one would expect small firms to need outside vendors more than large ones would, and thus the average sizes of firms should be inversely proportional to the sizes of the cities in which they are located. Evans shows that this is indeed so. Furthermore, since various firms providing various products and specialized services combine in various ways and proportion their required bundles of activities, we have a persuasive argument for variously sized cities.

Suppose a manufacturing firm uses specified quantities of floor space, labour, business services, and capital to produce its output. The prices of these inputs vary with city size . . . By calculating the cost of each output as a function of city size and adding the various costs together, the firm will be able to find the city size which minimizes its costs.[25]

Figure 7.4 shows one possible set of cost curves that produces a minimum

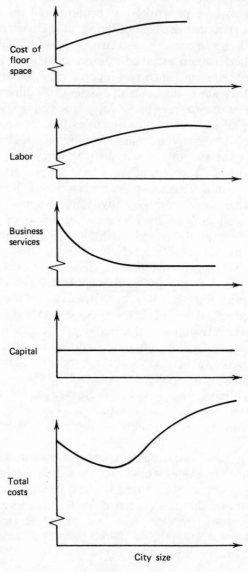

Figure 7.4 One possible set of manufacturing costs that produces a minimum total cost at a finite population. (SOURCE: after Evans, *loc. cit.*)

total cost at a finite population. Given that the actual costs are as shown in Figure 7.4, one would expect labor-intensive and land-intensive firms to locate in small cities, with those intensive in their use of outside specialized business services tending toward larger cities.

Evans also points out there is no reason to assume that a particular size city will be both economically optimal for a firm and socially optimal. Richardson[26] discusses this question as well, and we will follow his approach. Richardson adapts the standard theory of the firm to urban size by considering cost and product curves versus population rather than the more familiar cost and revenue curves plotted as a function of units of production. Consider the case in which the average product (AP) and the marginal product (MP) (i.e., productivity per capita and rate of change of productivity vs. population) are rising. Richardson claims that this is true for many firms because of agglomeration economies. Further assume that the average cost (AC) and marginal cost (MC) curves are concave upward.[27] In Figure 7.5 is shown this case of the continually rising average product (AP) curve and the U-shaped average cost (AC) curve. The intersection of the average cost with the average product occurs at population p_1. This is the minimum threshhold population below which the city cannot operate permanently. The minimum average cost occurs at p_2. But neither p_1 nor p_2 is an optimum population. There are, however, several optimal (O_i) each reflecting, as Richardson points out, a particular perspective.

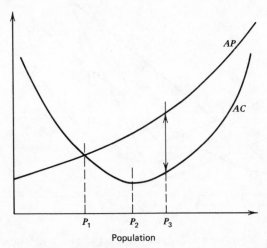

Figure 7.5 A case in which the average product curve for a city is a continually rising function of population (i.e., increasing productivity), and the average cost curve is U-shaped. This is a not unrealistic situation, according to many economists.

For the average resident, the optimum population occurs at p_3, the point at which the difference between AP and AC is a maximum.

$$O_1 = \text{Max}(AP - AC) \tag{7.1}$$

For the planner there are several optima. In Figure 7.6 the marginal product and marginal cost curves are added to the average curves shown in Figure 7.5. The first planning optimum occurs at p_4, where marginal cost and marginal product are equal, for "here the city maximizes its contribution to total output provided there is no more productive locality elsewhere for an increase in population."

$$O_2: MP = MC \tag{7.2}$$

A second social optimum occurs at p_5 (and possibly p_5'), the point (or points) at which MP exceeds MC by an amount equal to the opportunity cost of relocating the population in other cities.

$$O_3: MP = MC + \text{opportunity costs} \tag{7.3}$$

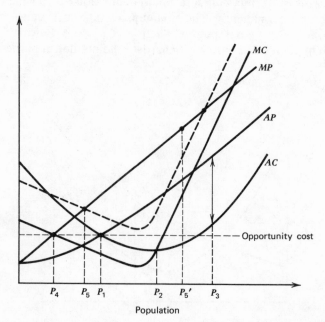

Figure 7.6 Marginal product and costs curves added to the average curves given in Figure 7.4. The sign of the marginal curve is neglected by convention. Thus marginal curves report magnitude only.

For the single firm, still a different size may be optimum.

$$O_4 = \text{Max (Agglomeration economics for that firm}$$
$$- \text{cost of services in that city)} \tag{7.4}$$

Evans arrives at the same concept by a slightly different approach.

There is little to argue about concerning these definitions, but beyond them exists an area of considerable controversy. Some of the arguments advanced by Richardson and others as to why these optima are meaningless and possible responses are as follows.

- *Free migration makes it impossible to fine-tune population numbers.* But there is no evidence that fine tuning is needed. The optima may be quite flat.
- *Because different interest groups have different optima, the concept is meaningless.* Not so; the concept means what it means. Only those seeking a single, unitary supremum have to be disappointed.
- *Social optimum points are controversial and difficult to measure.* True, but the idea still may be worth trying.
- *The social optimum may not be the economic optimum.* True, and indeed Evans shows that it is not. But unconstrained growth may push well beyond all optima. An optimal *range*, though weaker than a point, is preferable to no knowledge at all.
- *The economic theory used to derive these results is restrictive.* True; the theory assumes a closed economy and a static model. Thus one must consider the results only as a rough approximation of reality.
- *The concept of optimum size is unlikely to lead to an efficient system of cities.* We discussed this fallacy in a precoding section. Indeed, as we have said, Richardson himself, later in the same paper, is his own best opponent.
- *Total population is a gross statistic and too insensitive to be a suitable idea for optimality.* True; a simple population count is a gross thing, and hopefully in the future more evidence will be available on a desirable demographic mix. In the meantime let us use what we have.

Richardson concludes by saying that, although he believes the search for a single optimum size is as idle as the quest for the philosopher's stone, persuasive evidence supports the view that a minimum city population of 200,000 to 250,000 is needed to provide a comprehensive range of services, while for certain specialized services a population of 1 million may be necessary. Thus after fire and fury we arrive at a totally reasonable conclusion.

7.8   The Petaluma Decision and Rational Planning

An assault on the concept of optimum city size has developed recently
from an unexpected source: the courts of law. The legal status of growth
regulations and urban population limitations has been challenged in recent
Federal District Court rulings and, in particular, the now-famous (among
planners and urban officials) Petaluma case. "Hard cases make bad law"
goes the old saying, and the Petaluma case is hard. At stake, on the one
hand, are the constitutional rights of the individual and, on the other,
individual property rights and the whole concept of planned regional
development. It is clear that *all* zoning is restrictive, and most planners
would agree that zoning and other ordinances can be used unfairly to
restrict entrée to a region. But the question hinges on the word "unfairly." This is an axiological term and almost totally subjective. Unfortunately, however, arguments from all sides seem to develop in absolutist
terms.

Petaluma is a bedroom community for San Francisco, lying 25 miles
north of the Golden Gate Bridge. Its 1970 population was approximately
25,000 and growing explosively. The rate of construction more than
doubled in the early 1970s with over 2000 building permits being issued. In
1972 the city enacted various ordinances designed to slow the rate of
growth to a maximum of 500 units per year, a typical annual rate before
the late 1960s and early 1970s. These ordinances limiting the rate of
construction were to have expired by 1977.[28] In addition the city adopted
a policy of controlling the expansion of sewer and water facilities, as well
as a so-called urban extension line beyond which urban expansion would
be prohibited, in order to maintain a "green belt" surrounding the more
highly developed areas. All of these measures are in accord with conventional planning advice given to towns in the grip of fast-buck entrepreneurial developers and being pushed by them into a spiral of uncontrolled,
explosive growth.

In the typical explosive growth situation, builders and developers have
no concern for the heavy burden suddenly imposed on municipal facilities. Sewers and water supplies must be expanded, and police and fire
protection reorganized. Congestion develops in the downtown area, and
new suburban shopping centers draw trade away from Main Street. The
school system becomes stressed in the lower grades because the most
mobile families are those with small children. All these factors and others
cause social strain and severe economic costs. No wonder, then, that the
city fathers called for a growth rate limitation for Petaluma. Actually this
was considerably more "liberal" than the solution adopted by many other
towns in the same condition. Milpitas, California, and Boulder, Colorado,

for example, declared a complete moratorium on new subdivisions. San Jose, California, and Fairfax, Virginia, prohibited all rezoning of already overcrowded school districts. San Raphael, California, stopped all new development entirely. Black Jack, Missouri, banned multifamily housing, and Boca Raton, Florida, has imposed an absolute limit on total housing units.[29] Like the Petaluma ordinances, a number of these decisions are under challenge, and some have already been overturned by the courts.

Set against the need felt by residents and elected officials to control and regulate urban development is the right of individual access. There exists a constitutional right of an individual to travel into a region and to establish residence therein, and according to current legal interpretation this right cannot be abridged, by whatever subterfuge, simply for the convenience of existing residents. This does not necessarily mean that the right of access is paramount and can never be set aside, but it does mean that a community can be asked to show cause as to why this individual right should be abridged.

Thus far, perhaps, we appear to be not too deeply into conflict. Most Americans would agree with the right of individual access in the abstract. However, the right of access rather quickly collides in practice with the right to hold private property and the right of a community to regulate individual action for the common good. It is in the region of adjudicating among these conflicting rights that controversy lies. Justice Burke of the U. S. District Court of northern California made several declarations in his oral remarks of January 1974 on the Petaluma decision, and in his later written ruling on this matter, that, to say the least, appear controversial. The following (quotations from Burke, as cited by Scott, *loc. cit.*) are examples:

- "No city can regulate its population growth numerically so as to preclude residents of any other area from traveling into the region and establishing residence therein."
- "May a municipality capable of supporting a 'natural population expansion' [*sic*] limit growth simply because it does not prefer to grow at the rate which would be dictated by prevailing market demand? It is our opinion that it may not."
- Any policy or action of the city "which may have the effect, the intent, directly or indirectly, of placing any numerical limitation, whether definite or approximate, upon the number of persons permitted to enter the City of Petaluma in order to establish residence" is permanently enjoined.
- Existing limitations on sewer and water facilities may not be cited as a limit on growth even if citizens have failed to support bond issues for expansion.

- A city cannot stand in the way of growth dictated by market and demographic forces.

All this seems to say that a city is totally at the mercy of disjointed incrementalism and that all coordinated planning is illegal. This cannot be, of course. Nevertheless, that was the appearance of things as of mid-1974. At the very least, such an interpretation totally vitiates the concept of urban design based on an optimum fixed population and renders moot the question of Project Toroid. Perhaps, however, this is not the most serious obstacle in Toroid's path, since one has faith that, if Toroid proves feasible and in the best interests of the public, the principle of fixed size will be legalized, but Justice Burke's ruling if upheld would have a dampening effect on the idealism of planners. In fact Burke was overturned on appeal; nevertheless the courts have not had their last word.

7.9 Conclusion

We have examined the concept of a "natural size" for a city and concluded that in the absence of economic imperatives a population of less than 50,000 may be socially desirable. On the other hand, economic and other factors seem to indicate an optimum in the range between 250,000 and 2 million. Thus a population of 800,000 to 1.2 million appears to represent, as well as can be determined with the crude tools presently available, the optimum size for a freestanding new city. We must bear in mind when using this optimum range, however, that it is at or beyond the maximum limit of the purely social optimum range. Thus it would be well to examine the subject of urban form with the following question in mind: Is it possible to so arrange the form of the new city as to obtain the social advantages generally thought to be associated with a population of less than 200,000 while at the same time obtaining the advantages generally associated with the city population of 1 million or more?

Notes and References

1. *Business Week,* January 26, 1974, p. 27. Burke has since been overturned on appeal. However, a further appeal is still possible.
2. F. J. Osborn, A. Whittick, *The New Town: The Answer to Megalopolis,* M.I.T. Press, Cambridge, 1969. See especially Ch. 1 and Introduction by Lewis Mumford.
3. Except More, whose "Amaurote" would contain about 150,000 persons, I calculate. However, More's *Utopia* is an allegory, not a textbook in regional planning. It is an amusing exercise to estimate the size of his cities—nothing more.

4. P. Merlin, *New Towns,* Methuen and Co., London, 1971.

5. The "neighborhood" as a basic planning module has a long and honored history in American planning practice, and, perhaps because of the appeal of its simplicity and unity (and salability?), it dies hard. Take a case in point. James Rouse's Columbia began in 1962 and featured the neighborhood concept. See M. Hoppenfeld, "A Sketch of the Planning–Building Process for Columbia, Maryland," *Journal of the American Institute of Planners,* Vol. 33, No. 6 (November 1967), pp. 398–409. Rouse planners held strongly to this neighborhood ideology through 1973 in the face of developing evidence of failure of the concept, and despite reports of the British experience. See D. R. Godschalk, "Competitive New Community Design," *Journal of the American Institute of Planners,* Vol. 33, No. 6 (November 1967), pp. 371–387. Only informally and not for attribution would Rouse planners admit as late as mid-1974 that the neighborhood unit concept does not work at Columbia.

    As pointed out in Chapter 6, the Columbia approach has had a strong influence on HUD and its planning preferences, as expressed by the proposals approved for guarantees of the Title VII new towns.

6. J. V. Lindsay, *The City,* W. W. Norton and Co., N. Y., 1968.

7. S. Greer, *Governing the Metropolis,* John Wiley, N. Y., 1962.

8. Note that this is a repetition of the process that became necessary in classic times as ancient Class A regional trading centers became Class B centers of empire. Wide streets suitable for horse-drawn vehicles were made by opening up, often by force, the network of alleys in the village chosen by a leader for his capital.

9. Approximately 4000 persons per square mile.

10. R. Cobb, "Urban Size by Others—A Graphic Approach," internal memorandum, Battelle Memorial Institute, Columbus, Ohio, 1973.

11. D. N. Wentz, "A Survey of the Literature of Optimum City Size," Urban Systems Group Report, School of Engineering and Applied Science, Univ. of Virginia, Charlottesville, Feb. 1976.

12. G. K. Zipf, *Human Behavior and the Principle of Least Effort,* Addison–Wesley, Reading, Mass., 1949.

13. H. W. Richardson, "Theory of the Distribution of City Size: Review and Prospects," *Regional Studies,* Vol. 7, No. 3 (September 1973), pp. 239–251. This paper with its extensive bibliography is an excellent starting place for the reader interested in the question of urban size distributions.

14. W. Christaller, *Central Places in Southern Germany,* Prentice-Hall, Englewood Cliffs, N. J., 1966 (original German, 1933).

15. See, for example, M. J. Beckmann, *Location Theory,* Random House, N. Y., 1968.

16. See, for example, W. F. Lever, "A Markov Approach to the Optimal Size of Cities, Etc.," *Urban Studies,* Vol. 10, No. 3 (October 1973), pp. 353–365.

17. See, for example, J. B. Parr, "City Hierarchies and the Distribution of City Size, Etc.," *Journal of Regional Science,* Vol. 9, No. 2 (1969), pp. 239–253.

18. A. Rapoport, "Rank-Size Relations," *International Encyclopedia of the Social Sciences,* Vol. 13, Macmillan, N. Y., 1968.

19. E. S. Mills, "Welfare Aspects of National Policy toward City Sizes," *Urban Studies,* Vol. 9, No. 1 (February 1972), pp. 117–124.

20. It would appear that the concept of population-rank ordering or of geographical ordering of systems of cities in a region is considerably more sophisticated than the notion that there may be an optimal size for a given city and a specific criterion. Yet the

former concepts are dealt with rather routinely on an analytic basis by regional theorists, whereas the latter usually fails to attract this same sort of objective analytic treatment. See, for example, H. W. Richardson, "Optimality in City Size, Systems of Cities and Urban Policy: A Sceptic's View," *Urban Studies,* Vol. 9, No. 1 (February 1972), pp. 29–48.

21. Several ways of exporting services occur to one. Tourism is obvious, and insurance and banking, for example, are exportable service-oriented activities.

22. H. W. Richardson, "Optimality in City Size, Systems of Cities and Urban Policy: A Sceptic's View." loc. cit.

23. Perhaps this is too strong, but there is an indication of heavy emotional content in contentions that tampering with the natural processes of cities is dangerous. See, for example, E. S. Mills, "Welfare Aspects of National Policy toward City Sizes," *Urban Studies,* Vol. 9, No. 1 (February 1972), pp. 117–124.

24. I. Hoch, "Income and City Size," *Urban Studies,* Vol. 9, No. 3 (October 1972), pp. 299–328.

25. A. W. Evans, "The Pure Theory of City Size in an Industrial Economy," *Urban Studies,* Vol. 9, No. 1 (February 1972), pp. 49–77.

26. H. W. Richardson, "Optimality in City Size, Systems of Cities and Urban Policy: A Sceptic's View." loc. cit.

27. The usual term used by regional analysts is "U-shaped."

28. R. W. Scott, "The No-Growth Explosion and Petaluma," *Urban Land,* June 1974, pp. 20–23.

29. J. Roberts, L. Bush, "Managed Growth Overview and Analysis," *Environmental Comment,* The Urban Land Institute, March 19, 1975.

8

Urban Form

Actually, it is absurdly easy for an "open-ended" activity like city planning to play the dilettante through superficial contact with activities which matter greatly to people, or the mandarin through an exorbitant preoccupation with matters, which, however precious to the professional, elicit at best a tepid ardor from people as a whole. In spite of the rapid growth and intellectual advances of the field, these are lively perils for city planning today . . . ."

H. PERLOFF and L. WINGO, JR.
Journal of the American Institute of Planners, May 1962

8.1 Introduction

Winston Churchhill's famous remark on the effect a building has on its regular occupants can be extended to the effect a city has on its people. One could say, "First we mold our cities and then our cities mold us." Frank Lloyd Wright's most quoted dictum is valuable for pointing out that form is not the plaything of the architect; it is not to be used in an egocentric way to display the vanity of the planner or the client. "Form follows function." This is as true as when it was said, but it is only half the truth. Form should follow function, but then function will follow form. And McLuhan says that you can't change the frame without changing the picture. All of these are more or less striking ways of saying that the psychological and sociological behavior of people will be influenced by their physical surroundings.

The form and structure of a city subtly shape and change the way its residents go about living. Until recently, however, architects and designers have concerned themselves almost solely with single buildings and their immediate surroundings. And even today, single buildings sometimes are designed with no concern for the environment into which they will be placed. Little or no thought has been given to the overall spatial organization of the city. Each freeway, each urban renewal project, each new building is superimposed on an already formless agglomeration. Neighborhoods change their functions without plan under the assault of entrepreneurs as the tragedy of the commons (see Section 8.4) is reenacted daily.

One must not be persuaded, however, that lack of concern for the overall organization of the urban environment is a recent deficiency. The classic cities so loved by Mumford and other antiquarians suffered from the same ills. The Greeks and Romans sometimes planned their new provincial trading centers, but in Athens and Rome growth was chaotic. Reconstructed views of these capitals show a jumble of buildings. Classical cities gained their grandeur seemingly by accident and surely through destruction.[1] The reconstruction of Paris, visualized by Napoleon I and carried out by Napoleon III and Haussman in the 1850s and 1860s, and Wren's rebuilding of London after the great fire of 1666—these grew out of great destruction, not clear foresight.

One can go farther and say that the charm of the classical cities of Europe may be more in the eye of the modern beholder and arise more from his disgust with modern cities than from "objective" considerations. Take eighteenth century Bath, for example. Mumford, among the foremost of the modern-day urban critics, heaps the following praise on Bath, in a widely quoted comment:

Even now, after a century and a half of change, the heart of Bath has qualities of design that even the best examples in Paris, Nancy, London, or Edinburgh do not surpass. The excellence of Bath shows the advantage of a strict discipline, when it is supple enough to adapt itself to challenging realities, geographic and historic. The placing of the Royal Crescent on a height that commands the whole valley, protected by the bank that spreads below, shows that it was no mere application of an arbitrary geometric figure; and while nothing in the rest of the eighteenth century city reaches this level of planning, the further building of Bath, right through the Regency, never fell too short of its standard.[2]

Less picturesquely, perhaps, but more accurately, Morris describes the rebuilding of Bath as due to the influx of fashionable money to that resort town, triggered by the interest and patronage of Queen Anne and the consequent speculation of entrepreneurial builders. Starr contrasts the Mumford quotation above with one by Tobias Smollett in 1771 on the same development.

The rage of building has laid hold on such a number of adventurers, that one sees new houses starting up in every outlet and every corner of Bath contrived without judgment, executed without solidarity, and stuck together with so little regard to plan and propriety, that the different lines of the new rows and buildings interfere with, and intersect one another, in every different angle of conjunction. They look like the wreck of streets and squares disjointed by an earthquake, which hath broken the ground into a variety of holes and hillocks; or as if some Gothic devil had stuffed them altogether in a bag, and left them to stand higgledy piggledy, just as chance directed. What sort of monster Bath will become in a few years, with those growing excrescences, may be easily conceived; but the want of beauty and proportion is not the worst effect of these new mansions; they are built so slight, with the soft, crumbling stone found in this neighborhood that I shall never sleep quietly in one of them.

Can Mumford and Smollett possibly be talking of the same city and the same buildings? Yes, they are. But we should not shrug, murmur "non gustibus . . . ," and pass on. We can conclude that the same sort of short-run profiteers were active as entrepreneurial builders in eighteenth century Bath as in the late twentieth century United States and that somehow, by accident, what posterity considers "good design" may grow out of this, although all too seldom to count on. We might also conclude that this situation provides convincing evidence of the proposition in Chapter 7 on the time dependence of values as applied to urban design. Finally we hope that the Bath example will caution us to be slightly humble in our own pontificating on "good" design.

Recognizing that form and good design are not settled for the ages but grow out of the same sort of value questions as those examined in Chapter 7, we proceed with our discussion of the desirable form for the new city of a million people.

8.2 Definition of the Term

What precisely do we mean by "urban form"? Possible synonyms are "spatial organization" and "geography," but these are hardly more illuminating. Let us define form, then, by listing the factors to be understood as included within it, and then enlarge on several of these factors in turn.

- *Size*, both in geographic extent and in population.
- *Population density.*
- *Geometric arrangement*, in particular, the organization of streets and open places.
- *Grain*, that is, the comingling of various activity centers as discussed below.
- *Accessibility*, of one activity to other points.
- *Character*; this is a synonym for "ambience," "aesthetic impact," "soul," and so forth.

8.3   Urban Densities

There are several ways to approach the question of the proper density of land use. First, a descriptive approach utilizing historical data might be desirable; then a more normative scheme could be added. Clark[3] proposed to describe the density of large cities by a simple exponential distribution of population density as a function of distance from the center.

$$D(x) \triangleq D_0 e^{-bx} \tag{8.1}$$

where $D(x) \triangleq$ population density at distance x from center (persons/miles^2)

$\quad D_0 \triangleq$ population density as extrapolated to center

$\quad b \triangleq$ population density gradient

$\quad x \triangleq$ distance from center (miles)

Figure 8.1 shows a plot of population data for London which Clark's hypothesis is claimed to match fairly well. Note that the maximum density at the center of London held relatively constant until the advent of the automobile and other rapid-transit devices but is now dropping. Thus the megalopolis is not simply growing up around the long-established core cities. Rather, in a sense, the megalopolis is eating away at its core for elements of its growth.

This is accomplished not only by the movement to the suburbs, but also by the change in the usage of space in the downtown core. Because of the change in mode of transportation, a premium is available to be paid for roads, auto service facilities, and parking space. It has been estimated

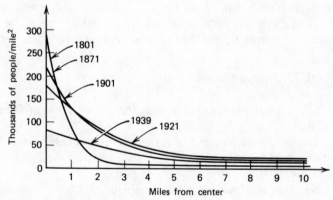

Figure 8.1   Population density in London as estimated by Clarke.

that 35 percent of the area in downtown Los Angeles is now devoted to such activities.

In Figure 8.2 is shown the best exponential fit, in a least-square error sense, to the population distribution of Detroit. We see that Clark's simple exponential rule does not match Detroit's population density. It is possible to suggest reasons for this lack of fit based on Detroit's nonsymmetry due to its river location. However, London is also on a river. If the negative exponential rule is viewed as merely suggestive of general trends, no problem is involved with this poor fit. However, modern regional analysts in their understandable eagerness to give their social science an analytic base sometimes press the point. Berry[4] says, for example, "No city has yet been studied for which a statistically significant fit of the [negative exponential] expression does not obtain." Even if we agree to ignore the decline near the center,[5] we are still not satisfied, since obviously, in a gross sense, *some* decreasing function must hold. Detroit's central business district (CBD) did not have a 4-mile radius in 1950 and a 7-mile radius in 1960. We cannot agree either that beyond these points the actual gradient is exponential; we are not satisfied

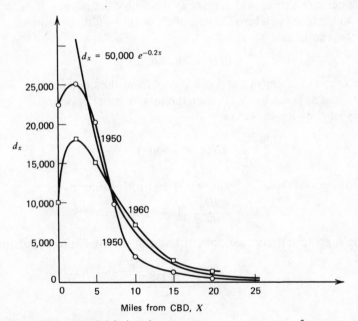

Figure 8.2   Best exponential fit in a least mean-square error sense of an exponential to 1950 census data for Detroit.

merely because the curves trend downward. By the very definition of a city the actual population gradient is generally downward, and there is an infinity of mathematical functions that are monotonically decreasing. Perhaps the quotation with which this chapter begins is relevant to this discussion.

Mills takes a balanced view on this question. In an excellent paper[6] he reviews the status of the exponential density approximation and provides perhaps the most complete data to date on U. S. cities. Mills says, "The justification for the use of the negative exponential density function in this and other studies is its computational convenience, its approximate accuracy at certain levels of aggregation, and its value as an easily understood descriptive summary." Who can argue with that? He points out that the precise method of determining the parameters D_0 and b from census tract data for a particular city is open to discussion, but then provides an intuitively appealing procedure.

Mills assumes the metropolitan area to be circular in shape except that a pie-shaped slice of $2\pi - \theta$ radians has been taken out. (See Figure 8.3.) This is an attempt to fit the circular model to the many cities centered near a lake, river, or other geographical object. Some very irregular cities or double-centered cities will not fit this model, of course. Then the population $n(x)$ enclosed in a torodial ring of elemental width dx centered x miles from the center is

$$n(x) = D(x)\,\theta x\,dx \tag{8.2}$$

where $D(x)$ is the density at a distance x from the center and is assumed exponential as given by (8.1). Then the total number of people $N(k)$ within k miles of the city center is

$$N(k) = \int_0^k n(x) \tag{8.3}$$

Substituting (8.1) and (8.2) into (8.3) and integrating by parts, we get

$$N(k) = \frac{\theta D_0}{b^2}\,[1 - (1 + kb)e^{-bk}] \tag{8.4}$$

Letting k go to infinity, we obtain the total metropolitan population N, where

$$N = \frac{\theta D_0}{b^2} \tag{8.5}$$

The parameter k can be any convenient radius. Then θ will be taken as the value yielding the area for a semicircular city of that radius. To solve (8.4) and (8.5) simultaneously for D_0 and b, we can substitute for N in (8.4)

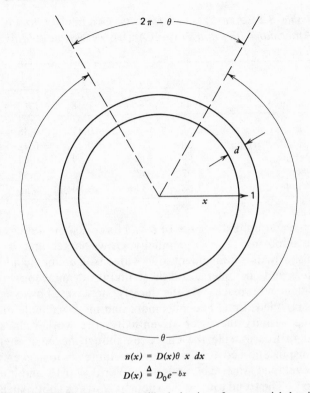

$$n(x) = D(x)\theta\ x\ dx$$
$$D(x) \stackrel{\Delta}{=} D_0 e^{-bx}$$

Figure 8.3   Definitions of terms for Mills derivation of exponential density curves.

from (8.5) and calculate for b by application of the Newton–Ralphson rule, for instance. Then, with b, we calculate D_0 from (8.5).

Mills provides estimates, calculated from available U.S. census data, for D_0 and b for population and for commercial activities in 18 U.S. cities varied as to size, age, and geographic distribution. The averages of the gradients are given in Table 8.1. The values for D_0 vary widely for cities of different size, and averages seem to have little meaning. For population, D_0 varies from 5748 for smaller cities such as Albuquerque in 1948 to 58,318 for Milwaukee in that same year. In general, these D_0 values fall with time, Albuquerque and San Diego being the only exceptions. The value for D_0 in Milwaukee was 31,123 people per square mile in 1963, for example. The D_0 value for Columbus, Ohio, was 31,710 in 1963, when the total metropolitan population was about 0.5 million.

Although the high-density CBD is probably a thing of the past, the trend to the suburbs will not continue to the point where a uniform density throughout a metropolitan region will prevail. Suppose that we think of

Table 8.1 *Averages of Density Gradient b for 18 American Cities and Various Activities (*SOURCE: *Mills, loc. cit.)*

	Year			
Category	1948	1954	1958	1963
Population	0.58	0.47	0.42	0.38
Manufacturing	0.68	0.55	0.48	0.42
Retailing	0.88	0.75	0.59	0.44
Services	0.97	0.81	0.66	0.53
Wholesaling	1.00	0.86	0.70	0.56

the city as a resultant of a number of social forces, some aiding each other and others opposing. The city initially grows larger and more dense because this growth is convenient to its citizens. Commerce and industry need workers and customers, and these find it advantageous to live and trade near their workplaces. As the density increases, however, a trade-off point is reached. Land becomes more and more valuable in the CBD as economic activity increases. Eventually, the worker finds it more economical to live outside the city even though he must then pay increased transportation costs. This trend was quite obvious even in mature and well-developed American cities after World War II, and it continued into the 1960s. The trend toward the suburbs slows as suburban land costs rise and the journey to work becomes unreasonably long and costly.

It would appear that the marginal appeal of the city will increase if apartment living in the suburbs is the only viable economic alternative. One may hope that, as city families realize escape to the suburbs is ruled out, they will devote their efforts to improving school systems and to civic betterment in the city.

Let us now consider a rationale for urban densities based on a normative social value structure. An early attempt (1934) at a new town design with an organic unity that grew out of a coherent value system was Frank Lloyd Wright's "Broad Acres City."[7] Unfortunately in a valiant though futile attempt to reintegrate agriculture and the urban life style, Wright chose the lavishly low density of one person per acre. Such a density means a very high physical infrastructural cost while still retaining the inefficient family-sized truck-garden farm. For these and other reasons the project never saw reality.

The Institute for Social Research in Ann Arbor, Michigan, has attempted through surveys to obtain a normative measure of resident satisfaction as a function of residential density.[8] The study covered 10 neighborhoods in which the median annual income ranged from $15,000 to $22,000, well above the national average. The surveys showed that the precise features of a neighborhood prized by its residents depended somewhat on the density. Not all people like the same things. Convenience to shopping and transport, privacy, green space, recreational opportunities, and other amenities are valued differently by different people, and this complexity of values makes it difficult to reach specific conclusions in social research. One conclusion, however, seems clear: there is little variation in satisfaction with one's neighborhood until the density exceeds 10 to 12 dwelling units per acre. This would mean a population of 25,000 to 30,000 per square mile for these affluent respondents. The survey did not include apartment dwellers, but detached single-family dwellings in Columbia and Boston, two to an acre, were not significantly more satisfying to survey respondents than were townhouses spaced 12 to the acre in Washington, D.C., and Detroit. How "well kept up" the neighborhood is, the authors report, rather than density or recreational opportunities or convenience, constitutes the single most significant predictor of neighborhood satisfaction.

A number of urban forms that we will discuss consist of various arrangements of high-density nodes surrounded by lower-density rings and green space. Governed by the normative considerations just covered, what maximum density distribution appears reasonable for such a high-density node? With a judicious mixture of apartment and high-rise dwellings at densities of 70,000 to 100,000 people per square mile near the center, then townhouses and garden apartments at densities of 20,000 to 30,000 persons per square mile, and then single-family dwellings much like those of Columbia and Reston with lakes and green space at 2000 to 5000 persons per square mile, approximately 150,000 persons could be located in a circle with a radius of 1.5 miles. A 3-mile-radius circle could contain almost 0.5 million persons. A small number of such high-density nodes could be spaced along the high-speed public transport of a ring city. Moving sidewalks or minitrams could move people within the node to connect them with the high-speed public transport terminal.

8.4 Geometric Arrangement

In Figure 8.4 are sketched some basic urban patterns. Mohenjo-Daro (circa 2500 B.C.) is the earliest known example of the rectangular gridiron shape, shown extended in Figure 8.4a. The dispersed sheet city, of which Los Angeles and Detroit are two examples, is quite common in the United States. Major north–south and east–west arteries are often spaced a mile apart and sometimes named for the mile distance from an arbitrary

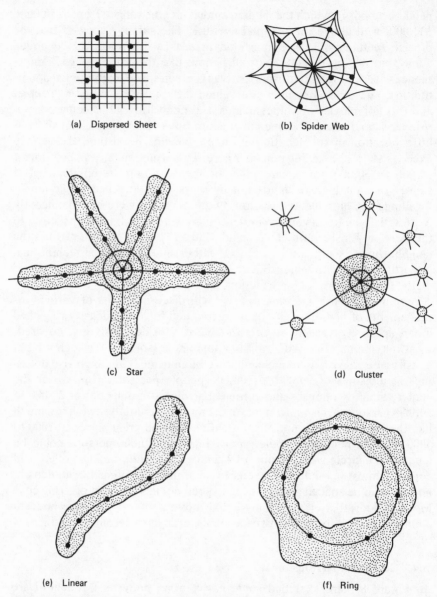

(a) Dispersed Sheet

(b) Spider Web

(c) Star

(d) Cluster

(e) Linear

(f) Ring

Figure 8.4 Six generic urban forms rarely, if ever, found in a pure state in nature. The dispersed sheet, spider web, and star can be produced by short-run, small-scale, individual entrepreneurial decision. The cluster, linear, and torodial forms require advance planning and careful control.

baseline. Shopping centers, industrial or commercial areas, and other clumpings occur seemingly at random. There usually is a central business district in existing dispersed sheet cities, but almost without exception, as mentioned in section 8.3, such CBDs are in decline. The ring-radial or spider-web city (Figure 8.4*b*) with major radials and circumferentials is less common in the United States, although Washington, D.C., is an example. The rectangular grid seems to imply an egalitarian sameness, whereas the web has a strong centrality or focus.

The star (Figure 8.4*c*) can evolve as high-speed transportation corridors are developed to articulate and control the growth of suburbs. In the nineteenth and early twentieth centuries, transportation corridors were commuter railways or street car lines. Lately one may note the corridor trend developing along the routes of urban expressways.

These first three forms are seldom if ever seen in a pure state, of course. But they are all "natural" in the sense that they grow without careful long-range planning. They develop by incremental optimization due to the favorable economics for each individual investor. The other three forms in Figure 8.4, on the other hand, are "artificial" in that they will not come into being by means of incremental entrepreneurship. These are planned forms, and to produce them individual developers must be prevented from taking actions that may be in their own short-run best interests but will be detrimental to the whole. Such a planned form should be adopted only if significant long-range advantages are assured, since constraining, insofar as growth is concerned, the natural market mechanism operative in an incremental city is a loss in itself.

This may be a suitable point at which to elaborate upon the concept that Garrett Hardin calls the "tragedy of the commons."[9] On overgrazed commons lands in sixteenth century England the profit of adding one additional animal was less than the cost. Yet, small though the benefit was, it was retained by a single individual while the cost was shared by all. Thus each individual's short-term rational policy was to add the extra animal even though this was destructive in the larger sense. We see this principle at work throughout the modern urban environment. It is an especially powerful, though hidden, rationale in location theory. We have referred above (rather caustically) to cost accounting on a narrow, selfish incremental basis, and the tragedy of the commons explains in part what we mean. In each of the final three urban forms shown in Figure 8.4, one can immediately see locations that will be highly profitable to the individual entrepreneur but that contribute to the destruction of the environment.

The cluster urban form (Figure 8.4*d*) was proposed by Ebenezer Howard in the 1890s. Howard was one of the earliest urban planners to attempt to design a city from the global point of view in order to obtain the advantages of urbanization while eliminating its disadvantages, and his *Garden Cities of Tomorrow* is a classic and prophetic work.[10] Howard's "town cluster" was to have 10 residential villages ("garden cities") connected to the commercial–industrial core by rapid transit, and the total population was to be about 300,000. It is apparent that the junction point of the rapid transit lines would be valuable commercial property and that the green belt surrounding the fixed-size core would soon be violated if regulations permitted.

The linear city (Figure 8.4*e*) could be 50 miles long and four blocks wide but square in time. If the spinal cord consisted of an urban mass transit (UMT) line that operated at 250 miles per hour, one could go from one end to the other in about the same length of time required for a person to walk a few blocks out into the green fields and woods running alongside. This green belt would be a prime target for violation, especially near the middle of the linear strip, by suboptimizing entrepreneurs.

The ring city (Figure 8.4*f*) is the logical extension of the linear city but is a real improvement since it reduces the maximum-length journey to one-half the circumference. Here the green space in the center of the ring becomes an attractive target for development. The clever entrepreneur would not even need to expose his plans directly. He could advocate a public but high-intensity use of the center, such as an airport or sports facility. Then public transport would follow, and commercial development would be demanded by the very citizens whose overall best interests might suffer most. The ideal solution might be to build the ring city around a lake. A large ring city would be practical only if a UMT system were an integral part of it.

It appears that Howard's cluster concept and the ring city are the two forms best designed to provide all the urban advantages with the minimum disadvantages. Of the two, the ring seems superior in one respect. The junction point in Howard's core is a natural bottleneck and will cause crowding and traffic jams. It will be necessary for all vehicles to stop at this junction point, and most passengers will need to switch cars. This is the single most disliked attribute of conventional urban mass transit systems. With the ring form, however, there is no junction point. No intermediate stops need be suffered, and the maximum-length journey is one-half the circumference.

Is there an objective mechanism for choosing one urban form over another? One obvious fact is that the form adopted should complement the site, yet even this simple precept seems to be violated more often than not. How many American cities does one know that turn away from a magnificent lake or river or mountain in order to focus on a railroad station or interstate highway?

In the absence of a site-dominant element how can one choose among forms? Here is one mechanism for assisting in the choice.[11] To assess directly how well various forms serve desired urban functions may be possible in principle but in practice this opens the process to grave errors due to prejudgments and subjective biases. To counter these difficulties it seems advisable to have the rating panel adopt a multistep process. The real performance criterion for an urban form is how well it meets such human functions as shopping, recreation, and socializing, but in order to assess these social values it may be desirable to establish first how well the form meets such intermediate technical criteria as access, cost, and growth potential.

To illustrate the proposed process, let us define the following technical criteria:

Access: How convenient, safe, simple, and economical is it to move from a residential zone to other activities?

Cost effectiveness: Is the cost effectiveness of the physical infrastructure high, medium, or low?

Image: Is there a well-defined focus? Does form follow function? Is it easy to tell where you are, or do you lose your way?

Growth potential: How well does the form adapt itself to continued growth? Calculate the ratio of area added to unit accessibility cost.

Environment: How well does the form relate to natural surroundings? Does it encourage contact with parks, playgrounds, recreation?

Other.

This method permits a separate consideration of the question of the importance of each of these factors. It may be difficult to be confortable initially with a finely differentiated rating. One feels, however, that it will be possible to classify a given form as high, medium, or low with respect to the chosen technical factors.

In Figure 8.5 is shown the arterial design for three simple forms for a given population. We will tabulate for these forms, in a so-called criterion matrix (8.6), a subjective weighting by one individual or an agreed-upon consensus by a group of the effectiveness of a given technical criterion for

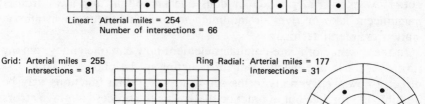

Linear: Arterial miles = 254
Number of intersections = 66

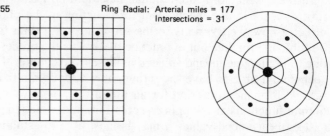

Grid: Arterial miles = 255
Intersections = 81

Ring Radial: Arterial miles = 177
Intersections = 31

Figure 8.5 Three basic forms with equal populations. Heavy dot represents CBD, while light dots are suburban centers. Average distance of a cell from CBD and number of intersections provide a measure of accessability.

a specific form. The following meanings for the weights are assumed: high = 3, medium = 2, low = 1.

		Technical Criterion			
Form	Access	Cost Effective-ness	Image	Growth Poten-tial	En-viron-ment
$[C] =$ Grid	2	3	1	2	0
Ring radial	2	2	2	1	1
Linear	1	1	2	2	2

$$(8.6)$$

Next, we relate the technical criteria and urban functions by a so-called urban function matrix (8.7), using the same weighting scale. It seems easier to take these two steps separately than to attempt to relate form and function directly. The procedure can be used to determine the consensus of a group or rating panel. Each rater asks himself how important each technical criterion is in aiding him to accomplish each desired urban function. The rating panel must agree on the names of the functions to be considered, but they need not agree on their importance. Note that geometric form does not enter into this $[F]$-matrix evaluation.

		Function				
Technical Criterion	Shop- ping	Work	Recre- ation	Educa- tion	Social- izing	
Access	3	2	1	2	1	
Cost effectiveness	1	3	2	2	1	
$[F]$ = Image	2	1	3	2	2	(8.7)
Growth potential	1	1	1	1	1	
Environment	2	1	3	2	2	

By multiplying the criterion matrix and the urban function matrix, we relate the geometric forms and the social functions. But one further step is desirable. Not all of the social functions are equally important to each critic. Therefore we next write a column vector of weights W to account for the importance of the various functions. For example:

$$\{W\} = \begin{matrix} \text{Shopping} \\ \text{Work} \\ \text{Recreation} \\ \text{Education} \\ \text{Socializing} \end{matrix} = \begin{Bmatrix} 2 \\ 3 \\ 1 \\ 2 \\ 2 \end{Bmatrix} \qquad (8.8)$$

Now by matrix multiplication we obtain the overall effectiveness of each form as seen by this group of raters.

$$(8.6) \times (8.7) \times (8.8) = \text{ranking}$$
$$[C] \times [F] \times \{W\} = \{R\} \text{ (ranking)}$$
$$(8.9)$$

$$\begin{bmatrix} 2 & 3 & 1 & 2 & 0 \\ 2 & 2 & 2 & 1 & 1 \\ 1 & 1 & 2 & 2 & 2 \end{bmatrix} \times \begin{bmatrix} 3 & 2 & 1 & 2 & 1 \\ 1 & 3 & 2 & 2 & 1 \\ 2 & 1 & 3 & 2 & 2 \\ 1 & 1 & 1 & 1 & 1 \\ 2 & 1 & 3 & 2 & 2 \end{bmatrix} \times \begin{Bmatrix} 2 \\ 3 \\ 1 \\ 2 \\ 2 \end{Bmatrix} = \begin{Bmatrix} 133 \\ 140 \\ 130 \end{Bmatrix} \begin{matrix} \text{Grid} \\ \text{Ring radial} \\ \text{Linear} \end{matrix}$$

Each of these three geometric forms could be further classified as concentrated or diffuse. A city with a well-defined high-density zone and a downtown would be called concentrated, whereas a diffuse city has no single main focus.

Let us now apply the same weighting process to the four planned urban forms shown in Figure 8.6. "Epcot" is the name suggested for a planned

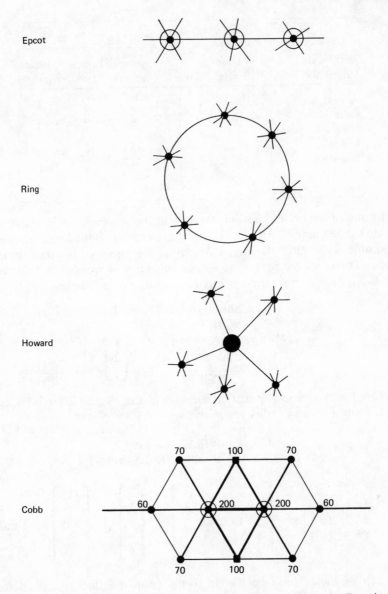

Epcot

Ring

Howard

Cobb

Figure 8.6 Four non incremental urban forms. EPCOT is an acronym for Experimental Prototype City of Tomorrow proposed for Disney World. The ring form is discussed in some detail in this text. Howard is the generic Garden City of Tomorrow form proposed by Ebenezer Howard and Cobb consists of a number of nodes around a main arterial and with transport links of carrying capacity in proportion to node populations.

linear city with three concentrated nuclei near Disney World near Orlando, Florida. The ring city and Howard's cluster concept have been discussed previously. "Cobb" is a planned city with nuclei distributed roughly as suggested by central place theory to maximize accessibility. The transportation links between nuclei in Cobb will have a designed carrying capacity in proportion to the populations they connect. Here are the results obtained by a different rating panel from the one that ranked the forms shown in Figure 8.5:

			Technical Criterion		
	Form	Access	Cost Effective-ness	Image	Growth Potential	Environ-ment
$[C] =$	Epcot	2	2	3	2	2
	Ring	3	2	3	1	3
	Howard	1	2	3	1	2
	Cobb	3	2	1	1	2

(8.10)

and

			Function		
	Technical Criterion	Shop-ping	Work	Recre-ation	Educa-tion	Social-izing
	Access	3	2	1	3	1
	Cost effectiveness	1	3	1	2	1
$[F] =$	Image	2	1	3	2	1
	Growth potential	3	1	1	2	1
	Environment	1	1	3	2	1

(8.11)

Then, with the same weighting for functions as before, we get:

$$[C] \times [F] \qquad \times \quad \{W\} \quad = \quad \{R\}$$

$$\begin{bmatrix} 22 & 17 & 21 & 24 & 11 \\ 23 & 19 & 24 & 27 & 12 \\ 16 & 14 & 19 & 19 & 9 \\ 18 & 16 & 15 & 21 & 9 \end{bmatrix} \times \begin{Bmatrix} 2 \\ 3 \\ 1 \\ 2 \\ 2 \end{Bmatrix} = \begin{Bmatrix} 186 \\ 205 \\ 149 \\ 159 \end{Bmatrix} \begin{matrix} \text{Epcot} \\ \text{Ring} \\ \text{Howard} \\ \text{Cobb} \end{matrix}$$

(8.12)

The particular weighting entries are subjective, and the reader is invited to perform his own weighting to determine his own preferences.

8.5 Urban Grain

Among the critics of modern American cities, Jane Jacobs is especially influential. Her *The Death and Life of Great American Cities*[12] must be classed as a pivotal book in the reevaluation of government policies on urban renewal. Perhaps it stretches the meaning of the word to call her insights a theory, but social theories cannot be expected to have the simplicity of laws in physical science. In the sense that it represents a point of view, explains many phenomena, is susceptible to proof, and permits extensions and extrapolations, Jacobs' work is a body of theory.

Jacobs points out the theoretical functions of sidewalks, neighborhood parks, and diversity of use in neighborhoods. "Quantifiers" have generally ignored her insights thus far, to society's disadvantage. Jacobs is quite explicit about the functions of diversity in the urban environment and, indeed, goes further to list the four necessary (she calls them indispensable) conditions to achieve proper neighborhood diversity.

1. The district, and indeed as many of its internal parts as possible, must serve more than one primary function; preferably more than two. These must insure the presence of people who go outdoors on different schedules and are in the place for different purposes, but who are able to use many facilities in common.[13]

Jacobs proposes to intermix residences, commercial shops, small factories, and bars and other recreational facilities in the same neighborhood, indeed on the same block. As she points out, this provides not only convenience but also safety, since neighborhood residents will be present and on watch at all hours. The relation to Lynch's concept of urban "grain" is apparent.

2. Most blocks must be short; that is, streets and opportunities to turn corners must be frequent.[13]

Jacobs refers here to the interest or surprise and variety that corners provide with new vistas opening to each side. Short blocks break up the "trapped in a canyon" feeling. Moreover, it can be shown analytically, using Manhattan or taxicab geometry,[14] that Jacobs' insight is eminently practical. From a corner location it is possible to cover a maximum grid distance for a given length span. Furthermore, the smaller the grid spacing, the greater is the grid distance to be covered for a given length span.

For both these reasons one wishes to provide as many corners as possible. This is one half of the analytic optimization process. Why not push to the limit, then, one may ask? If the grid lines themselves are of zero width, it is obvious that, for any given finite length span, one covers an infinite grid distance if the grid is spaced infinitely close. But, of course, streets do have finite width and buildings alongside the streets require more space. Thus one reduces either the grid spacing or the building space between the street grids. Now we have the other side of the optimization process: find the balance between these two conflicting requirements to obtain the optimum block length.

3. The district must mingle buildings that vary in age and condition, including a good proportion of old ones, so that they vary in the economic yield they produce. This mingling must be fairly close-grained.[15]

Here Jacobs makes a reasonable use of the economic facts of life. She does not wish to turn her back on these aspects but rather to use economics for good social purpose.

If some older buildings are available at lower rents, struggling new enterprises are thereby aided in gaining a foothold. It seems likely that these new enterprises will substitute "sweat equity" and ingenuity for capital if they are to survive. Thus the likelihood exists that the struggling enterprise will endeavor to preserve the structure it inhabits as well as its neighborhood. The ideal neighborhood of Jacobs is not one with buildings all of the same age and offered at the same floor rent, since such a neighborhood does not grow old gracefully. It demands premiums when new and then rapidly gives way to some other, still newer area. After a few more years all of its buildings move toward the rather steep downward slope of depreciation and deterioration. To halt this trend and reverse it requires a heroic effort. It cannot be done on a building-by-building basis. Jacobs argues for a slow and graceful degradation rather than this catastrophic collapse.

4. There must be a sufficiently dense concentration of people, for whatever purposes they may be there. This includes dense concentration in the case of people who are there because of residence.
   The necessity for these four conditions is the most important point this book has to make.[15]

This last requirement may sound circular to the analytic mind, but Jacobs elaborates in the text to help one grasp her meaning. She was among the first, for example, to point out the fallacy in the statement, "I wouldn't go out alone in the street at night. There's crime in the streets."

Jacobs suggests that crime in the streets does not cause deserted streets. Rather, deserted streets cause crime. If a street is deserted at certain times of the day or night except for an occasional pedestrian, there is no one to notice a street crime if committed. Moreover, the city cannot afford to station foot patrolmen in lightly traveled areas. The low density and single usage of certain areas makes them susceptible to crime.

The notion that Jacobs' theory is susceptible to testing has occurred to others. Weicher[16] has applied the theory to neighborhoods in Chicago and reports that his data fail to confirm Jacobs' neighborhood attributes as fundamental to residents' perceptions of success or nonsuccess, but further study is needed to establish or disprove the Jacobs thesis.

Kevin Lynch is preeminent among urban geographers who emphasize the importance of urban "grain" in determining the form of the city.[17] All of the conditions suggested by Jacobs as necessary for urban viability are included in the concept of urban grain. Jacobs advocates a fine or close grain mixture of urban activities. Implicit in a close grain structure is a higher urban density. But it also means more than merely high density. High-rise, low-cost housing developments such as the infamous Pruitt-Igoe of St. Louis represent high-density land utilization, but Pruitt-Igoe is not fine grained because it is single-purpose land usage.

Close urban grain implies a mixture of land usages within the same neighborhood. Jacobs argues that on a given block one might see commercial and retail activities on the street floor and apartments on the floor above. Still higher one finds artists' lofts. Behind the streetfront buildings there might be located light manufacturing and warehousing. Such a fine grain as this can still be found in New York City, although it is growing rare elsewhere in the United States. Carried to this extreme, the Jacobs concept may not be practical, yet the single usage that has become so common in U.S. land-use planning does not work either.

The grain with which one is comfortable is almost entirely embedded in his cultural matrix. Americans transplanted to European cities find themselves quite comfortable with an urban grain rather more fine than that to which they were accustomed. The grain of European cities, moreover, is becoming more coarse as the automobile becomes more common. Asian cities have both a higher density and a closer grain than most westerners find comfortable. Interestingly enough, the converse is also true. About 10 years ago the Republic of China commissioned an American architectural firm to plan a new provincial capital city for Taiwan. This new capital, Chung Hsin, is laid out on much more spacious lines than is customary in the Far East. The government buildings, recreational areas, shopping centers and freestanding homes are set down along broad winding roads that remind one of suburban developments in southern California. Automobiles, although very rare even among the middle-level managerial class, are almost a necessity in Chung Hsin. Ten years after completion, Chung Hsin must be judged a failure. It is unpopular with all social levels. Top-level managers who can afford two homes and a car continue to live in Taipei and commute several hours each way to work. Almost all others whose job assignment is in Chung Hsin prefer to live in Taichung, an older city 25 miles away, and to commute by bus. All economic groups complain that Chung Hsin is dull, that there is no place to go within walking distance, that there is no public transport, that there is no brightly lighted shopping district, and that the freestanding houses do not permit one to bring his relatives in to live with him. Chung Hsin stands as a monument to the arrogance of American planners who assumed, perhaps without even thinking about it, that their own values would be accepted by the Chinese.

8.6 Accessibility

"Accessibility" in the urban environment is a descriptor for the ability of people, goods, and information to move from a source to a point of use. One obvious measure of accessibility is the time and distance involved in the individual journey to work. Current design doctrine for all urban transportation elements is based on this single criterion. It is apparent that here land use and transportation links are the determinants. It is also apparent that a particular land-use philosophy cannot be chosen independently of the transport modal mix if accessibility is to be maintained without excessive cost.

The present crisis of American cities has been caused in large part by a refusal to accept this apparently self-evident fact. In Figure 8.7 is given an estimate of the proportion of urban land use devoted to six major categories in America's seven largest cities. Streets and highways occupy, on the average, 25 percent. It has been estimated, however, that the proportion of land use devoted to streets, gas stations, and parking lots in Los Angeles, a large disbursed sheet city devoted to the automobile, is well over 50 percent. In a series of publications Smeed[18] has analyzed the amount of land required for a rush-hour trip, depending on the mode of transportation. Although we will not present his analysis in detail here, certain of his results seem especially valuable. In Table 8.2 is shown the data for cities of circular shape in which essentially all the residents live outside the CBD and workers journey into the CBD for employment. It is apparent that the private automobile occupies approximately half the total available space, and to provide for parking is expensive in either land or

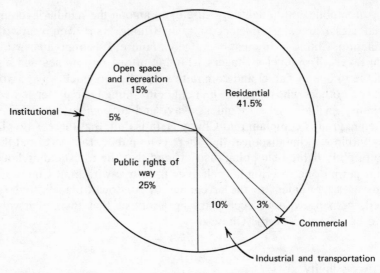

Figure 8.7 Land use in seven largest American cities distributed into six categories.

Residential Proportion, Example Calculation

Raw %		Weight by Population of City	Total
46.6	×	2.97	138
51.3	×	2.60	133
52.3	×	4.60	241
38.5	×	7.59	298
44.3	×	1.65	73
33.2	×	5.17	167
39.8	×	16.10	640
		40.68	1688

The weighted percentage of 41.5% is the total (1688) divided by the total weight by total population (40.68).

capital[19] or in both. The additional space required for urban structures in a city of given size if all workers use private automobiles increases the distance between activity centers, thus decreasing accessibility. Transportation-link congestion further decreases accessibility, and moderate congestion is necessary if the transport link is to be used efficiently and the cost is to be reasonable.

Although all of this may be evident to the planner, he is loath to accept the strong attachment of the public to the automobile. The planner de-

Table 8.2 *Percentages of Land Devoted to Roads, Parking, and Other Uses for Two Values of Working Population as a Function of Transportation Mode Used in the Journey to Work* (SOURCE. *Smeed, loc. cit.*)

Travel Mode	Parking Mode		Working Population in Town Center	
			50,000	500,000
Urban railway	None	Roads = 0.3		4
		Parking = 0		0
		Other uses = 99.7		96
Urban expressway	Multilevel	4		13
		11		10
		85		77
Urban expressway	Ground	3		9
		55		52
		42		39
44-Foot street	Multilevel	11		31
		10		8
		79		61
44-Foot street	Ground	8		23
		53		44
		39		33

signs mass transit for "the worker," but he himself counts on using his own car. He argues for mass transit downtown but locates his planning office in the suburbs to avoid congestion. Banning private transport in high-density areas by legislative fiat may not be politically feasible. It may be more rational simply to assign actual costs to the use of private vehicles in high-density areas and to permit citizens to allocate their own resources as they see fit.[20]

8.7 Form of the New City

The high-density core of conventional American cities can be made compatible with private transportation modes only with concomitant acceptance of extremely high costs. Yet there appears to be no objective reason for authorizing the expenditure of higher per capita sums on the new city than are permitted elsewhere. Therefore we can conclude that the new city will not look like a conventional present-day American city.

It is evident that major value choices are necessary in selecting the form of the new city. Thus the designer must be very careful. Several guidelines seem useful.

- Only constraints that are absolutely necessary for successful operation of the city should be imposed on architects, builders, and individuals.
- Maximum participation by the individuals concerned should be encouraged in choosing various design formats.
- Continuous revitalization will be necessary if the city is to keep pace with changing values.

One possible design scenario will be put forward below for purposes of illustration and discussion. There is no reason to demand, however, that this scenario be adhered to in later design iterations.

- The ring form with a limited number of high-density nodes surrounded with lower-density satellites and by green space will be adopted. Call this Project Toroid. (See Figure 10.7.)
- Each high-density node for Toroid will be designed for a total population of 200,000 to 250,000 persons. Each will provide the normal urban opportunities for a city of that size. In addition, each node will have located in it one or more of the singular activities suitable for a city of 1 million. Our planning designations will reflect those special activities.

Terminus: This will contain the major airport for Toroid, along with transcontinental high-speed ground-transport connections.

Senatus: Here will be located the major governmental offices and space for elected officials.

Universitas: Each node will provide educational facilities through the junior college level, but the University of Toroid will be located at this node.

Colosseum: Although provisions will be made for sports participation and spectating throughout Toroid, the major sport complex will be located here.

Centralis: All nodes will provide retail trade and service outlets. Major banking, major finance, and central office facilities, however, will be located here.

Factoris: Light industry will be encouraged at all nodes, but Factoris will be the high-energy node. The nuclear reactor and heavy manufacturing will be located here. By concentrating heavy industry and eliminating residential areas, Factoris will provide agglomeration economics and ease the task of industrial security.

- Transportation between nodes will be by means of high-speed, fixed-guideway vehicles operating at peak speeds of 150 to 200 miles per hour. The nodes will be approximately 10 miles apart, and with no intermediate stops a maximum-length trip center to center will take about 10 minutes with acceleration and deceleration. Within a high-density node, transport will be by moving belts, possibly at several different speeds. Accessibility to satellite communities from a central node will be by means of small personal rapid transit (PRT) vehicles or so-called horizontal elevators. Total elapsed time for a maximum-length journey from one suburb to another at a different node should be 20 minutes or less.

  Private vehicles under personal control will be welcome to operate between satellites and outside the city. No private vehicles, however, will be permitted in town centers or in the high-density nodes.

- Environmental zoning will control land use in the green space between the nodes and in the interior of the ring. No high-density activities will be permitted within the ring, and no hard-surface roads will be allowed. Personal recreation, picnicking, farming, amateur sports, and similar activities will be encouraged in the outer portion of the central space, while the inner portion will be designated a wilderness area.

- Attempts will be made to provide for various living styles in various satellites. Heavy participation will be expected in local governance. Central planning will not be imposed on architectural styles or social arrangements. Satellite communities will be aided in articulating their values to help newcomers choose compatible arrangements.

- In the first node to be constructed, provision will be made for determining personal preferences for living accommodations. As a first approximation it might be assumed that half the population will prefer apartment or condominium living in the high-density node, while the remainder will prefer a more small-town or suburban style in one or another satellite. As costs and personal preferences become clear with experience, adjustments in this mix will be simple.

The transition scenario for Project Toroid is important and must be given considerable attention by designers. If a 10-year construction plan is expected, approximately 80,000 to 100,000 new residents must be handled each year. Construction of 20,000 housing units annually is a large industry in itself, and simultaneously to design and put into place all services is to be viewed as a major system planning effort, possibly larger and certainly more complex than the NASA moon mission. See Chapter 10.

Exercises

8.1. Given a marketplace for a single good, apply central place theory to predict the distance between retail outlets for the good in the equilibrium state. Use the following assumptions: (1) The area under consideration has uniform population density S; (2) The demand curve for individual consumers is a straight line with a price intercept at zero demand of $2 and a quantity demand at zero price of five units; and (3) the shipping charge is (*a*) 10 cents per mile, (*b*) 5 cents per mile.

Reference. B. J. L. Berry, *Geography of Market Centers and Retail Distribution*, Prentice-Hall, Englewood Cliffs, N. J., 1967, pp. 62, 63.

8.2. On a logarithmic scale plot the size of the largest 100 U. S. cities (SMSA) versus rank, using the 1970 census. Make a best least-squares straight-line fit to the data to determine q, and find the correlation coefficient.

8.3. Calculate the values of D_0 and b for Baltimore from 1970 census data, and compare your results with the historical values given by Mills.

Year:	1948	1954	1958	1963	1970
D_0:	51,159	42,693	37,481	34,541	. . .
b:	0.48	0.40	0.36	0.33	. . .

8.4. Calculate a measure of accessibility for the typical urban forms: ring radial (spider web), linear, and rectangular grid.

Assume: (1) Population of one million; (2) Density of 4000 persons/ mi^2; (3) One central node (where applicable); (4) Average distance to neighborhood shopping nodes independent of forms; (5) Linear form has one central artery plus orthogonal cross arteries; (6) Ring radial has radial and circumferential arteries; (7) Grid has rectangular artery pattern; (8) Maximum distance to artery is independent of form and equals ½ mile.

Suggested measures of accessibility: (1) Number of shopping centers required; (2) Number of intersections; (3) Number of miles of arteries.

Notes and References

1. The Goths and Vandals did less damage to Rome in the fifth and sixth centuries than did the eleventh century Norman invasion, earthquakes, the Black Death, and the loss of law and order following the removal of the popes to Avignon in the fourteenth century. The return of the popes and the construction of Christian Rome in the fifteenth and sixteenth centuries sounded the death knell of the classical city. Contractors for Christian shrines were given free rein to pull down classical structures for building material. A. E. J. Morris, *History of Urban Form*, George Godwin, London, 1972, pp. 120–132.

2. L. Mumford, *The City in History*, Harcourt Brace & World, Inc., N. Y., 1961. This excerpt quoted by A. E. J. Morris, *History of Urban Form*, p. 208, and R. Starr, *The Living End*, Coward-McCann, N. Y., 1966, p. 157.

3. C. Clark, "Urban Population Densities," *Journal of the Royal Statistical Society*, Vol. 114 (1951), Pt. 4, pp. 490–496.

4. B. J. L. Berry, "Cities as Systems within Systems of Cities," *Papers and Proceedings of the Regional Science Association*, Vol. 13 (1964), pp. 147–163. Item 10 in Leahy, McKee, Dean, *Urban Economics*, Macmillan, N. Y., 1970.

5. This decline is usually finessed by defining D_0 as the central density "as extrapolated into the city's central business district."

6. E. S. Mills, "Urban Density Functions," *Urban Studies*, Vol. 7, No. 1 (February 1970), pp. 5–20.

7. F. L. Wright, *The Living City*, Horizon Press, N. Y., 1958.

8. J. B. Lansing, R. W. Marans, R. B. Zehner, *Planned Residential Environments*, Institute for Social Research, Ann Arbor, Mich., 1970.

9. G. Hardin, "The Tragedy of the Commons," *Science*, Vol. 162 (December 13, 1968), pp. 1243–1248.

10. Sir Ebenezer Howard, *Garden Cities of Tomorrow* (1902), F. J. Osborn (Ed.), M.I.T. Press, Cambridge, 1966.

11. Suggested in a private communication by J. M. Griffin, Battelle Institute, Columbus, Ohio.

12. J. Jacobs, *The Death and Life of Great American Cities*, Random House, N. Y., 1963.

13. Jacobs, *loc. cit.*, p. 150.

14. These picturesque terms describe a simple geometry in which the only distances defined are those mutually orthogonal. This corresponds to a rectangular grid of streets.

15. J. Jacobs, *loc. cit.*, pp. 150, 151.

16. J. C. Weicher, "A Test of Jane Jacobs' Theory of Successful Neighborhoods," *Journal of Regional Science*, Vol. 13, No. 1 (1973).

17. K. Lynch, *The Image of the City*, M.I.T. Press, Cambridge, 1963.

18. See, for example, R. J. Smeed, *The Traffic Problem in Towns*, Manchester Statistical Society, 1961.

19. In 1970, cost estimates for minimum preparation of ground-level parking space averaged $300 per car and parking structures cost $1500 per car, exclusive of land costs.

20. Disclosure of the full costs of operating private automobiles is met with universal disbelief. It may be estimated that in late 1974 the minimum total operating cost of an automobile was over $2000 annually or more than $0.20 per mile. A moderate-length auto journey to work from suburb to CBD costs well over $6 daily.

9

Site Location

When you tell a location analyst that a firm is where it is because its founders prefer to live there, he throws up his hands. Such cases, he claims, are outside his domain. Our own experience suggests that for many industries cost is almost invariant with location.

B. CHINITZ
American Economics Review, May 1961

A fundamental difficulty has been that the theory of regional economic growth has little reference for the development of regions in America. Not only does the sequence of stages outlined by the theory bear little resemblance to American development, but its policy implications are also fundamentally misleading.

D. C. NORTH
Journal of Political Economy, Vol. 63 (June 1955)

Sec. 702(C) To promote the general welfare and properly apply the resources of the Federal Government in strengthening the economic and social health of all areas of the Nation and more adequately protect the physical environment and conserve natural resources, the Congress declares that the Federal Government, consistent with the responsibilities of State and local government and the private sector, must assume responsibility for the development of a national urban growth policy which shall incorporate social, economic, and other appropriate factors. Such policy shall serve as a guide in making specific decisions at the national level which affect the pattern of urban growth and shall provide a framework for development of interstate, State, and local growth and stabilization policy.

Title VII
Housing and Urban Development Act of 1970

9.1 Introduction

Conventional site location theory is dominated by economic considerations and is restricted almost exclusively to the location of industrial sites.

We have argued that jobs provide the basic stimulus for immigration to a region. Thus the economics of industrial location play a dominant role in the location and growth of present American cities. On the other hand, there are compelling reasons for not restricting our attention to this single consideration. Among them are the following:

- Although cheap transport determined the location of many existing U.S. cities, it will not play the same role in the future. With interstate highways and reliable motor truck transport available such concern is less important than it was when transportation was restricted to certain corridors.
- The percentage of those employed in industrial and production type jobs will continue to decline in future U.S. society; the number is already less than 50 percent in the U.S. economy. Thus industrial location theory cannot be allowed to be the sole deciding factor in site location of the new city.
- In the postindustrial age, narrow bookkeeping principles based on the economic man will be rejected as guiding principles for society. For example, location on rivers and streams was attractive to some industries in the past because they could dump heat, solid, and chemical wastes into the water supply at no apparent cost. This will not be true in the future.
- There is growing interest in a national growth policy. Such a policy would count the total cost and the total benefit to the nation of various proposed urban locations and would regulate future growth through tax level adjustments and the awarding or withholding of government contracts. This approach manipulates conventional accounting principles to encourage industrial location in the national interest.

After introducing the concept of a national growth policy (NGP), we will concentrate in this chapter on the development of a site selection methodology for Project Toroid and the application of this methodology to Appalachia.

9.2 Industrial Site Location

Considerable divergence exists between industrial site location theory and practice. There is a well-developed theory of optimum industrial site location, such as that of Weber,[1] which is based on transport costs of raw materials to the processing site and the cost of transporting the finished goods to market, but this theory seems somewhat abstracted from practical business reality. There exist firms whose sole activity is the search for optimum plant locations,[2] and their recommendations more often hinge on such intangibles as regional preferences of owners and political cooperation than on theoretical considerations. The most important tangible consideration is often the local tax structure. Putting these items aside, the following elements are among those that enter into an industrial site optimization process.

Labor

A so-called labor-intensive industry is one in which a major portion of the final cost of the product is due to the cost of labor. The availability of a supply of appropriately skilled labor is an important component in the site location equation for such industries. Moreover, the concept of availability has general components within itself. These are, first, the total number of competent persons in the region; second, the absence of restrictive practices such as closed-shop rules; third, the going wage rate for the given skill in the area; and, finally, the cost of training unskilled persons and their availability.

Raw Materials

A materials-intensive product is one in which the cost of raw material is a significant component of the final product cost. It may be possible to locate a plant so as to take advantage of the lowest-cost supply. Some raw materials are perishable, others require extractive effort, a third group is in limited supply. All these factors will be influenced by the manufacturing location.

Transport

The transport of raw materials to the factory and the transport of the finished product to centers of distribution fall within this category. Because of complex regulations covering freight rates, this calculation cannot be limited to simple ton-mile considerations.

Energy

Reduction of raw ore to aluminum ingots is an electric-energy-intensive process; thus plants are generally located to minimize this factor.

Distribution

Distribution costs constitute a large portion of the total price of such products as newspapers, magazines, bread, and milk. Thus bakeries and pasteurization plants are located to minimize this cost. Obviously, retail sales of all sorts must be located conveniently near the customer.

Environment

Minimizing environmental impact at minimum cost is rather a new consideration, but it is of increasing importance. The environment also affects heating and cooling costs and is important in providing outdoor recreation for workers. By federal law an environmental impact statement must be filed with the Environmental Protection Agency before construction of nuclear power stations, roads, dams, canals, airports, and other large projects will be approved.

Safety

Safety factors are important in such matters as nuclear reactor site location.

Other

Table 9.1 shows a breakdown of the major cost categories in a number of basic industries. Industrial site location has absorbed the efforts of regional analysis theorists for at least two reasons. First, the problem can often be quantified on a dollar basis, thus providing a consistent index for comparing the multitude of various factors. Second, there exists at least a potential market for such studies. Businessmen (sometimes) are guided by profit optimization and should thus be interested in minimum-cost site location studies. It is less easy to find a buyer for a site location study aimed at minimizing the environmental impact or maximizing the psychic incomes of residents.

9.3 Nonindustrial Job Site Location

Daniel Bell, a Harvard sociologist, is among those who hold that the United States is moving into the "postindustrial" phase of society.[3] Bell argues that for several decades now in the United States more workers have been in nonindustrial jobs than otherwise. This trend will continue, he says; thus we should not let a minority consideration overinfluence urban site location or other major societal decisions. In 1960, for example, goods-producing jobs in manufacturing, mining, and construction amounted to 30 percent of the 66 million jobs in the United States. By

Table 9.1 Cost Allocations for Several Representative U.S. Industries

	Value of Shipments (%)	Value of Shipments - Profits (%)	Wages (%)	Capital Investment (%)	Materials (%)	Energy (%)	Other[a] (%)
Food and tobacco	103.3	100.0	12.1	2.0	64.2	1.2	20.5
Textiles and apparel	103.2	100.0	25.0	2.4	47.9	1.0	23.8
Lumber and wood products	b	100.0	28.4	3.5	47.8	1.5	18.9
Chemicals and plastics	106.4	100.0	18.9	7.0	41.2	3.7	29.3
Paper	106.3	100.0	22.1	7.4	50.5	3.7	16.2
Metal fabricating	103.6	100.0	26.5	3.3	48.9	0.9	20.5
Primary metal	107.3	100.0	29.1	7.7	53.3	4.7	5.2
Electrical equipment and instruments	106.0	100.0	31.4	3.9	41.6	0.7	22.5
Petroleum and coal	108.2	100.0	26.7	6.3	41.3	5.3	20.3

[a]Covers a wide range of expenditures including, but not limited to, (1) taxes, (2) R and D costs other than wages and plant, (3) marketing, (4) shipping, (5) unsold products, and (6) subcontracted manufacturing.
[b]Actual profit not available; assumed 4.0% of value of shipments.

1973 total employment had increased to 85.3 million, and goods-producing jobs had risen 3.6 million to 23.6 million but had dropped to 27 percent of the total number. Although Bell's position is accepted by the intelligentsia, a few influential observers such as Peter Drucker believes that the purported trend away from industrial jobs has been overemphasized and may even be entirely nonexistent. Granting such caveats, it still seems clear that in the future more Americans will be able to choose their places of residence on grounds other than the availability of industrial employment than could do so in the past. Jobs in the service sector of society will be far more numerous than formerly, and such jobs will be located for entirely different reasons. We introduced the concept of the center of communication previously, for example, and will not repeat that argument here.

Postindustrial society holds other implications as well. Already regional differences are narrowing as the whole nation becomes one marketplace under the influence of national television networks and nationally distributed magazines.[4] As tastes become homogenized, so also will wage rates and the need for national distribution of products.

9.4 National Growth Policy: Present Status

The Housing and Urban Development Act of 1970 called for the development of a national growth policy (NGP) to supplant the existing hodgepodge approach to national development. Section 703(a) of that Act called for a biennial report on the development of such policy. This task was assigned to a federal interagency task force and coordinated by the President's Domestic Council. Reports were prepared[5] in 1972 and 1974, and both contain a considerable amount of valuable information. But it must be emphasized at the outset that an NGP as called for under Section 702(c) of the Housing and Urban Development Act of 1970 presently does not exist, nor is one likely to come rapidly into being in any operational sense. To report to the Congress on broad social trends and to supply growth statistics once every 2 years, along with a list of possible policy considerations for developing a growth policy, is one thing. But to elaborate, on the basis of an accepted value structure, a set of guidelines that will discriminate between various proposed actions is quite another. The Domestic Council is no doubt wise in approaching the question with caution. In some circles even mere knowledge of the existence of the intent to develop an NGP would be controversial. Nevertheless it has become increasingly evident that an incremental approach to growth based *solely* on short-run private entrepreneurial return to the individual cannot be long continued.

The early history of the Tennessee Valley Authority (TVA) in the 1930s gives a successful pattern for regional development. Appointed by President Franklin D. Roosevelt soon after the TVA was organized, David Lillienthal was an energetic and creative director. The flood control projects and the development of cheap energy sources through dam building were the most obvious early accomplishments of the TVA, but the Authority also engaged in rural and urban development of other sorts. Opposed from the beginning by private electric utilities of the region and embroiled in political controversy in later years, the TVA became less venturesome and today exists primarily as a government-owned electric utility. Later regional development agencies such as the Bonneville Power Administration in the Northwest never ventured far beyond the building of dams and the generation of electric power, which was sold to privately owned utilities.

Not for more than three decades, until the Appalachian Regional Commission (ARC) was created by Congress in 1965, was the overall development of a region again considered. The Appalachian region includes parts of 13 states and a population of 18 million. Approximately $2 billion of federal funds, matched by an equal amount of local funds, has been expended since the ARC came into existence. Since then, seven additional regional commissions have been formed under the Public Works and Economic Development Act of 1965, but all exercise more limited authority and operate with less funding than does the ARC. See Figure 9.1.

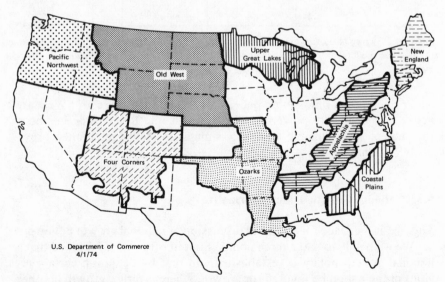

Figure 9.1 The eight economic development regions organized under the Public Works and Economic Development Act of 1965. (SOURCE: U.S. Department of Commerce: reproduced in *National Growth and Development*.)

Patterned more closely after the TVA regional development than the economic regional development areas, are the 21 river basin and water resource regions now in existence. See Figure 9.2. Perhaps some of these

Figure 9.2 River basin surveys water resources regions established by Water Resources Council and Federal Interagency Committees. (SOURCE: *National Growth and Development.*)

water regions exist mostly on paper, but those in the more arid West are active and politically powerful. The Susquehanna River basin has been the subject of a dynamic computer simulation study, mentioned previously[6] in Chapter 3.

9.5 National Growth Policy: Normative

This is not the place for a general discussion of national growth policy per se. We wish only to make three points. First, it is the law of the land that a national growth policy be established and that by definition certain regions of the nation be favored for growth, whereas future growth in other ones is to be discouraged. Second, this seems directly to imply that

federal policies which have an effect on growth should be put into force
with this (perhaps incidental) effect in mind. Thus we need not depend
exclusively on the market mechanism for the establishment of the new
city. Third, there exist in practice a number of instruments with which the
federal government can influence growth in accordance with a national
growth policy. Among these are the following:[7]

- *Grants and loans to state and local governments.* Presently, various
  federal acts influence growth and development in many conflicting
  ways because such grants ($50 billion in FY 1975) are categorical and
  specific, with their long-range influence on growth seldom if ever
  considered. The interstate highway system is perhaps the most obvious example of this deficiency. If an NGP were in effect, it could be
  used to guide such specific enactments to gain a consistent effect on
  development.
- *Federal construction.* Although highway funds are allocated to the
  states for expenditure, approximately $13 billion was spent directly
  by the federal government in FY 1975 on other federal construction
  programs. These include projects addressing flood control, beach
  erosion control, irrigation, water conservation, navigation, power
  generation, and recreation. "Though economic growth is used to
  justify these programs, many of them are conducted without reference
  to any broad economic development strategy."[8]
- *Procurement of goods and services.* Approximately 90 percent of the
  total FY 1973 Defense-NASA-AEC outlay, amounting to $41 billion,
  was spent in metropolitan counties. These funds could be expended so
  as to influence development consistently with an NGP. Since a rational NGP would no doubt favor development in the less densely
  settled areas of the nation, this would seem to favor disbursal of
  defense and nuclear power activities, thus providing additional benefits.
- *Taxation.* The oil depletion allowance and capital gains provisions for
  land investments are ways in which the present tax policy influences
  regional development unevenly. Other arrangements could be investi-
  gated that would encourage development along the lines of an NGP.
- *Credit management.* A number of federal agencies have a stake in the
  availability of credit. Among them are the Federal Reserve System,
  the Federal Home Loan Bank Board, the Farm Credit Administration,
  the Government National Mortgage Association, the Federal Housing
  Authority, the Farmers Home Administration, and the Veterans Administration. Although the intelligent use of these credit instruments
  to accomplish predetermined NGP ends is presently nonexistent, it is
  apparent that they have had such effects accidentally. As we have

seen in preceding chapters, FHA mortgage loan policies have encouraged rapid suburbanization, as well as racial segregation in housing patterns and the decline of the urban core. Such naive disjointed incrementalism is not the only way to go.

- *Regulatory activities.* The Clean Air Act of 1969 as amended, the Water Pollution Control Act of 1971 as amended, the National Environmental Policy Act of 1969, and the Disaster Relief Act of 1974 will have major impacts on the future growth of our nation in some obvious ways and in still other ways as yet unforeseen. Perhaps less apparent is the effect on development of such regulatory agencies as the Federal Power Commission (dam location and river-water-level control), the Civil Aeronautics Board (economics of air service to small communities), and the Interstate Commerce Commission (rail, water, and highway freight rates). Control of maritime commerce, strip mining, interstate natural gas rates, and so on is another example of ways in which an NGP could be implemented indirectly.

It is apparent that many and varied instruments presently are available to influence the development of regions along the lines of an NGP should one be developed.

9.6   Why Appalachia for Project Toroid?

The location of Project Toroid should be consistent with the NGP. Although this policy does not yet exist, it seems likely that Appalachia will be one of the regions of the nation indicated for development by such a future NGP. Among the factors that support this assumption are the following:

- The population of Appalachia is poorer, less well educated, and less likely to have job opportunities than the average U.S. population.
- The real income in Appalachia consistently runs at about 75 percent of the U.S. mean income.
- Unemployment consistently is greater in Appalachia than the U.S. average.
- Population growth in Appalachia consistently lags overall U.S. growth (2.7 vs. 13.3 percent growth for the decade of the 1960s) because of heavy out-migration.
- Central Appalachia has *lost* 13 percent of its population during this period. Of course, it is the younger, more energetic persons having the most to contribute to development who find it easiest to migrate.

9.7   General Considerations in a Site Selection Process

Metaphysics may be defined as the study of the first principles that guide the formation of the sciences (truth, beauty, symmetry, causality, etc.). In that sense a metapolicy is the set of principles by which policies are constructed. This is what is meant by saying we must discuss for a moment the metapolicy for developing a site selection process. It might be supposed initially that, to find an ideal site location, we merely need to put into action the "will of the majority." In other words, a group of informed and interested citizens or their conscientious representatives, after consideration, rank-order various site candidates, and the median of the individual rankings will indicate the overall preference. Unfortunately, as Arrow and others have shown,[9] this is not necessarily true.

Concordet's paradox can be illustrated quite simply. Suppose that there are three evaluators or voters and three site candidates, a, b, and c. It will be assumed that individual rankings are transitive. In other words, if voter 1 prefers site a over site b, written as

$$aP_1b \tag{9.1}$$

and voter 1 also prefers site b over site c:

$$bP_1c \tag{9.2}$$

then it follows by transitivity that he prefers a over c, that is, (9.1) and (9.2) imply

$$aP_1c \tag{9.3}$$

or

$$aP_1bP_1c \tag{9.4}$$

Let us suppose that voter 2 prefers

$$bP_2cP_2a \tag{9.5}$$

and that voter 3 prefers

$$cP_3aP_3b \tag{9.6}$$

Simple majority voting indicates that site a is preferred to site b by two out of three or, in general, aPb. Similarly, b is preferred to c by two out of three, thus bPc. Therefore, by the transitive rule, we have aPc. But actually the majority prefer cPa. This paradox should cast doubt on the whole procedure, since a set of simple transitive preferences has produced an intransitive result. Farris and Sage[10] review the axioms proposed by Arrow and the modifications given by later authors for ameliorating this paradoxical situation and provide an additional methodology of their own. We must recognize that, given a number of site candidates and a number of voters representing different constituencies, we are vulnerable to the Concordet paradox in combining individual preferences to form "the will of the majority."

Now let us consider the development of a voter ranking, given a set of site candidates. If transitivity is assumed, it would be possible to produce a complete table of ranks by asking an individual to make pairwise comparisons and to express a pairwise preference. It would never be necessary for a voter to consider the candidates as a whole. But what does "prefer" mean? Voter 1 may "prefer" the job opportunities at site a over those at site b, but he may "prefer" the recreational opportunities at site b over those at site c. What is the meaning, then, of aP_1bP_1c in such a case? Would it not be desirable to help a voter to consider a given factor such as jobs for each site and then to do the same for recreation? This would help the voter to deal with the very complex problem of handling many factors and many sites.

Such a process would also have the added value of illuminating the reasons for voter selection, thus permitting remedial action on a site that was initially unattractive for certain isolated reasons but is consistent with an overall NGP. This suggestion is open, of course, to the charge of manipulation. And that is exactly what it is. But think about it. By definition Appalachia and other underdeveloped regions are not now undergoing balanced development. The question is how to change this. What could be more reasonable than asking the citizens to say how to make Appalachia, for example, more attractive to them? What factors should be changed to move Appalachia up in the ranking?

The three-step process described in the next section is aimed at forcing an objective process on the voter and making it more difficult for him to rate a site high for undisclosed "subjective" reasons. We are not persuaded that this is an ideal approach or that it is impossible to thwart or evade it. Rather, we merely claim that it makes an "objective" or at least repeatable process somewhat more practical.

9.8 A Three-Step Site Selection Process

Here are the steps of the proposed three-step process.

1. A number of "technical criteria" are defined, and each site is rated with respect to each of them.

2. A number of "urban functions" are defined, and each technical criterion is rated with respect to each of them.

3. The urban functions are weighted for personal value to the voter. By a mechanical process these ratings are manipulated to yield a site ranking.

Technical Criteria

The members of the rating panel agree to consider a number of site descriptors called technical criteria. These criteria may be demographic, such as age and skills of the existing population; may be geographic, such as soil conditions, gradient, rainfall, and temperature ranges; may pertain to physical infrastructures such as roads and railroads; and may have other characteristics. No agreement among the voters is needed on the importance of a particular criterion. If a given voter feels that a particular criterion is irrelevant, no argument is necessary. That voter merely rates all site candidates as average for that criterion.

It is possible in principle, perhaps, for a rater to rate each site for all the technical criteria before moving on to the next site. We find in practice, however, that this procedure tends to produce a halo effect. A rater decides that he "likes" or "dislikes" a given site and then proceeds systematically to grade that site high or low on all categories in order to produce the desired result. It is impossible in principle, of course, to prevent subjective feelings from entering into this rating process because this is precisely what the rating is about. Nevertheless, objective agreement is easier to reach on the rating of a site for technical criteria, because of the high objective content, than it would be for an urban function. Furthermore, by focusing on a single criterion rating for each site candidate in turn, the rater tends to focus on the criterion rather than on the site. For these reasons I recommend that one technical criterion be applied to the series of site candidates before moving to the next criterion.

Most raters feel more comfortable with a limited number of discrete choices. A three-point, a five-point, and a seven-point scale seem the most popular. For initial processing of many sites and many factors, I favor a three-point scale: high, medium, and low. But other people may disagree. The raters may choose the number of points on the scale to suit themselves. Any individual rater who feels uncomfortable with a finely divided scale, say a seven-point scale, may ignore intermediate values. Table 9.2 gives an example of 10 possible technical criteria for site rating. These 10 criteria are highly agglomerated. It is desirable, perhaps on a second iteration with a smaller number of site candidates, to disagglomerate these general features. Table 9.3 gives some examples of this process for three of the factors in Table 9.2.

Table 9.2 Ten Technical Criteria or Site Descriptors—Geographic, Topological, Geologic, Demographic, Physical and Social Infrastructure, Etc.

1. Exploitable natural resources
2. Land and natural environment
3. Climate
4. Buildability
5. Economic climate
6. Transportation
7. Ecological stability
8. Land acquisition cost
9. Social and political climate
10. Potential labor force

Table 9.3 More Detailed Characteristics for Three General Technical Factors Given in Table 9.2

Buildability
  (a) Suitable for bearing heavy structures (marshy)?
  (b) Suitable for drainage (clay)?
  (c) Suitable for excavation (rocky)?
  (d) Suitable for earth moving and construction (hilly)?
  (e) Other (ravines, valuable crop land)?
Land acquisition cost
  (a) Land tightly held (small parcels, many owners)?
  (b) Already in productive use?
  (c) Government land available?
  (d) Price relative to other areas?
  (e) Clear titles available?
  (f) Other (mineral rights)?
Land and natural environment
  (a) Clean air, water?
  (b) Recreational opportunities?
  (c) Hills, mountains, oceans, etc., nearby?
  (d) Presently crowded?
  (e) Presently polluted with old factories, strip mines, etc.?
  (f) Other (temperature extremes, precipitation)?

Urban Functions

The technical criteria describe the sites, but they do not indicate what people want to do in a city. The urban functions are designed to serve this purpose. Once again, the panel need agree only on the overall list and not on the value attached to any of the elements.

A typical list of urban functions is given in Table 9.4.

Table 9.4 *Urban Social Functions*

---

1. Employment
2. Recreation and outdoor activity
3. Health care
4. Social welfare
5. Education
6. Shopping
7. Cultural activities
8. Waste disposal
9. Entrepreneurial opportunity
10. Other

Some of these social functions may seem at first to be independent of the technical site descriptors, and this intial opinion may withstand a more detailed examination. On the other hand, climate does affect shopping, for example, and transportation to other cities does influence cultural opportunities. No doubt, the political climate of the region may be such that public higher education is of low quality. There are other, similar examples. The important point is that the voter is asked to rate a particular social function with respect to a technical descriptor but *not* with respect to a site candidate. Thus, for example, a rater cannot say, "I like the Pacific Northwest for recreation." But he may say, "I like a cool, mountainous, seashore area for recreation." Thus he is allowed to express a personal preference but not an irrational prejudgment.

Weighting Functions

Not all urban functions are equally important to an individual, nor are they the same for all people. Thus we wish to provide an opportunity for the voter to express his evaluation of the importance of each of the urban functions.

The Mechanical Procedure

Two rating matrices and a rating vector must be filled in by each voter. The [C] matrix expresses the value of each technical criterion for each site candidate. For illustration, suppose that we choose a limited number of sites and criteria and rate them on a three-point scale. We will select three of the economic development regions shown in Figure 9.1 plus the region for the proposed Minnesota Experimental City. The specific numbers in the [C] matrix shown in Table 9.5 are only one individual's opinion and not to be taken too seriously.

Next we form an [F] matrix, which relates the importance of a specific technical criterion to a given urban function. Table 9.6 gives one voter's rating of the six criteria of Table 9.5 in respect to five sample urban functions.

Note that we have permitted zero ratings on the [F] matrix in Table 9.6. This may be a mistake because it enlarges the rating scale and may distort the overall process. One might also argue, of course, with the specific numbers. With the rising price of gasoline it may not be apparent that energy has zero effect on accessibility, education, and socializing. It is intended that the [F] matrix ratings be site independent. Thus, to minimize the halo effect mentioned above, it would make good sense to ask voters to complete the [F] matrix before revealing to them the list of site candidates in the [C] matrix.

Finally, each voter is asked to rate the subjective importance of each urban function. Table 9.7 gives one such weighting for the five urban functions used in Table 9.6. Once again the rating scale has been expanded, and this may be a second procedural error. To be consistent, perhaps the voter should have been forced to rate each function only as high (3), medium (2), or low (1).

Now the site ranking is obtained by the following matrix multiplication:

$$\{R\} = [C] \times [F] \times \{W\} \tag{9.7}$$

For the values in Tables 9.5, 9.6, and 9.7, Equation 9.7 yields

$$\{R\} = \begin{Bmatrix} 349 \\ 222 \\ 337 \\ 327 \end{Bmatrix} \begin{matrix} \text{Appalachia} \\ \text{Four Corners} \\ \text{Pacific Northwest} \\ \text{Minnesota} \end{matrix} \tag{9.8}$$

Thus we see that this voter prefers Appalachia.

One must understand that site ranking should not be a "popularity" contest in the sense of a choice for a vacation trip. The availability of water in the Four Corners region is not a matter of the will of the majority. It may be, therefore, that the elements of the [C] matrix and the actual C_{ij} ratings should be determined by a panel of experts, possibly operating in the Delphi process.[11]

The essence of the Delphi process seems to be to provide sufficient social distance among the participants during the ranking to prevent

Table 9.5 *A Sample [C] Matrix*

			Criterion			
Site	Land and Environment	Regional Transport	Political Cooperation	Energy and Raw Materials	Water	Labor
Appalachia	3	1	3	2	3	3
Four Corners	2	1	2	3	1	1
Pacific						
Northwest	3	2	1	3	3	2
Minnesota	2	2	2	3	3	2	= [C]

[1 = low (bad), 2 = medium, 3 = high (good)]

Table 9.6 *A Sample [F] Matrix*

Criterion	Function					
	Work	Recreation	Accessibility	Education	Socializing	
Land and environment	2	3	1	1	2	
Regional transport	3	1	3	2	3	
Political cooperation	2	1	1	1	0	
Energy and raw materials	3	0	0	0	0	
Water	2	3	1	0	0	
Labor	3	1	0	1	1	= [F]

Table 9.7   *A Sample* $\{W\}$ *Vector*

Work		5	
Recreation		4	
Accessibility	$\left\{\right.$	2	$\left.\right\} = \{W\}$
Education		3	
Socializing		1	

verbal, domineering, or persuasive raters from influencing other raters, while at the same time permitting logical positions and objective information held by one rater to be made known to the other participants.

It must also be admitted that the proper values in the $[F]$ matrix are not always self evident. In the first place it is not clear that the impact of a particular technical criterion upon a given urban function is a matter of popular sovereignty. Energy at the proper price and in the proper form is essential for an industrial base and thus for jobs or "work." Yet why should a worker concern himself with this problem? Finally, is the relative importance of various social functions to urban dwellers apparent to these people? Would it not be preferable to assess the relative importance by asking a skilled specialist to provide a ranking on the basis of observed behavior rather than on the expressed, but possibly unconsidered, aspirations of individuals?

All of the caveats expressed as we have developed this three-step process are meant to provide possible discussion topics for further refining of the process, rather than to raise doubts concerning its effectiveness. Although clearly not without fault, this three-step process appears to represent an advance in the state of the art.

9.9   An Appalachia Site Selection for Toroid

Having laid a foundation for the three-step site selection process, we will now apply it to a site selection for Toroid in Appalachia. In a report by M. B. Schoultz a more complete justification for Appalachia as a possible location for Toroid, in terms of its people, its problems, and its potential, has been given. Schoultz also integrates a strategy for development of the region with a projected national urban growth policy.[12] We will not elaborate further on the points made above concerning these matters.

First Iteration

There are 397 counties in the Appalachian region. A number of these are in or contiguous to existing SMSA regions; see Figure 9.3. In addition, a

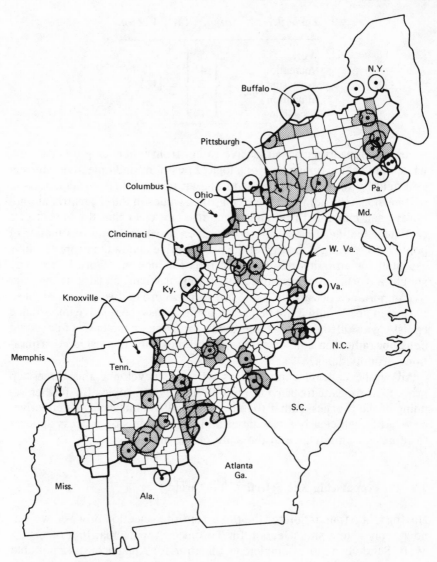

Figure 9.3 Appalachian counties in proximity to existing cities.

number of counties form urban corridors between existing cities. A total of 158 counties must be eliminated as possible sites for Toroid on these grounds of urban proximity. An additional 53 counties were eliminated because they are in extremely rugged terrain that would make construction very expensive; see Figure 9.4. Thus a total of 211 counties was eliminated in this first iteration, leaving 186 counties for further examina-

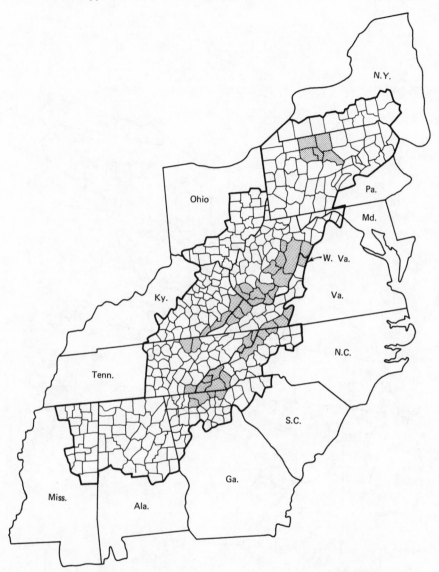

Figure 9.4 Rugged areas not suitable for construction in Appalachia.

tion. The next step was to agglomerate closely adjacent two- and three-county groups to yield 81 remaining site candidates; see Figure 9.5. Note that these 81 first-iteration candidates are spread throughout northern, central, and southern Appalachia and represent a number of different kinds of opportunities. We seem to have arrived at this result rather smoothly and rapidly, but the reader should recognize that a number of

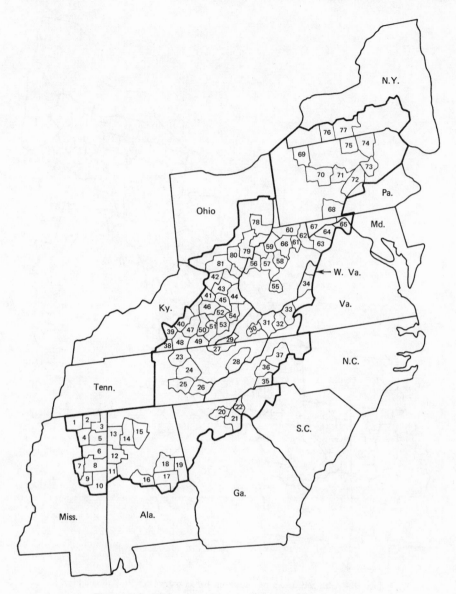

Figure 9.5 Eighty-one sites resulting from first iteration.

man-months are represented by this effort. This first phase could be carried out without a heavy investment in developing a data base, however, and we view this as an important point.

Second Iteration

An in-depth study of 81 site candidates would represent an incredibly expensive process if not carefully controlled. It is here, we believe, that the balance provided by the three-step process begins to prove its value. A five-point rating scale was utilized by Schoultz, and his technical factors and urban functions are shown in Table 9.8.

Table 9.8 *Technical Criteria and Urban Functions Used in the Second-Iteration Site-Selection Process for Toroid* (SOURCE: Schoultz, *loc. cit.*)

Technical Criteria	Urban Functions
Land resources	Employment
Natural environment	Recreation
Energy resources	Accessibility and communication
Water resources	Education
Other natural resources	Social and community
Man-made resources	Health care
Manufactured products	Retail shopping
Political Cooperation	Housing
Transportation resources	Government
Labor resources	Security

Each technical factor was carefully applied to each site candidate, utilizing the data provided in the *National Atlas of the United States*.[13] Schoultz quotes Appalachian Commission reports to the effect that local tax structures, government, and so forth are not as important at this stage as they will be in the final elimination process. Here, in this iteration, geographic considerations predominate. Many of the technical criteria of Table 9.8 seem self explanatory. "Man-made resources" is perhaps an exception. This item relates, for example, to the supply of petroleum and natural gas pipelines. The three-step process was applied to the sites as described in Section 9.8. The 12 top-ranking sites are shown in Table 9.9.

An informal sensitivity analysis was performed on these candidates. Multipliers were applied to various of the technical criteria to reflect a weighting of the importance of each. This weighting is given in Table 9.10. These weightings did not change the results. There is no claim that this is

Table 9.9 *Twelve Sites Selected in the Second Iteration (See text for significance of asterisks)* (SOURCE: Schoultz, *loc. cit.*)

Site Number	Counties	State	Score
69*	Warren, Forest	Pennsylvania	2103
70*	Jefferson, Clearfield	Pennsylvania	2079
78*	Guernsey, Monroe, Noble	Ohio	2049
79*	Morgan, Athens, Meigs	Ohio	2030
28	Cocke, Greene, Washington	Tennessee	1846
16*	Bibb, Chilton	Alabama	1839
41	Bath, Menifee, Montgomery	Kentucky	1848
48	Clinton, Russell, Wayne	Kentucky	1806
1	Marshall, Benton	Mississippi	1691
31/32	Tazewell, Symth, Bland, Wythe	Virginia	1628
66	Doddridge, Harrison, Lewis	West Virginia	1595
36	Burke, McDowell	North Carolina	1545

a definitive ranking, however, since the rating jury represented only a narrow slice of American society. Nevertheless we seem to have demonstrated a certain robustness in the results.

In the first iteration, care was taken to define rather strictly urban proximity and unbuildability; that is, it was recognized that elimination of a county is irreversible. No matter how high that county would have

Table 9.10 *Technical-Factors Weighting Used to Test Sensitivity of Sites Given in Table 9.9*

Technical Criterion	Weighting
Land resources	2
Natural environment	1
Energy	3
Water	3
Other natural resources	2
Man-Made resources	1
Man-Made products	2
Labor	1
Transportation	3
Political cooperation	2

scored in a later evaluation, if removed it could not be reconsidered. Now, having completed the second iteration, it appears appropriate to interpret this requirement more broadly. Of the 12 sites, 5 appear to warrant disqualification on the grounds that they are located in corridors between existing cities, and to build in these counties is to encourage urban sprawl. The 5 sites listed in Table 9.9 with an asterisk were deemed susceptible to this problem and were thus eliminated from further consideration.

9.10   Third Iteration and Final Triad

We have maintained that a properly conducted system study should grow more complete as the field of candidates is narrowed. Thus we would not expect merely to reapply on a mechanical basis the same process to the remaining candidates in the third iteration; a deeper and more intensive study seems appropriate.[14] First, let us reevaluate the implication of the technical criteria used in the previous iteration. By comparing the results of the first iteration and those of the second, we see that the process seems to discriminate against rural sites and for sites in high-population-density areas, especially those in industrially developed regions. Four criteria, namely, "transportation," "labor," "man-made resources," and "man-made products," contribute to this bias. "After all," as Shoultz says, "one of the major reasons for the New City is to contribute to a national growth policy. But by stressing those criteria which correspond to urban regions, we are contradicting this policy." To restore the balance, Schoultz recommends that the "man-made resources" criterion be merged with "energy resources" and that "man-made products" be more broadly defined as a general "market potential" criterion. In addition we explicitly define a criterion for "supports NGP," as well as one for "supports regional needs and requirements." Schoultz also adds criteria for "recreational resource potential" and "natural environment."

Table 9.11 shows the technical criteria to be used for the third iteration.

Table 9.11   *Technical Criteria to Be Used in Third Iteration* (SOURCE: Schoultz, *loc. cit.*)

Land resources	Supports NGP
Energy resources	Supports regional needs and requirements
Water resources	Recreational resource potential
Raw materials	Natural environment
Market potential	Labor potential
Transportation resources	State incentives for development

One may reasonably ask whether, if this perfected set of technical criteria was applied to the 81 candidates in the second iteration, would we have a different group of seven semifinalists? This would be a suitable way in which to test the sensitivity of our results.

Although a number of steep mountainous counties were excluded initially, the buildability of the remaining site candidates must not be ignored in later iterations. Such factors as soil drainage, geological faults, foundation characteristics, flood conditions, excavation, and grading characteristics, along with general topological conditions, are included in the "land resources" criterion. We have shown in Table 9.2 and 9.3 how each of the general criteria can be broken down for more detailed consideration, and this is an example of that process.

In the second iteration "transportation" was measured by the existence of a railroad in the country and an interstate highway. At this level of analysis a more detailed consideration is warranted. The miles of track and the cities to which the railway directly connects, as well as its links to the natural resources, are considered. In addition the availability of ocean access is included.

"Energy resources" includes the availability of coal, petroleum, natural gas, and oil shale, as well as installed and potential hydroelectric generating capability. "Water resources" includes the presence of surface reservoirs, rivers, lakes, and aquifers.

In previous iterations "natural environment" was a weak criterion in that the simple measures employed failed to provide significant site differentials. Thus we will add to this criterion a consideration of deviation from ideal temperatures, mean heating and cooling degree days,[15] number of frost-free days, forecasted high-pollution days, and normal precipitation.

"Raw materials" includes the availability of agricultural products, timber, nonmetals, metals, sand and gravel, and manufactured construction products. To estimate "market potential" we measure the market demand in cities of 100,000 population within a 200-mile radius. The availability of a specific report of the Appalachian Commission has eased the problem of rating the "recreational resource potential" of our site candidates.[16] To rate "labor potential" we use the same 14 selected two-digit, SIC code, basic industries used previously to measure value added in manufacturing. Here we count the number of blue collar employees available in the state in these industries.

It is doubtful that "state incentives for development" is important in an initial broad-sweeping site search. However, as a fine tuning device to select from among a few finalists this criterion has its place. Schoultz measures six categories of state financial assistance plus seven tax incentives plus several special legal items (right to work, air pollution code, water pollution code, and pollution reduction incentives) plus four special services offered by states to industry. Applying all of these criteria along with the urban functions and weightings of these functions resulted in the following final triad:

- Site 48: Clinton, Russell, Wayne counties in southern Kentucky
- Site 36: Burke, McDowell counties in North Carolina
- Site 41: Bath, Menifee, Montgomery counties in northern Kentucky

These three sites rated clearly superior to the remaining four. When other jurors repeated the selection process using their own urban function weights, these three sites continued to be selected. Moreover, variations in the weights and number of technical criteria used did not alter the triad membership. Thus we conclude that this triad is robust and is relatively impervious to individual variations of the jurors. This is not to say, however, that a more cosmopolitan jury or jurors with a widely divergent set of values would necessarily select the same sites.

Schoultz in his report[17] proceeds to provide additional background on the three finalists gathered by further data analysis and personal site visits. He does *not*, however, proceed with a final site selection. This termination point for the process was chosen in advance for the following reasons:

- Final selection should be made by a representative panel of citizens in an open fashion rather than by technical experts. Analysts are not decision makers.
- Political cooperation is essential for the success of Toroid. Thus some room for bargaining must be left to NUCOM. To designate the final site is to relinquish a powerful lever for extracting state and county cooperation.
- The final triad represents an area of 2516 square miles. Clearly this is too large to influence significant anticipatory land purchases by selfish entrepreneurs. To proceed further, however, is to run this risk and thus to jeopardize the success of Project Toroid.

Notes and References

1. For an excellent introduction to modern economic site location theory see the collection of papers edited by R. D. Dean, W. H. Leahy, D. L. McKee, *Spatial Economic Theory*, The Free Press, N. Y., 1970. The standard textbook in the field is W. Isard, *Methods of Regional Analysis*, John Wiley, N. Y., 1960.

2. For an interesting discussion of a study that resulted in General Foods locating a new

factory in Dover, Del., see E. S. Whitman, W. S. Schmidt, *Plant Relocation*, American Management Association, N. Y., 1966.

3. D. Bell, *The Coming of Post-Industrial Society*, Basic Books, N. Y., 1973.

4. These influences are perhaps best seen from the outside. Criticism currently rages in Canada about the ubiquitious influence of American television and magazines. Legal steps are contemplated that would raise tariff walls against such "foreign" influences.

5. *National Growth and Development 1974*, HUD-386-CPD, December 1974.

6. H. R. Hamilton et. al., *Systems Simulation for Regional Analysis*, M.I.T. Press, Cambridge, 1969.

7. *National Growth and Development 1974*, pp. 21–26.

8. *National Growth and Development 1974*, p. 23.

9. K. J. Arrow, *Social Choice and Individual Values*, 2nd ed., Yale University Press, New Haven, 1963.

10. D. R. Farris, A. P. Sage, "Worth Assessment in Group Decision Making," *IEEE Transactions on Systems, Man and Cybernetics*, Vol. SMC-5 (May 1975), pp. 346–358.

11. T. J. Gordon, *The Future*, St. Martin's Press, N. Y., 1972.

12. M. B. Schoultz, "An Appalachian Region Site Location Analysis for Project Toroid," Report of Urban Systems Group, School of Engineering and Applied Sciences, University of Virginia, November 1975.

13. U. S. Department of Interior, Geological Survey, Washington, D. C., 1970.

14. At the same time the reader should be mindful that we are condensing Schoultz's 150-page report into these few pages.

15. Defined as departures from 65° Fahrenheit.

16. "Recreation Potential in the Appalachian Highlands: A Market Analysis," *Appalachian Research Report* No. 14, Appalachian Research Commission, March 1971.

17. M. B. Schoultz, *loc. cit.*

10

A Transition Scenario for Project Toroid

Family well-being is not possible without good housing. Good housing is not possible without good town planning. Good town planning is not possible without good regional planning. And good regional planning is not possible without a national program for urbanization.

H. VON HERTEN
Executive Director for Tapiola, Finland
in *Building a New Town*
M.I.T. Press, 1973

[We] learned that plans must be realized fairly rapidly, for plans become obsolete quickly, and their cost becomes a loss. [We] learned the importance of firm discipline and control over all operations during the building period so that plans would not be spoiled. [We] had to guard against expedient alterations that were demanded daily, alterations that compromise the plan unnecessarily.

H. VON HERTEN
loc. cit.

10.1 Definition of the Term

The ultimate state defined by the normative plan is without question more important than the process of transition per se, but one ignores either at great peril. The system analyst must describe as precisely as possible the process of moving from the status quo to the normative solution. This narrative we call the transition scenario.

The transition scenario should include consideration of all of the classic trifold planning components, physical, economic, and social. We will concentrate here on the development of the physical infrastructure, simply because of the limitations of space. This is not to say, however, that one may design the physical elements of a city without influencing economic and social factors, since, as we have repeatedly shown, this is not so.

The term "physical infrastructure," of rather recent usage, clearly emphasizes the unity of all the physical elements of the city and correctly concentrates on this unity rather than emphasizing the separateness of the various components. The dictionary defines "infrastructure" as the underlying foundation or basic framework, and again this conveys a correct impression. But can we be more specific? What exactly goes to make up the urban "physical infrastructure"? One could develop a "laundry list" of all the various classes of physical structures existing in a typical American city. Another approach might be to take the functions performed by an individual in a city, such as work, education, shopping, and recreation, to add the word "facilities" after each, and then compile an appropriate list. But it will be necessary to leave the detailed and systemic study of the interactions of all the various physical systems of the city, one with another, to the next, more detailed iteration of this study. It is already apparent from the studies thus far, however, that three components of the physical infrastructure impact on the totality of the city with particular force.

Housing has been shown by our preliminary economic estimates to be the largest single cost factor in the city. Thus, if Toroid is to provide less expensive living or, alternatively, more amenities for the same cost, housing is the single highest leverage item on which to concentrate.

Interaction studies of the dozen or so major urban design sectors show consistently that transportation has the highest score. Of course it should not be surprising that transportation has the highest interaction index, since by definition it knits together all other sectors and makes possible most individual urban functions. Project Toroid is particularly sensitive to effective mass transit, since the toroid form was chosen with this in mind. One of the putative strengths of the toroidal form is savings to individuals in the cost of transportation. Thus transportation benefit/cost ratio studies have a special place in the transition scenario for Toroid.

Finally, the recent rapid increase in the cost of energy has cast doubt on many previous design decisions concerning elements of the urban infrastructure. Almost every design decision made in the past has been based on the assumption of cheap energy. The list is endless. Suburban sprawl flourished because, in part, of cheap gasoline. Home appliances are bought on the basis of first cost with never a thought given to operating costs. Homes are not properly insulated, and office buildings have acres of glass. The energy costs of packaging the goods bought at retail in American stores alone are not negligible. Modern high-intensity agriculture as practiced in the United States is extremely lavish in its use of energy.[1] Project Toroid provides an opportunity for an integrated systemic introduction of minimum energy design alternatives, and thus energy consumption must receive a special place in the transition scenario for Toroid.

10.2   Phase I: Preplanning

Before detailed project planning for Toroid must come a consensus building phase. The need for revitalizing urban America must be recognized and brought to the attention of persons of influence. Is there any evidence that policy leaders have recognized a need for a new initiative in revitalizing urban America, and specifically is there evidence that a large new freestanding city could be one element of this program?

- There is widespread recognition that past and present urban policies have failed. Consider, for example, George Romney, former President of American Motors, former Governor of Michigan, and former Secretary of the U.S. Department of Housing and Urban Development. Romney is generally regarded as an honest, rather dynamic manager. Although he is not considered to be an ideologue or particularly socially conscious, it is accepted that his own self-view is that of a moralistic, success-oriented, Calvinistic business man. He would be unlikely to permit himself knowingly to acquiesce to corner-cutting or easily to admit defeat. Thus it is particularly significant that such a person declared shortly before leaving HUD that our present urban policies are bankrupt and that it is foolish to suppose that spending more federal funds is the answer. Romney admitted failure when he said, "The truth is, we don't know what to do." This crucial speech was discussed in more detail in Chapter 4.
- There is a growing recognition that a national growth policy should be instituted in place of incrementalism. The concept of an overall NGP is accepted in the Housing Act of 1970. The Congress has required the executive branch to publish biannually a report on the state of the nation. Thus far, the reports have not been met with widespread approval, but the need for an NGP is becoming recognized.
- The Academy for Contemporary Problems, an action-oriented organization recently founded in Columbus, sponsored jointly by Ohio State University and Battelle Institute and headed by Ralph Widner, former executive of the Appalachian Regional Commission, chose as the first problem to be addressed by the new academy the development of a national growth policy.

- The Rains report discussed in Chapter 1, published by Praeger under the editorship of Canty and entitled *The New City*, specifically called for the construction of a number of new cities, some of them in the freestanding, 1-million-population class. Although the initiative was supported by the Nixon administration early in its first term, it soon fell into disfavor.
- In 1971 David Rockefeller, Chairman of the Board of Chase Manhattan Bank, in a speech widely reported in the national press,[2] called for raising $10 billion of private funds to finance the construction of 100 new cities.
- In 1971, in response to a decline in the national economy and widespread cutbacks in the aerospace industry, U.S. Senator Edward Kennedy called for the establishment of an "urban NASA," a federal agency that would apply aerospace system techniques to solving the problems of the cities and guiding the design and construction of whole new ones. Although Kennedy introduced legislation, it was not passed into law.
- A number of books, of which this is one, and journal articles have appeared that debate the new city concept; but since they are not necessarily representative of the views of policy makers, they need not be further reviewed here in detail, although a number are mentioned elsewhere in this text.[3]

Despite these isolated examples, it would not appear that there exists a widespread and developing consensus among policy makers that the new city would provide a suitable vehicle for revitalization of U.S. urban society in the closing decades of the twentieth century.

The DELTA chart shown in Figure 10.1 gives one possible sequence of events, beginning with the recognition of the national need for revitalizing urban America. We will not elaborate further on this preplanning phase, fascinating though it may be, since it is beyond the central focus of the text. Rather, we will assume that by one means or another the New Community Development Corporation (NUCOM) has been formed and the planning phase is about to begin.

10.3   Phase II: General Project Planning

In Figure 10.2 is shown the DELTA chart for the major activities involved in planning, constructing, and placing into operation a freestanding new city of 1 million persons. Let us discuss the activities shown in this chart in some detail.

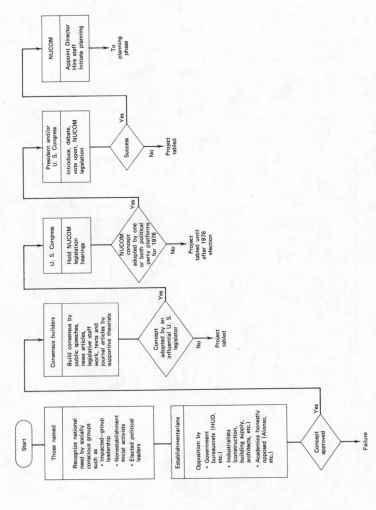

Figure 10.1 DELTA chart for preplanning phase of New City Project, Phase I.

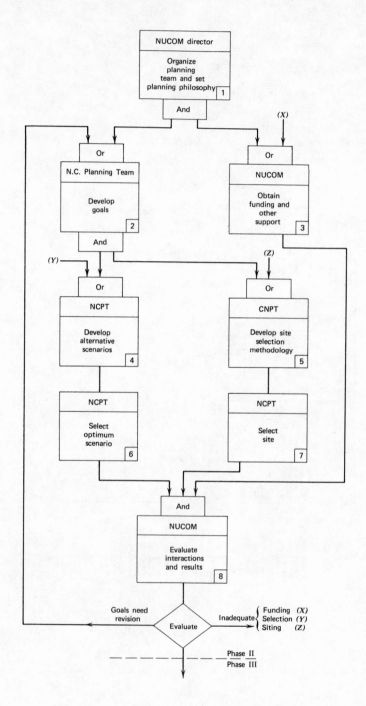

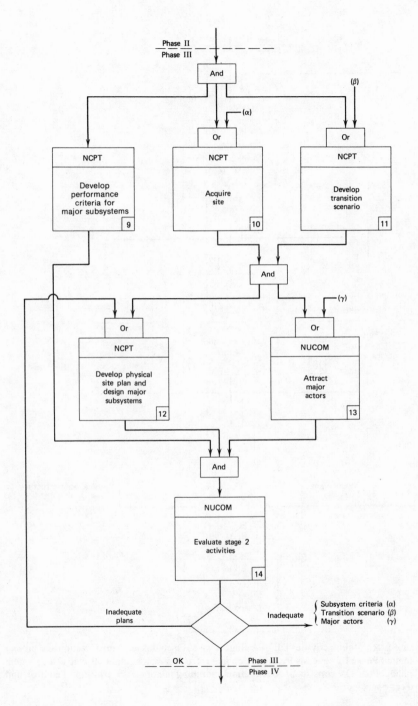

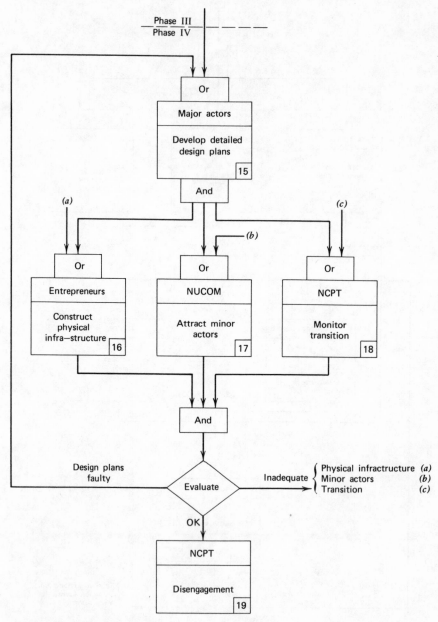

Figure 10.2 Major activities DELTA chart. Phase II includes team organization and project planning. Phase III covers site acquisition and recruiting major actors, as well as subsystem planning. Phase IV consists of construction, recruiting minor actors, transfer of control, and project phase-out.

1 Organize Planning Team

An early activity for the director of NUCOM will be to initiate the organization of the New City Planning Team (NCPT) by hiring the team leader and working with him to develop the overall philosophy under which the team will work. Other activities of NUCOM will be congressional liaison, public relations, and evaluation of the planning team effort.

2 Develop Goals

An early task of the planning team will be to initiate the goal development phase of a systemic planning process. Consultants are a vital part of this process, and validation by citizens must be obtained. Key activities are the development of the descriptive and normative scenarios, the elaboration of the axiological component (value structure), and the development and validation of specific planning objectives.

3 Obtain Support

The federal government role in supplying initial funding, site acquisition aid, zoning changes, environmental impact statements, and so on must be explored. Some of these external activities will be retained by NUCOM central offices; others will be assigned to the NCPT. State government interfaces must be explored and contingency policies developed.

4 Develop Alternative Solutions

This activity by the NCPT produces several alternative project definitions consistent with the goals developed in activity 2. The discussion of the eightfold way in Chapter 6 is a part of this activity.

5 Develop Site Selection Methodology

Site location is a politically sensitive issue. Moreover, land speculation must be forestalled. Thus development of an objective site selection process is an early priority target. Options on several sites may be necessary to avoid premature commitment in the planning process. Site selection was discussed in Chapter 9.

6 Select Optimum Solution

Project management, external consultants, an independent review committee, and government sponsors should review the leading candidates developed in activity 4. Feedback to a redevelopment of the performance indices and a reevaluation of the requisite level and kind of governmental support is included in this activity. The expected outcome of this activity is a consistent and accepted project definition.

7 Select Site

The process developed in activity 5 is applied. The accepted indices are applied, and a few choice sites are retained. Two options present themselves at this point. The indices may be revised and new site candidates obtained, or the rank ordering is accepted.

8 Evaluate Interaction and Results

The interactions between prime site candidates, planning solutions, goals, and available support are examined. Revisions and modifications of goals and other factors are in order at this point, but after approval by NUCOM Phase II is locked up.

10.4 Phase III: Site Preparation

Phase III of Project Toroid consists of site acquisition and the recruiting of major actors such as developers, financiers, and planners of the major subsystems. It also includes the overall planning of the major subsystems. See the DELTA chart shown in Figure 10.2.

9 Develop Performance Criteria for Major Subsystems

The major subsystems of the city are identified. Examples might be health and welfare services, education, safety and security, transportation, and government. Indices for the successful performance of each must be developed.

10 Acquire Site

In activity 7 the primary site was chosen. In this activity that choice is reviewed and confirmed, and a strategy for acquiring the land developed. This activity is complete upon obtaining the necessary land options.

11 Develop Transition Scenario

A narrative description of the project from beginning to steady-state operation is prepared. Crucial mileposts are identified, and attention is given to minimizing dislocations and transient effects by good planning.

Responsible groups are identified for initiating various activities and managing them until the permanent team is assembled and functioning. Such questions as construction worker housing, public relations, and the orientation of early immigrants to the undeveloped site, must be covered. The transition scenario is a step-by-step discussion of how to proceed from the status quo to the normative state.

12   Develop Physical Site Plan and Design Major Subsystems

This activity represents a greater investment of planning effort than all of the other planning sectors added together. The new city form must be chosen, and other design specifications consistent with performance indices must be developed. Interactions among various subsectors must be identified, and conflicts resolved. Plans must be approved by project management, the independent review committee, and the potential major actors.

13   Attract Major Actors

Large industries, government agencies funding sources, and major developers must be convinced to take part in the project. A major aid in this regard will be a well-developed planning activity, number 12.

14   Evaluate Stage II Activities

The interactions of goals, the transition scenario, physical plans, major actors, and so on are reviewed. A number of feedback paths are available. This evaluation is the responsibility of the project management, NUCOM, the independent review committee, major actors, and sponsors.

10.5   Phase IV: Construction and Occupation

In this final phase, which will occupy most of the term of the project and call for the major expenditure of funds, the new city is constructed and becomes a functioning, viable entity.

15   Develop Detailed Designs

In this activity the major actors develop the detailed designs of the commercial, industrial, residential, communication, transport, health care, education, government, and other sectors. Interactions are examined, and conflicts resolved.

16   Construct Physical Infrastructure

Worker facilities and services are provided, and the construction phase is implemented. Project management provides coordination and supervision to ensure compliance with goals and constraints.

17   Attract Minor Actors

Any participant whose activities do not influence a large number of other actors is designated as a minor actor. Citizens, small businessmen, shopkeepers, contractors, workers, and so forth are included in this category. Advertising campaigns are begun, and the selection of small entrepreneurs is accomplished. Orientation material is prepared, and the attraction of new city citizens begins.

18   Monitor Transition

Sensors are implemented, performance indices are evaluated, and feedback to the design and construction teams is included. Evaluation documents are prepared. This is a continuing process, of course.

19   Disengagement

Total self-government is in place, and steady-state sensing is set up and operating. The project history is documented. New city team members are placed in new jobs, and NUCOM pulls out.

More detailed DELTA charts must be prepared for each of the 19 general activities we have discussed. In one such exercise a number of the detailed charts had as many as 16 activities, and some as few as 6. On the average the detailed charts contain 10 or 12 activities.

10.6   Detailed DELTA Charts: An Example

Since each of the 19 activities represented in Figure 10.2 is highly generalized, the next step is to prepare a more detailed chart for each.[4] At this next level of disagglomeration, some 240 activities are defined, and for detailed planning each of these must be carried to still another level of detail. We will choose only one activity, number 15, for discussion here as an example. Figure 10.3 shows the detailed DELTA chart for activity 15.

Figure 10.3   Activity 15.0 in the DELTA chart of Figure 10.2, "Develop NC Detailed Design Plans," broken down to the next level of detail as an example. (SOURCE: J. D. Owens et al., *loc. cit.*)

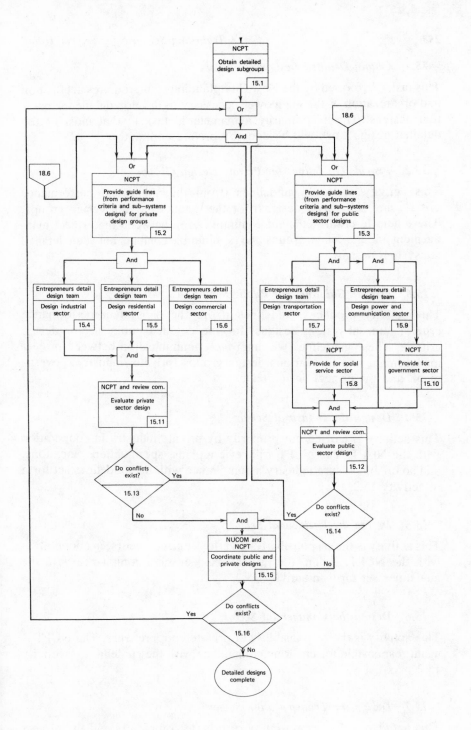

15.1   Obtain Detailed Design Subgroups

This task, performed by the New City planning team, requires acquisition and organization of the manpower necessary to develop detailed subsystem designs. This is primarily a managerial task in that most of the detailed design work will be done by private contractors.

15.2   Provide Guidelines for Private Design Groups

This activity produces guidelines (from the subsystem performance criteria and subsystem designs) for the detailed private design groups. These help to ensure efficient communication between the project management and the design groups and to minimize conflicts between detailed subsystem designs.

15.3   Provide Guidlines for Public Sector Designs

This activity produces guidelines (from the subsystem performance criteria and subsystem designs) for the detailed public sector design criteria. These guidelines will improve communication between project management and the various design groups (private, industry, government, and the project design teams).

15.4   Design the Industrial Sector

This activity is carried out primarily by private industry in cooperation with the NCPT. The NCPT will review plans, specifications, locations, and so on and ensure industry's compliance with the guidelines set forth in activity 15.2.

15.5   Design the Residential Sector

This activity is the responsibility of various entrepreneurs, in cooperation with the NCPT. Again, the project team ensures compliance with the guidelines set forth in activity 15.2.

15.6   Design the Commercial Sector

This activity is the responsibility of private entrepreneurs. The NCPT is again responsible for ensuring compliance with the guidelines of activity 15.2.

15.7   Design the Transportation Sector

This activity is the responsibility of private contractors and the project team. The contractors will be given the subsystem design (developed in activity 12) and the guidelines (activity 15.2). They will then produce detailed designs and bids in cooperation with the NCPT.

15.8   Provide for the Social Service Sector

This activity is the responsibility of the NCPT in cooperation with the government and citizens of the city. Included in the social service sector are churches, parks, lakes, youth centers, museums, libraries, and other amenities.

15.9   Design the Power and Communication Sector

This activity is primarily the responsibility of private enterprise. Close communication with the project design team must be maintained to ensure compliance with the guidelines set forth in activity 15.2.

15.10   Provide for the Government Sector

This activity is primarily the responsibility of the NCPT and the government in cooperation with city residents. Included are schools, police and fire stations, and sanitation facilities.

15.11   Evaluate the Private Sector

This activity reviews the detailed designs submitted by private enterprise, and conflicts between the subsystems are evaluated and resolved. This activity is the responsibility of project management, the independent review committee, and private industry.

15.12   Evaluate the Public Sector Design

This activity reviews the public subsystem designs for conflicts and compliance with the subsystem guidelines. It is primarily the responsibility of project management, the independent review committee, and the government sponsors.

15.13 and 15.14   Do Conflicts Exist?

If conflicts exist, the detailed designs must be revised. This decision is the responsibility of NUCOM and the independent review committee.

15.15   Coordinate the Public and Private Designs

The public and private designs are coordinated into a single overall design, and conflicts between the two sectors are evaluated. This activity is the responsibility of NUCOM along with the NCPT and the independent review committee.

15.16 Do Conflicts Exist?

If conflicts exist between public and private sector designs, the designs must be modified. This decision is the responsibility of project management and the independent review committee.

One can see from the high level of generality of many of the activities just outlined that several additional levels of detail will be required before accurate time and manpower needs for transition can be estimated with precision. The DELTA chart concept appears to be effective for the organization of this effort.

10.7 Toroid's First Export Industry: A Crucial Milepost

The developers of Ebenezer Howard's new town, Letchworth, at the turn of the century and the Rouse Company at Columbia more than a half-century later faced the same crucial milepost, as will Toroid in its turn. After all the full-color renderings and artists' views help to obtain front-end financing and even after the first roads and sewers are installed, the project is still in doubt. The first few homes may be constructed and the retail shops to service them may be in place, but the project can still fail. The city has not yet shown that it can be financially self-sustaining. The first indicator of future solvency occurs well before financial stability is assured, but without this first indicator we know that failure lies ahead. This key indicator of future financial solvency is the selection of Toroid as the location of a major export industry.

Cadbury Chocolates located a new plant at Letchworth, and the issue of Columbia was resolved when General Electric agreed to locate a major home appliance plant there. The new city developer is not without bargaining counters, of course. In the case of Columbia, Rouse is reported to have paid for the cost of routing utility lines and a railroad siding, as well as providing land at a bargain price for the G. E. plant. Crucial in the decision as well, perhaps, was the agreement that G. E. would be given the exclusive rights to supply all built-in appliances for housing in Columbia. The Bendix Corporation was next attracted to Columbia by similar arrangements and the exclusive right to supply people-mover public transit to the town. Perhaps a local business opportunity in the new